Couture and Consensus

Cultural Studies of the Americas
George Yúdice, Jean Franco, and Juan Flores, Series Editors

(continued on page 224)

COUTURE AND CONSENSUS

Fashion and Politics in Postcolonial Argentina

Para mis amigos
June y Cliff
con agradecimiento
y admiración

REGINA A. ROOT

Regina
Root

Cultural Studies of the Americas Series, Volume 24

University of Minnesota Press
Minneapolis
London

MINNESOTA

An earlier version of chapter 3 was published as "Fashioning Independence: Gender, Dress, and Social Space in Postcolonial Argentina," in *The Latin American Fashion Reader,* ed. Regina A. Root (Oxford: Berg Publishers, 2005), 31–43; reprinted with permission of Berg Publishers. An earlier version of chapter 4 was published as "Tailoring the Nation: Fashion Writing in Nineteenth-Century Argentina," *Fashion Theory* 4, no. 1 (2000): 89–118 (Oxford: Berg Publishers, 2000); reprinted with permission of Berg Publishers. Chapter 5 reprints material from Regina A. Root, "Searching for the Oasis in Life: Fashion and Female Emancipation in Late Nineteenth-Century Argentina," *The Americas* 60, no. 3 (January 2004): 363–90; reprinted with permission from the Academy of American Franciscan History. Portions of the Epilogue are based on "Urban Expressions of Solidarity: Fashioning Citizenship in Argentina," in *The Politics of Dress in Asia and the Americas,* ed. Louise Edwards and Mina Roces (East Sussex, U.K.: Sussex Academic Press, 2007); reprinted with permission of Sussex Academic Press.

Published by the University of Minnesota Press
111 Third Avenue South, Suite 290
Minneapolis, MN 55401-2520
http://www.upress.umn.edu

Library of Congress Cataloging-in-Publication Data
Root, Regina A.
    Couture and consensus : fashion and politics in postcolonial Argentina / Regina A. Root.
        p. cm. — (Cultural studies of the Americas ; 24)
    Includes bibliographical references and index.
    ISBN 978-0-8166-4793-4 (alk. paper) — ISBN 978-0-8166-4794-1 (pb : alk. paper)
        1. Clothing trade—Argentina—History.   2. Fashion—Argentina—History.
    3. Consumption (Economics)—Argentina—History.   4. Argentina—Politics and government—1810-   I. Title.
    HD9864.A7R66 2010
    338.4'76870982—dc22

                                                                    2010006650

Printed in the United States of America on acid-free paper

The University of Minnesota is an equal-opportunity educator and employer.

18 17 16 15 14 13 12 11 10   10 9 8 7 6 5 4 3 2 1

To my father
James R. McDuffie
in memoriam

Contents

Acknowledgments

Writing this book has been an incredible journey spanning years, continents, and cyberspace. The generous spirits of many people dance along each page of *Couture and Consensus*. Any errors, however, remain solely my own.

While I was a scholar in residence at the Argentine National Library, the kind attention of former director Héctor Yanover, Ignacio Martín Cloppet, Agustina Ganglof, Silvia Ganglof, and Hugo Acevedo allowed me to spend almost two years culling through that library's special collections. Colleagues at the Centro de Estudios de la Moda, National Fine Arts Museum, the National History Museum, the Brigadier General Cornelio de Saavedra Historical Museum, the Mitre Museum, and the Police Museum were extremely helpful in locating documents and additional sources. Ricardo Rodríguez Molas and Eugenio Rohm generously lent me materials from their personal libraries. Natalia Kohen graciously opened her home so that I might study firsthand many of the nineteenth-century fashion lithographs discussed in this book. Isidoro Blaisten, Claudia Kohen, and Eduardo Paz Leston brought me into an intriguing discussion on Romanticism and nation-building.

Support from the J. William Fulbright Foreign Scholarship Board made it possible to work with colleagues at the University of Buenos Aires Schools of Architecture, Design, and Urban Planning, and Philosophy and Letters. Laura Novik and Carlos Macchi helped me understand the narrative of culture from the designer's perspective. Silvia Delfino, Jorge Panessi, Ariel Schettini, Silvia Tieffemberg, and David Viñas were hospitable and generous with their time and materials. I had the great fortune to visit historical sites of intrigue with Natalia and Flor Truchi, my Argentine sisters. The U.S. Information Agency granted me funds for travel to special collections in Córdoba. For all these experiences and many more, I am grateful to Norma González and Laura Moraña of the Argentine Fulbright Commission for their unwavering support of interdisciplinary collaborations and cultural exchange.

Over the years, my colleagues, students, and friends posed brilliant questions about material culture in the Americas that led me to several of the artifacts that inform this project. Several anonymous reviewers inspired connections that ultimately made this work all the stronger. Colleagues at the University of California at Berkeley and the College of William and Mary deserve special mention and heartfelt thanks. This project, which grew out of my doctoral dissertation, flourished with the support of Francine Masiello, Gwen Kirkpatrick, Antonio Cornejo Polar, Tulio Halperín Donghi, Josefina Ludmer, J. H. R. Polt, and Emilie Bergmann. The University of California Regents and the Lesley Byrd Simpson Fellowship funded initial stages of archival research. As I expanded the scope of this project, the Old Dominion University Research Foundation and the College of William and Mary Alumni Foundation, Wendy and Emery Reves Center for International Studies, and Department of Modern Languages and Literatures offered additional support.

Many others offered inspiring words or guidance that helped shape this book: Néstor Aúza, Catherine Barrera, Arnold Bauer, Ksenija Bilbija, Judith Ewell, Fabricio Forastelli, Elizabeth Garrels, Nancy Hanway, June Henderson, Luisa Igloria, Yasushi Ishii, William Katra, Sharon Larisch, Christopher Larkosh, Felicitas Luna, Seth Meisel, Jorge Meyers, Sujata Moorti, Lía Munilla Lacasa, Elías Palti, Isabel Quintana, Rubén Quintana, Kathleen Ross, Silvina Sazunic, Diana Sorensen, Mary Beth Tierney-Tello, Barbara Weissberger, and Enrique Yepes. Contemporary artists María Silvia Corcuera Terán and Enrique Breccia and designer Flavia Angriman generously allowed the reproduction of their works. Sara Gilmer and Sarah Smith, alumnae of the College of William and Mary who traveled with me to Argentina under the auspices of a Jack L. Borgenicht Identity and Transformation Grant in 2004, kindly provided two contributions to the kaleidoscope of urban images that the Epilogue seeks to represent. Michael Blum assisted with the preparation of images for publication. Richard Morrison has been a most thoughtful and compassionate editor. He and his team at the University of Minnesota Press demonstrate a kind professionalism that is not easily matched. Adam Brunner offered encouraging words and helped me secure permission requests. Dawn Stahl and Nancy Sauro edited the manuscript with great care. Two anonymous reviewers for the Press, to whom I am greatly indebted, offered important advice that helped expand significantly the depth and scope of *Couture and Consensus*. I am also grateful for the kind words and unparalleled vision of series editors Juan Flores, Jean Franco, and George Yúdice.

My family, friends, and neighbors have given new meaning to the phrase "it takes a village." David provided great moral support. Audrey, coloring by my side as I wrote most of these pages, gleefully pronounced that a tortoise like me would one day finish the race.

A journey completed inevitably reminds us of a path not realized. This book is dedicated to my father, the late James R. McDuffie, whose life was taken unexpectedly in 2006. The son of sharecroppers in rural Mississippi, he grew up in dire poverty, served valiantly in the Korean conflict, and became the first in his family to attend college. Believing in the power of education to transform lives and avert war, he became a lifelong educator who instilled in me the importance of learning, community, and global citizenship. I believe he would have taken great pleasure in seeing this book in print.

Finally, I acknowledge you, the reader, for all the connections and conversations you are sure to inspire.

Interrogating Fashion

A T THE HEIGHT OF THE PROTESTS in economically devastated Argentina, on December 20, 2001, several prominent authors waited in front of television cameras at the Clásica y Moderna bookstore in Buenos Aires for a special cultural event organized by the Secretaría de Cultura de la Nación and the Cámara Argentina del Libro. For weeks, television advertisements had promoted a "buy one book and get the next free" offer alongside the opportunity to meet with the country's most celebrated authors. As *La Nación* would report, not one reader showed up.[1] The authors, who included Federico Andahazi, Juan Forn, Dalmiro Sáenz, Leopoldo Brizuela, Miguel Vitagliano, and Carlos Gamerro, initiated an impromptu talk on their country's political ills. Before reporters, the group quickly came to a consensus: The history of Argentina seemed to have the structure of a *folletín,* a novel in episodes, with a plot that unfolds slowly, chapter by chapter, leaving its reader in suspense and, at times, in despair. "One cannot foretell anything. You have to go chapter by chapter. May we one day know the whole story," they agreed.

The choice of the word *folletín* to describe Argentine history was certainly an interesting one. As a nineteenth-century term, it brings to mind the antiquated custom of the reader who laboriously cut, assembled, and bound together a narrative from the serialized sections of a favorite newspaper or magazine. *Folletín* also recalls the very forum in which many of the guiding fictions of the region appeared, such as the masterpiece by one intellectual who would become an Argentine president, Domingo Faustino Sarmiento, first translated into English as *Life in the Argentine Republic in the Days of Tyrants, or Civilization and Barbarism*.[2] Like other guiding fictions from Argentina, this study of the tyrannical practices of the military caudillo appropriated the vocabulary of color and fashion to shed light on the psychology of civil war in the River Plate region following independence from Spain. In this work, crimson, then a legalized color, and the gaucho's indigenous poncho represented the barbarians whose brute military force pushed open the gates of power and then proceeded to destroy the political opposition. The appearance of European-style clothing, in turn, represented the persecuted and more "civilized" minority who, like Sarmiento, initiated a struggle that was *against* dictatorship yet *for* interpretive supremacy.[3] In the pages of the guiding fictions, the nineteenth-century reader found the very fragments that spoke to the heart of national constitution—however elusive those goals might have seemed at the time—and proceeded to collect and order them in some logical fashion. Responding to debates already in the realm of popular culture and helping foster patriotic sentiments, these at times contradictory and tension-filled fragments reflected on questions of national identity and worked to unite readers in a kind of consensus-building endeavor.

Back at the Clásica y Moderna bookstore, a chapter continued to unfold. Expressing their solidarity with the protesters who risked their lives in the streets of Buenos Aires and before the Casa Rosada,[4] the authors admitted to feeling torn about producing and attempting to sell their work at a time of crisis. "If someone comes to loot books," Juan Forn reportedly said, "I will tell them to take one of mine and not one by Isabel Allende." Carlos Gamerro was deeply concerned: "The problem will be if the reports present a montage of images of the country being torn apart with intercalated ones of a few writers chatting passively in a bookstore. And that would be a complete fabrication. We are not in an ivory tower." In reference to the authors' discussion, *La Nación* would add a subtitle to contextualize these fears. It recalled a Peronist slogan, "Alpargatas sí, libros no" (Yes to espadrilles, no to books), that sought to undermine intellectual pursuits by privileging working-class interests—as evidenced by the espadrilles and overalls flaunted by the masses. In the 1940s and 1950s, during the first wave of Peronism, mobilized workers often sported "bizarre costumes," writes Daniel James, "in settings other than the workplace or the barrio." Some identified the *gente bien* (the well-to-do) by mocking their fashionable clothing and hairstyles.[5] Although gathered at the bookstore of choice for intellectuals and many a *gente bien,* the authors at this media event clearly sided with the voices of the Argentine people on December 20, 2001, who demanded accountability from their political leaders in the wake of massive corruption and economic devastation.

Dalmiro Sáenz, who signed only one copy of his *Yo te odio, político* (I hate you, politician) that day, would argue that Argentine politicians have long preoccupied themselves with image-making apparel rather than the interests of their constituents. In the 1980s, Carlos Menem, the Peronist president who first sported sideburns and ponchos to appeal to the working classes, claimed to represent the interests of all citizens. His government policies over the next ten years favored overwhelmingly the Washington Consensus, especially when it came to privatizing for economic development. It was not long before Menem moved to tailored Versace suits and boasted higher cheekbones and a surgically moved hairline.[6] In 1999, at the brink of the twenty-first century, Fernando de la Rúa had won over people by wearing conservative suits, which eventually came to represent a passive stance in the face of chaos. In response to Argentina's political crisis, Sáenz engaged a word play with *vestidura* (clothing) and *investidura* (investiture):

> Until now, the transfer in power seemed only to have occurred at the level of "dress." We came from well-cut and iridescent Versace suits and went on to dark and sober suits made by hand by an untiring tailor who conserves in his notebooks the stable and proportionate measurements of a trusted client, right down to his bodily contours.[7]

Formal investiture in Argentina is often equated with the presentation of a presidential sash—its light blue and white stripes as a backdrop for a yellow sun—and a gold cane uniquely fashioned for each president. The crisis of December 2001, however, led to a succession of four interim presidents after the resignation of La Rúa. Citizens at large, accustomed with the tailored suits of politicians and bankers, began to regard "status" clothing in Argentina with suspicion. This kind of representation was not new. Argentine politicians had long been represented as "parasites of their clothes" at previous historical junctures, as when Ezequiel Martínez Estrada observed that they needed to dress better than those citizens who ordinarily wore their Sunday best in the business district. Dress, he believed, "should be in accord with one's economic state and his manner of thinking; it should not merely keep pace with other dresses."[8] Martínez Estrada's particular view of the heart of Buenos Aires's banking district, with the British department store Harrod's situated along its pedestrian mall on Calle Florida, seemed almost fetishistic. These same places, where luxury items are sold, have since become emotionally charged symbols of excess that hammer-brandishing protestors destroyed and looted during the recent economic crisis after banking institutions converted and dissolved their life savings.

If dress had always been implicated in the project of national politics, how would one interpret its signs during crisis? In the 1990s, an angry song titled "Martín Fierro está furioso" (Martín Fierro is furious) surfaced on the Internet and linked, in rhyme, the poncho-clad gaucho and the average Argentine citizen suffering from economic hardship in an insolvent debtor nation: Rather than facing the threat of forced military conscription, the contemporary version of the gaucho now found himself the victim of banks, the International Monetary Fund (IMF), and slick political figures who had long abandoned their country's ideals.[9] In this context, the politician's clothes reflected allegiances to those forces blamed for the political and economic disenfranchisement of others. Although European styles had once announced revolution during a period of nation-building, those who now dared don such clothing went against the trend. As sectors of the population focused on the reversal of neoliberal slogans and objectives, and a shift in the representation of the working classes now highlighted *piqueteros* rather than *descamisados*,[10] the urban billboard fiction of luxurious consumption appeared to corrode. Perhaps like the nineteenth-century authors of the *folletín,* Sáenz imagined an Argentine body politic obsessed with appearances and projected an

image of limitation and political incompetence. The crimson cover of
Yo te odio, político further evoked the coded signs of dress in the nineteenth century and the aggressive waves of civil unrest that would follow Argentine independence.

At a time when Argentines are reassessing the "fracturing of memory" that makes up the present-day process of national reconstitution,
artists and authors have appropriated the historical vocabulary of color
and fashion to reformulate the tenets of collective identity. Fashion,
after all, can provide powerful visual and narrative force within which
to place the body politic. As a profoundly social process, fashion invites individual and collective bodies to assume certain identities and,
at times, to transgress its limits. Turning to the dynamics of couture
and consensus, some contemporary artists have asked their public to
take on the wounds of Argentina's past, in particular the plight of the
"disappeared" and the collective pain of human rights violations and
abuses from the Dirty War that targeted its own citizens (1976–83).
The "disappeared" refer to the 30,000 people who the military regime
labeled as subversives, kidnapped, and then executed, with little to no
details left behind of their whereabouts.[11] Fashioning works from ink,
paper, wood, string, rusted nails, and other found materials, visual artists have recovered the dignity of the human subject when transforming postcolonial fashion icons into symbols for human rights issues.

During the transition to democracy in Argentina, María Silvia
Corcuera Terán located the politics of memory in national forms of
dress when she began to register artistically the dynamics of active
memory, collective identity, and everyday life in her native Buenos
Aires. She challenged the politics of seduction that characterized the
neoliberal period when she began to incorporate in her work one
forgotten cultural icon in particular, the exuberant *peinetón*. Worn by
women of the 1820s and 1830s to distance themselves visually from the
customs of Spain, this comb of one meter in height and length quickly
emerged as a site of resistance in the annals of popular poetry and the
press. As part of the independence movement, it became an accessory
that women used to assert their presences in public, a kind of fashionable statement against the political vanity of nineteenth-century male
leaders who had fought Spanish oppression but then denied women

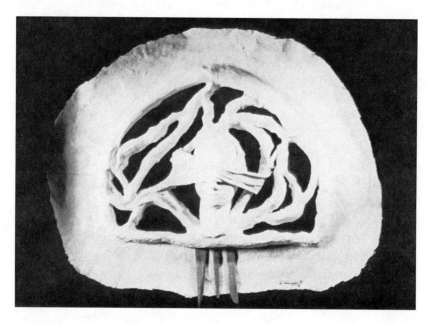

María Silvia Corcuera Terán, *Peinetón,* 1993. Paper, cloth, wood; 1.10 x 0.90 x 0.19 meters.
Exhibited at Centro Cultural Borges, Buenos Aires, Argentina, 1997. Courtesy of the artist.

their emancipation. In the 1990s, at a time when magazines like *Gente* (People) or *Caras* (Faces) showcased the exuberant lifestyles of the rich and famous, Corcuera Terán deliberately used this icon from the past to expose the nation's dead, its migrations, and unresolved conflicts. "Art," as the artist attributes to Jorge Luis Borges, "should be the mirror that reveals to us our own face." Her 1998 exhibition titled "Voluntad de desmesura" (Desire for excess) presented blindfolded female subjects embedded within the frames of combs with nail-like teeth. Corcuera Terán imagined one possible relationship with the viewer of the works, hoping to encourage her fellow compatriots to wear the past and thereby initiate a collective healing process: "Put it on. It hurts you and it hurts me. If I feel pain, so do you."[12] Several years later, Corcuera Terán has inverted the comb, creating a cityscape with arches and teeth that represent vessels bringing immigrants to the port of Buenos Aires at the turn of the nineteenth century or totemic towers that ascend toward the sky from the forces of global migration below. The use of menacing colors, forty hues of red in the case of one sculpture, ground her most recent works in the foundational tensions on which the Argentine collective identity often rests: the elitist ideals of city dwellers and the populist forces from the countryside that first made themselves apparent during the regime of Juan Manuel de Rosas (1829–52). To capture the subtleties of Corcuera Terán's work, one gazes as if to examine the layers of a sacred garment: The viewer must piece together the fragments of historical memory and contemplate the cultural imaginings that may have survived.

In Ricardo Piglia's *La Argentina en pedazos* (Argentina in pieces), the comic art of Enrique Breccia represents the violence of tyranny through the visual portrayal of a gentleman in European styles overtaken by crimson-clad gauchos. Piglia, who assembled this volume of artistic renditions of Argentine literary classics in 1993, began the work with Breccia's vision of a haunting tale set in the Rosas period, "The Slaughterhouse."[13] Throughout this rearticulation of horror, Breccia uses black ink and a combination of thin and choppy lines to narrate the civil conflicts of an emerging Argentina. The artist presents the butchers in uniforms, whereas he outlines the appearance of the revolutionary Unitarian as if to indicate a hollow figure objectified by the degrading slurs of onlookers and the gaze of the contemporary reader. The illustrations of competing dress practices are indeed politically charged and meaningful. The reader of this comic art finds the force of color only in the words used by a crowd that manifests its support of authoritarianism, fashion ultimately becoming like the kind of defiant statement made by those protesting dictatorships in the 1970s and 1980s, when men risked long hair and women short skirts to defy prevailing dress codes. This contemporary vision of the slaughterhouse, in which the victim's traces are sketched with lines and somber shadows, presents a kind of colorless epitaph, not unlike those black and white photographs carried by the Asociación Madres de Plaza de Mayo (Mothers of the Plaza de Mayo) to commemorate their loved ones who disappeared at the hands of repressive regimes. Through an exploration of dress, subjectivity, and difference, Breccia remembers.

With this fusion of couture and consensus at the heart of national politics, it should not surprise us that historical fiction, and particularly revisionist histories that detail the dress and habits of the

Enrique Breccia, sequence from *El matadero,* 1993. Paper and black ink. Originally created for *La Argentina en Pedazos,* ed. Ricardo Piglia (Buenos Aires: Ediciones de la Urraca), this was published as the companion illustration to Esteban Echeverría's foundational text of the same title. Courtesy of the artist.

postcolonial period, line the shelves of Argentine bookstores. A panel on "Rearticulations: Contemporary Argentine Culture and the Politics of Memory" at the 2001 Latin American Studies Association posited that the effects of collective silencing during the Dirty War made it very difficult for the public to explore the dynamics of active memory in a purely twentieth-century context.[14] It was as if "Argentines continue to refer to their national dilemma through a narrative desire for an all-encompassing history," writes Francine Masiello.[15] Luis Roniger affirms in another context: "It was insisted that these events be placed in the context of previous periods, related even to the founding moments of these societies. The European conquest, the colonial period, the struggle for independence, the ensuing civil wars and the processes of modernization, all could be questioned in terms of their connections to a particular pattern of social formation and shaping of collective identity."[16] Contemporary representations of postcolonial dress reveal similar conflicts, as the historical object embodies a realm of the collective imaginary still in the process of being recovered and articulated. Collective memory, as Susana Rotker reminds us, serves as a tool that obliges us "to conform to the configurations of the present."[17] Reconfigurations of historical fashion can register failures and betrayals, as do the representations of styles used to denote absence in the poetry of Néstor Perlongher[18] or the fragmented chronology of an infant's rose-colored garment that surfaces and disappears throughout a novella by César Aira.[19] On the other hand, rearticulations can also evoke hope and elicit change, as do the postcolonial accessories converted into brightly colored pull toys by Corcuera Terán or the kaleidoscopic views of dress and Argentine cultural identity as exhibited at the Museo de Arte Latinoamericano de Buenos Aires (MALBA). As scholars of many disciplines unravel the political history of fashion in the Americas, we might find that dress has always been intimately connected to the workings of culture, identity formation, and social change.[20] The multivalent characteristics of dress in Argentina certainly reflect larger cultural processes at work.

Material culture in Latin America has long been the domain of archeologists, Arnold Bauer writes, even though it also refers "to the creation of more well-known items such as haute couture or cluster bombs."[21] Although archeologists have unearthed many fragments of cultural significance, Bauer believes that scholars have been "less successful in interpreting their meaning because there is a limit to the knowledge that can be squeezed from stones."[22] Furthermore, possessions that might have been significant to households in centuries past are rarely found in excavations, such as wood and cloth.[23] In situating the material culture of Latin America, Ross Jamieson encourages scholars to question consistently their interpretations: What one finds in the rear of the house, for example, may not necessarily have been hidden or discarded.[24] Yet other objects may never have been registered in a will or other probate matter because the period did not deem them of significant value. Regardless of such tangible pitfalls, Bauer and Jamieson confirm that material culture in Latin America was an integral part of human agency and that individuals defined their identities and at times redefined their role in society with their possessions.[25]

These same aspects of "agency, practice and performance" have yet to be unraveled fully in the context of Latin American fashion studies.[26] In *The Latin American Fashion Reader,* an international group of scholars discovered that fashion in this world culture region is a cultural process in which individual and collective bodies assume, alter, and transgress certain identities. To appreciate fashion's transformative qualities, one must remember that the concept itself is grounded in particular social frameworks that are temporal, sensory, and spatial in nature. Many theoretical paradigms in cultural studies have neglected these facts until only recently, having treated clothing as an "accessory in symbolic, structural or semiotic explanations"[27] rather than acknowledging the meaning it generates. As Karen Tranberg Hansen explains in her insightful review of global fashion scholarship, clothing and other aspects of material culture are emerging as significant objects of critical inquiry despite complicated disciplinary distinctions.[28] Often these complications arise because our research on fashion also registers the invisible sides of a garment, such as the terms of its production, sale, use, circulation, and disposal.

Fashion is often situated in discourses that circulate as a "general social institution"[29] and that impact individuals and their communities. This is a somewhat fortunate circumstance in the context of postcolonial Argentina: Although samples of cloth and garments are not generally available, discursive registers abound in the archives that can help shape our interpretations. A scholar may access quite readily the variances in contemporary dress; samples from the nineteenth century, however, are rare. For this reason, Susana Saulquin asserts that it will never be possible to ascertain a full register of historical styles in Argentina. She points to the existence of only one nineteenth-century dress in the collection of the Historical Museum of the City of Buenos Aires. This dress belonged to Remedios Escalada de San Martín, the wife of independence leader General José de San Martín, and apparently was the only garment in her possession that was not burned when she died.[30] To construct a more comprehensive history of postcolonial material culture in Argentina, scholars must rely on the printed word to reconstruct more fully the history of dress, culture, and identity. Portraits certainly give us some sense of what might have been worn and under what circumstances. Fashionable images, however, tended to emphasize the opulence of the upper classes in urban areas and do not necessarily represent those social and political identities documented in fashion writing, political pamphlets, advertisements, song, and other forms of popular culture.

Couture and Consensus examines a pivotal moment in Argentina's nation-building project through the lens of fashion and political culture. When one culls the archives for materials related to the nation-building process, it quickly becomes clear that Benedict Anderson's theoretical outline of the nation as a limited, sovereign, and horizontal comradeship[31] does not address sufficiently the tensions—in particular, the sexual and racial exclusions—that linked future citizens of Spanish American nation-states to a new historical consciousness.[32] The "socialized image of the national community," as Antonio Cornejo Polar proposed in his analysis of proclamations for Peruvian independence and other founding fictions, often presented the terms of national identity without acknowledging the heterogeneous basis of the new nation.[33] In most cases, postcolonial school textbooks projected "the new world that Columbus gave us,"[34] thereby integrating the colonial past into a narrative of heroic deeds that promoted the values of a "strong" national identity based on the domination of others. Thomas C. Holt emphasizes that the nation was more than the creation of any one particular shared identity; it remains part of a consensus-building process that is constantly reimagined.[35] In terms of cultural production, a "creative outlook" emerged from the instability that accompanied independence.[36] Following these perspectives on cultural practice in the Americas, *Couture and Consensus* argues that dress served as a critical expression of political agency and citizenship during the struggle to forge the Argentine nation.

In postcolonial Argentina, fashion engaged a battlefield of signifiers. The dress of young, nation-building patriots distanced political subjects from the relics of Spanish colonialism, a period when dress served as a visual register that complemented the caste system and its notions of European privilege and construction of cultural, racial, and ethnic differences.[37] Under the colonial system, Creole descendants of Europeans had been designated inferior social status, although some boldly dared to appropriate subtle details to imitate their Spanish superiors.[38] As tensions mounted, Creoles moved to anti-Spanish styles that symbolized the legacy of "Liberty, Equality, and Fraternity" espoused by the French Revolution and advocated a society based on merit rather than inherited privilege. Creole leaders such as San Martín designed American uniforms for troops.[39] Dress represented emerging political interests that would play a significant role in shaping the future Argentine nation; in fact, fashion appears to have reflected uniquely national concerns long before any consolidation process had been enacted. Even the rhetoric of fashion served as a forum through which to engage the configuration of a national identity.

Carlos Morel, *Carga de caballería del ejército federal* (The Confederate army's cavalry in combat), ca. 1839. Oil on canvas; 44.5 x 53.5 centimeters. Courtesy of Museo Nacional de Bellas Artes, Buenos Aires, Argentina.

At a time when the political panorama found itself divided between two tendencies, the Unitarians and the Federalists, individual appearances identified particular affiliations. Led by the intellectual elite of Buenos Aires, the Unitarians were progressive, European-centered, and liberal. Noted for their tailored French suits, Unitarian colors incorporated light blue and white, reminders of the flag of independence from Spain, and much later, hues of green. From 1824 to 1827, the Unitarians had a brief stay in power under President Bernadino de Rivadavia, who established Buenos Aires as the capital of Argentina to overcome growing tensions over the annexation of territory in today's Uruguay. The provinces revolted, and civil strife quickly ensued outside Buenos Aires. William Katra identifies these tensions appropriately as the great paradox of the Rioplatense revolution, when "the oligarchic and aristocratic spirit of the Europeanized and educated forces of the city embraced liberalism as the ideological basis for their struggle, while they were opposed by the radically democratic spirit of the autochthonous, rustic masses of the countryside."[40] In an attempt to install order, an interim government supported the rise to power of Federalist Rosas, who had the support of caudillos from the country's interior and some landowners based in Buenos Aires. According to John Lynch, Rosas had served as an ammunition boy during the British invasion of 1806, worked on the estancia of his parents during the May Revolution of 1810, and rose to economic power as a cattle baron whose growing business partnership in the pampas exported jerked beef to slave markets in Brazil and Cuba.[41] As the self-professed "Restorer of the Laws," Rosas ruled the Argentine Confederation from Buenos Aires between 1829 and 1852.

Shortly after assuming power, Rosas legalized a civilian uniform in the province of Buenos Aires, with severe penalties for those who did not follow such mandates. On February 3, 1832, a decree legalized crimson as the national color of faith in the Federation. This happened at a time when "the percentages of men who wore the traditional ponchos and *chiripás* [gaucho dress trousers worn over pantaloons] and of women dressed in coarse cotton and woolen clothes increased in step with the concentric regions radiating outward from the Plaza de Mayo and its immediate vicinity."[42] In a violent push toward homogeneity, authorities of the Confederation prohibited the light blue and green hues of Unitarian factions. Unsure of the hostile political climate, some men resorted to conveying opinions and political messages secretly, placing their ideas on round cards within their top hats, which they extended to one another when taking a salutatory bow.[43] The ebbs and flows of civil war continued until Rosas was deposed in 1852, when the Unitarians finally defeated the Federalists at the Battle of Caseros.

This book initiates its exploration of postcolonial fashion and political culture with a chapter on establishing consensus. Using poetry chapbooks, police records, and other sources of political intrigue revealed in the archives, "Uniform Consensus" documents the theatrical nature of conformity and rebellion following independence. As a sign that "stands still," the postcolonial uniform affirmed hierarchies as much as it allowed regime authorities to police the society at large. Rosas legislated an obligatory crimson insignia that organized citizens under the tenets of a Confederation. As the regime sought to strengthen and maintain its power base, popular culture projected a unified Federal family cloaked with the accessories of war. Descriptions of civilian uniform further politicized the transactions of daily life, promoting a warrior prototype whose dominance relied on stereotypes of male aggression and female passivity. In multiple contexts, the Confederation subjugated an effeminate Unitarian body to its power. Because this sexualized dichotomy of war threatened to overshadow the contributions of other marginalized sectors, and especially women, the Rosas regime astutely appropriated popular female voices to inspire complicity with its political goals. For this reason, the next chapter analyzes the evolution of "beautiful roles" during the early years of the nation-building process.

"Dressed to Kill" details representations of women called on to participate actively in the war effort and whose significance in the independence process has often been overlooked. Many nameless women pieced together uniforms of coarse linen for the battlefield and, in a few cases, assumed the uniforms themselves. Although the ideals of Republican motherhood afforded new roles to women, in particular the raising of future patriots, the idea of female political subjectivity threatened political hierarchies. The Rosas regime depended on a cult of male leadership, with the caudillo as the ultimate authority figure. Any notion of female agency was thereby subservient to male power and subject to manipulation. Material culture emphasized this relationship. Popular literature suggested that women should attract and mobilize others—men, that is—to support the Confederate cause. While this emphasis initially granted some sectors, most notably African Argentine women, more visibility and hinted at their political inclusion, I argue that the romanticization of subservience to the regime—and the identification of all who did not conform to such service as Unitarians—ultimately represented women as beautiful "possessions" dominated by male authorities. Any potential for female political agency was quickly contested by the practices of sexual and sometimes racial exclusion.

The third chapter, "Fashion as Presence," sheds light on the practice of exaggerated head dressing through an examination of its relationship to debates on the status of women and the limits of citizenship. Following independence, women of the River Plate region began to wear horizontally elongated hair combs to distance themselves from those who wore the vertical Spanish mantilla. During the Rosas period, these combs grew into elaborate three-foot-square accessories that fashionable women used to obstruct the very public sphere in which men professed the goals of independence without granting all inhabitants the privilege of citizenship. My research in the archives reveals that the *peinetón* became a metonym for the politically engaged woman. The representation of active presence in the streets of Buenos Aires, however, became the subject of satirical caricatures that undermined the potential of women's political participation. Appropriating fashion as metonymy to bar women from access to critical public events, popular culture reminded women that their fashionable crowns granted them reign over only their domestic obligations. Until recently, most historical references to the comb seemed like brief, identity-inspired quotations in a sea of trends, as when *Vogue* appropriated it to evoke the spirit of Buenos Aires when marketing the fashions of French designer Jean Paul Gaultier.[44] This unique headdress has also been the subject of exhibitions that attract large numbers of museum visitors; the Argentine Ministry of Culture has initiated an online catalogue of material culture that registers those samples that have survived the test of time.[45] Some artistic allusions to the *peinetón,* for example, in the works of Corcuera Terán or in the short stories of Eduardo Gudiño Kieffer,[46] further link this fragment of postcolonial material culture to the charged legacies of authoritarianism. "Fashion as Presence" locates and examines the historical conditions that helped create and shape the emblematic and politically significant Argentine headdress.

To regain control of the body politic, the forces of philosophical enlightenment in postcolonial Argentina responded through the unlikely forum of "Fashion Writing," also the title of the third chapter. In an environment of extreme political repression, the rhetoric of fashion served to disseminate radical political agendas. A group of intellectuals known as the Association of the Young Argentine Generation founded a fashion magazine titled *La Moda* (Fashion) after the audacious *La Mode* that had served as a force of violent opposition in revolutionary France.

Realizing that few associated fashion writing with politics and using female pseudonyms to disguise their identities, many of these future founding fathers of the Argentine nation risked their lives when asserting urban, democratic ideals. At this same time, women writers turned to fashion writing to establish a public space in which they could exercise more control over the perception of gender. "Ladies and gentlemen," a group of writers urged in 1830, "if men shield their identities when writing, we women should manifest ourselves."[47] Through fashionable representations of urban solidarity, women writers responded bravely to the ill-fitting constructions of masculinity and femininity as proscribed by the regime and dictated by society at large. Fashion writing was, quite literally, tailoring the political landscape, a concept that still predominates in contemporary Argentine fashion magazines, although the political realities addressed have changed. Ana Torrejón, the editor of *Elle* (Argentina), believes that the fashion magazine is still "good dressing with which to relay to women their rights and to show how they might tell their story."[48] Even in the era of globalization, when styles travel broadly and most Argentines dress as do the inhabitants of any other major urban area of the world, fashion continues to project new voices and agendas.

By the end of the nineteenth century, economic booms helped Buenos Aires earn the reputation of the "Paris of South America." The cityscape was transformed into an allusion of luxury, consumerism, and international capitalism. Newspaper chronicles "decorated the city" with a literary "make-up" or "window dressing" that covered the fragmented and heterogeneous nature of urban life, Julio Ramos writes.[49] With the massive influx of European immigrants to Buenos Aires, luxury took on a fraudulent role. To blend in and find work, members of the nouveau riche and new arrivals began to imitate the styles of the upper classes. With the emergence of the fashion lithograph, modistes copied European designs and then commissioned seamstresses who, enduring miserable working conditions, pieced garments together with the help of sewing machines. As sewing machines became more affordable, many women opted to purchase ready-made clothing or to fashion their own, more comfortable, styles at home. Encouraging readers to consider individualized designs and the prospect of female emancipation, women authors used the language of fantasy and self-transformation to enter a public debate on materialism and female economic autonomy. The final chapter, "Searching for Female Emancipation," details the liberating qualities of fashion at a moment of national reorganization and modernization. Popular magazines authored by women had long used images of beauty and fashion to reflect on the restrictive nature of their social roles. *Oasis en la vida,* a best-selling novel by Juana Manuela Gorriti, initiated a unique discussion that inspired alternative designs for the social fabric. As Argentina's first professional female author, Gorriti posed a question in the fashion magazine she edited, *La Alborada del Plata* (Dawn of the River Plate), a few years prior to her novel's publication: In women's daily lives, what constituted the oasis in life? Her magazine's columns revealed a diverse set of answers to this question, encouraging female readers to approach, think about, and experience life from multiple perspectives. Like Gorriti's book on the *Cocina ecléctica* (Eclectic kitchen) published in 1890, which helped establish networks among Spanish-speaking women throughout Latin American through the compilation of favorite recipes, fashion columns enlisted women to forge a pan-American enterprise that would lead to expanded rights and the goal of citizenship. Toward the end of the nineteenth century, the fashion narratives of María del Pilar Sinués de Marco, recognized as Spain's first professional female author, helped demystify the highly commercialized realm of fashion for middle-class women throughout Latin America. Best known for her early Christian conduct manuals, Sinués de Marco became a staunch defender of the professional rights of women authors and female autonomy. She was also well known in Argentina for her writings in *La Torre de Oro* (The golden tower), a fashion magazine that had its main offices in Sevilla, Spain, and Buenos Aires. The transatlantic approach to women's fashion suggests that the initial gap between Iberian and Argentine dress codes had waned. The lengthened bodices and uncorseted waists surfacing in urban areas revealed a more relaxed appearance and contrasted dramatically with the traditional dress of rural communities. Into the twentieth century, fashion writing continued to provide women with a unique forum from which to debate their domestic obligations and questions regarding their emancipation in an ever-expanding version of the public sphere.

At a time when digital images circulate in a flash, *Couture and Consensus* returns to the archival record to reassess the status of dress and political culture in postcolonial Argentina. The kaleidoscope of fashion consistently brings to light new interpretations for the field of cultural studies in the Americas. Given the speed with which scholars are often asked to publish their results, the process of this kind of recovery of material culture can seem painstakingly slow. Like the slow food or sustainable fashion movements, however, the interpretation of material culture begs us to slow down and ascertain the significance of artifacts and the larger cultural processes they reveal. Just like the museum conservator who, a few decades ago, discovered a crimson insignia hidden for the better part of a century during a restoration process that removed overpaint from the portrait of a prominent Argentine family,[50] the scholar of fashion studies turns to materials sometimes forgotten in dark and musty archives to recover and interpret remnants of cultural history.[51] Given the increasing value placed on the artifacts of everyday life, many libraries and museums have begun to reevaluate samples in their collections.[52] In Argentina, the mapping of dress and cultural expression will continue to entail a great deal of detective work, scholarly connections, and interdisciplinary collaborations. When I began researching *Couture and Consensus* in the 1990s, there were extremely few works documenting the cultural history of dress in Argentina, let alone Latin America. One can easily argue that this is still the case, although the field of fashion studies is increasingly aware of its skewed emphasis on the Western hemisphere and the historical omission of entire regions of world culture. This assessment of fashion and political culture aims to fill some of the gaps in our current knowledge of Argentine sartorial history. Piecing together the fragments of dress, *Couture and Consensus* carefully unfolds particular aspects of this sartorial history, chapter by chapter. May we one day know the whole story.

ONE

Uniform Consensus

I N THE POLITICAL ALLEGORY by Esteban Echeverría, "El matadero" ("The Slaughterhouse"), knife-wielding butchers reminiscent of some of Goya's more monstrous ghouls overpower an
elegantly dressed gentleman. Because of his European-style costume
and mannerisms, the young man is identified by a Federalist multitude as a Unitarian and is declared an enemy of the people. Under
the spell of religious fanaticism and patriotic fervor, Federalists prepare him for sacrifice. His well-groomed appearance contrasts with the
blood-stained rags of the spectators and the crimson uniforms worn
by Federalist soldiers. Restrained by his oppressors, the defenseless
body of the Unitarian is like a strip of territory that soldiers divide
into pieces. As a terrifying metaphor for the politics of an emerging
Argentina, the slaughterhouse functions as a kind of Confederate Hall
of Justice, the site at which a despotic system grants power to a truculent multitude.

In an instructive dispensation of law, a judge finds the Unitarian
guilty of political treachery. Why, the judge asks the gentleman, does
the accused not wear the Federalist crimson insignia? Such symbols
are not worn by free men, the Unitarian replies. Why does he not don
the black ribbon on his hat in a display of grief for Doña Encarnación,
Rosas's deceased wife? He wears his badge on his heart, he boldly declares, to mourn for the nation that Rosas has killed.[1] Having violated all
dress codes in order to express dissent, the Unitarian soon finds himself

forcibly shaved "a la federala," a ritualized act carried out by secret police at the time when authorities prohibited pear-shaped or closed beards, as they recalled the letter *U* for Unitarian. Through contrasting descriptions of uniform and dress, Echeverría wages the strongest accusation against the brutal methods employed by Federalist sympathizers to silence the opposition.

Revealing to us the precarious nature of power, this lesson from the past recalls the vocabulary of color and patriotic imagery that Echeverría's readers understood all too well. The portrayal of the harrowing scenes that took place alongside the emergence of identity politics in the Argentine confederation posited the cooked against the raw, the elite against the masses, civilization against barbarism.[2] Contemplating this framing of dress, subjectivity and national identity, the early twenty-first-century reader cannot help but connect the violence of this foundational text to more recent historical contexts. Written between 1838 and 1840, "The Slaughterhouse" was not published until 1874. Echeverría's first words imply that his historical narrative rejected the traditional framework of colonial history, or any chronology that began with the genealogical claims of Spanish colonizers. Understanding that authors and statesmen lacked basic historical data, as Doris Sommer suggests in another context, emerging national cultures projected their consolidation through fiction. "The Slaughterhouse" can thus be regarded as a kind of genesis of Argentine fiction, despite the fact that this political allegory was not assigned a fictional genre until the 1950s.[3] Following the human rights violations of the second half of the twentieth century, such as those committed during Argentina's Dirty War, in which tens of thousands of people "disappeared" in the late 1970s and 1980s (that is, were forcibly taken from their homes or places of work and tortured and/or killed), a return to this early imagining of Argentina reveals a nationalism grounded in the paradoxical opposition between the individual and the other, between civilized citizens and unruly barbarians.[4]

Echeverría's work also revealed the critical role attributed to fashion in the building of consensus following independence. Under the Rosas regime, one's grooming and overall appearance provided symbolic ammunition for the formation of local opinions and apparently national customs that emphasized rural values and Federalist policies.

Lawful male citizens wore crimson vests and insignias.[5] Cerulean blue, the color of independence and a recognized symbol of Unitarian partisanship, was shunned. Women incorporated hues of red and pink into their wardrobes—from ribbons in the hair to embroidered roses garnishing elegant dresses. Hoping to avoid public embarrassment and arrest, many Unitarians stopped wearing light blue altogether, purportedly turning to green, a symbol of hope. This color, too, became dangerously suspect, with Federalist soldiers even destroying green-colored objects in the homes of suspected Unitarians.

Since its creation, the uniform has enabled individuals to transform the power of their authority into the power of government. "Government would never have been possible had it not been for the invention of the uniform," argues Lawrence Langner.[6] In a similar fashion, it appears that the Argentine uniform developed alongside growing sentiments to unite the River Plate region into a nation. The Rosas regime instituted a crimson uniform to create an esprit de corps and foster a sense of belonging among all patriots. Federalist soldiers and civilians alike exalted the power of Rosas with this uniform, while relegating Unitarians to the margins. As this chapter shows, the depiction of patriotic dress in popular literature helped fashion a "Federal family," bringing to fore a familial configuration for the collective experience of nationhood decades before such a notion seemed possible. This Federal family perhaps even became the most prominent symbol of the *Santa Federación*.

Repeated enunciations of the uniform in traditional poetic forms, such as the simple, patriotic verse known as the *cielito patriótico,* further delineated Federalists from Unitarians. Many poems posited the masculine Federalist and his family opposite a feminized Unitarian. In this way, poetic dialogue created an imaginary public space in which to engage ideas on national identity and see them unfold. Patriotic verse functioned as a type of uniform when probing the vastness of Federal identity or engaging in simulated battle against the Unitarian opposition. In the realm of poetic representation, two kinds of bodies and uniform emerged. The desirable Federal body appeared shrouded in a poncho and scarlet insignia, exemplifying an obedient body easily prepared for war. The Unitarian body, on the other hand, represented sexual chaos and disease. Represented as effeminate and disorderly, the

Unitarian of patriotic poetry chapbooks was like the gentleman of "The Slaughterhouse" in the sense that he found himself subjugated to the power of the Federalist uniform.

In *Discipline and Punish,* Michel Foucault demonstrates how the uniform is an interpretation and an assignment of function, an ideological projection in which the body is broken down into parts to perform efficient acts of war. Assuming the uniform implies possessing a "bodily rhetoric of honor," an aspect of discipline that symbolically connects the body to the apparatus of power that oversees it. Foucault explains, "The individual body becomes an element that may be placed, moved, articulated on others. . . . The soldier is above all a fragment of mobile space, before he is courage or honour."[7] The soldier functions as a kind of synecdoche, or a part of a whole, his body organized strategically for the rigors of battle. Within this system of understanding, the uniform streamlines a soldier's identity and responds to precise historical contexts and even limitations.

The consolidated uniform of postcolonial Argentina faced several challenges, especially because its own fabrication depended on resources as basic as the availability of dyes and financing, both of which were scarce. Several soldiers in the battle for independence from Spain incorporated recycled fragments and accessories taken from the bodies of enemy casualties. The early war hero, therefore, maintained only the most basic of color codes adopted by his military superiors. On certain occasions, soldiers could opt for a more individualized approach. The veteran infantry of Buenos Aires, for instance, found itself in an unusual predicament in 1804 when the colors of the Spanish Army were unavailable. In response, the Marquis Rafael de Sobremonte ordered that soldiers don bright colors on their lapels and wear similar suits and hats. Thus, the first regional uniforms are likely to have varied quite drastically from person to person. Although subject to constant modification by military superiors, the early uniforms made known each soldier's private affiliations and bound him to service. The base for an Argentine military dress code is said to have emerged shortly after 1806, the first unsuccessful attempt by the British to invade the city of Buenos Aires. At this moment, citizen groups began to create militia units with unique styles, colors, and matching flags.[8] Units composed of Spanish soldiers appropriated the colors of the region of Spain to which its members belonged. Indian, mestizo, and black soldiers, who made up the largest artillery units, wore similarly patterned uniforms, distinguished only by the style of their hats and the colors of their jackets and sashes.[9]

Many historians credit Colonel San Martín with the design of the earliest Argentine uniform and its astute projections of social status. His narratives on the uniform, often a short list of adjectives and nouns detailing color and basic accessories, led to an institutionalized dress code as early as 1812. In a letter written in Buenos Aires and sent to General Antonio González Balcarce, he described the basis for the *Granadero* uniform.

> Plan for the uniform that the line-up squadron of Granaderos on horseback will use: Dress coat, padding, pants, cloak with sleeves, saddlebag, jacket, an all blue cap. Turned-up collar in rich crimson. White vest with knotted buttons. Helmet and strong spurs.[10]

As this description reveals, the early uniform fragmented the body of the soldier into many parts and left little room for individual expression. The clear-cut nature of San Martín's plan emphasized the readiness and strength of troops; he did not, however, detail the construction of any article. Their unity was instead left to the seamstress who would have worked collaboratively with other women to design what was required in battle, a topic addressed in the next chapter. The blue and crimson tones in San Martín's letter may have announced the symbols of rank on the battlefield, but they did not describe the actual style. In the end, dashing appearances matched the fighting abilities of soldiers.

Scholars have long studied the expressive qualities of color, from the Romantic sentiments captured by Goethe to the linguistic hierarchies proposed by Wittgenstein. Charged with meaning, the language of color reveals the emotive charges of an entire system of ideas. During the Rosas period, color separated visually the Federalists from the Unitarians on the battlefield and in daily life. As the struggle over the fate of power continued in the emerging republic, literary descriptions of the uniform marked affiliations and disclosed political ideals. Colors and styles that gained civilian recognition resonated in popular song and patriotic odes that told of the triumphs and losses of civil war.

Friar Cayetano Rodríguez (1761–1823) poetically recounts the successes of the Colorados del Monte (Red Soldiers of the Wild Country) in restoring public order, identifying them by the colors of their unique costume. Once Rosas emerged on the political scene in 1820, he had an established reputation as a military commander in the province of Buenos Aires. Subsequently, he was granted leadership of the Fifth Regiment, also known as the Colorados del Monte. Their guerilla-style warfare included attacks on property; soldiers avoided battle and, in the process, helped Rosas acquire more military power and land.[11] Rodríguez's sonnet, written the same year, became a popular tribute, sung to Rosas at several public celebrations.

> Soldiers of the South, brave heroes
> Dressed in crimson, purple and scarlet,
> Honorable American legion,
> Orderly and courageous squadrons.
>
> To the voice of the law your banners
> Triumphed with heroic feat
> Filling you with glories during the campaign
> And offering great lessons powerfully.
>
> Engrave forever in your hearts
> The memory and greatness of Rosas
> Who in restoring order informs you
>
> That the Province and its institutions
> Shall be saved if *law* is your enterprise
> And beautiful Liberty is your insignia.[12]

For many years, this sonnet circulated in loose sheet form and underwent a series of thematic transformations after Rosas took power in Buenos Aires, even aligning the colors of this regiment with the Santa Federación in the last verse: "*Confederation or death* as your insignia." With these changes, the term *Colorado* became synonymous for the Federalist soldier and his crimson uniform. Every detail—from the buttons to the carmine ribbons woven into the tails of red-haired horses—conveyed affiliation to the Argentine Confederation. As Foucault reminds us, "For the disciplined man, as for the true believer, no detail is unimportant, but not so much for the meaning that it conceals within it as for the hold it provides for the power that wishes to seize it."[13] With masculinity on parade, the regime created a sense of "strictly hierarchized and functionalizable collectivity."[14] In lieu of medals, soldiers received "lavish" land grants, ordinarily land confiscations of Unitarian properties, for their services.[15] Wherever rumors of dissent surfaced, Rosas reportedly dispatched a Colorado regiment to dispel the possibility. Newspapers also suggested that these uniforms aroused a great deal of attention from spectators, who lined up outside with curiosity and excitement to welcome the regiment into their neighborhood, perhaps intent on sighting a prisoner or witnessing protests.[16]

The camps that opposed Rosas sported attire in light blue and green tones, which symbolized liberty and hope, respectively, and which reputedly irritated Rosas.[17] Unitarian General José María Paz recounts the danger he ran when he inadvertently (and perhaps too innocently) wore green gloves to Rosas's house.[18] Arrested in 1831, Paz was taken to Buenos Aires in 1839, where he was allowed to walk the city freely provided that he not take arms or conspire against the regime. In his memoirs, Paz describes waiting in a courtyard for Rosas to receive him, suspecting that the dictator watches him, while hidden by a curtain, from an adjacent room, "I, who did not doubt this, tried to show the most complete indifference. As I paced with nonchalance, I played with my gloves held together with one hand. When my visit was over and Mr. Elizalde warned me that my gloves were of a dark green hue, he explained their inappropriateness and the danger I had faced. Even more, since it had already happened, we could remain calm but he advised me not to put this to the test again."[19] In this instance, General Paz likely used color to convey his defiance of the regime. While escaping the consequences at that particular moment, his memoirs acknowledged the severity of his actions. Color served as symbolic ammunition used by male political rivals for the purposes of psychological domination.

In his treatise on civilization and barbarism, Domingo Faustino Sarmiento's exploration of the tainted history of color in the Argentine Confederation exposes the undefined nature of the pampas as howling and wild. Sarmiento compares the crimson uniform of Federalist looters to eighteenth-century executioner's garb and Algerian flags.[20] He then extends this analysis to the Tartar-style reign of Facundo Quiroga, a local boss whose barbaric acts only Rosas seemed to surpass. In this hybrid historical text, crimson is the litmus test for loyalty to the Confederation, silencing all other visual territories. Sarmiento notes that the light blue and white flag of independence, which had experienced only minor changes since its creation in 1812 by Manuel Belgrano, had undergone significant transformations once Rosas's stay in power was reaffirmed in 1836. As Tulio Halperin Donghi explains, "The crusade against the color of the enemy did not even respect the national flag, that had its two sky-blue stripes replaced with two slate-blue ones."[21] A Federal cap had been woven into each corner of the flag and even the golden rays of the sun were now a deep red. Many responses to the change in the colors of the flag subsequently appeared in literary descriptions of the sky and the dichotomous presentation of stormy and peaceful weather.[22]

Juan María Gutiérrez reflected on the changed design of the flag in a series of images that appeared in poems that he published in 1841. "The Color Blue" exalted the beauty of cerulean blue as symbolic of the sky and sacred nation.[23] In "Scenes of the Mazorca," a group of women draped in the colors of independence stroll peacefully when the blood red uniforms of Federalist soldiers erupt from the landscape and disperse them.[24] "Rosas's Flag," another poem by Gutiérrez, evoked a similar palette for readers.

> The varied shades of color
> speak a mute and mysterious language;
> white speaks of affection,
> the chaste love of a virgin.
>
> Yellow interwoven with pink
> brings to light the doubt that disturbs the soul,
> and the light green of the airy palm
> kindly reveals a voluptuous hope.
>
> So it was that in the fights of the ring one day
> a floating troop of the steel breastplate
> sorrowful or loving words did say
>
> and the red emblem so slavishly respected
> fearfully disseminates the dementia of a tyrant,
> expressing blood that his hand has spilled.[25]

Through the mute world of color, Gutiérrez articulated the voice of hope and freedom. His sonnet began with an understated pattern of pale colors that symbolized more youthful and innocent times. The intermingling yellow and pink represented the emblem of war on the Confederate flag, which had promptly replaced its yellow rays from independence for red ones. The solid green of the swaying palm tree, growing from the battlefield, lifted one's gaze to the promise of a light blue sky.[26] This vertical, almost pious positioning of the gaze thus led the reader, albeit temporarily, from the earthly to the spiritual world or from the realm of Federal inhumanity to some transcendent ideal. The sharp edges of the final two strophes, which further dissected the national landscape, then gave way to a series of violent images depicting the cruelty of Rosas.

José Rivera Indarte charted the color of death under Rosas in his truculent *Tablas de sangre* (Bloody stalemate), an alphabetical outline of the names of guilty Federals and the gory details surrounding their victims' deaths. In these pages, Rivera Indarte accuses Rosas of incestuous behavior toward his daughter Manuelita and accuses both of serving salted prisoner ears at formal dinners. Furthermore, he accuses the Confederation's most fervent followers of vampirism. Fixing the association between the Colorado uniform and stains of blood, Rivera Indarte added to the appendix a manifesto-like corollary titled "Es acción santa matar a Rosas"(It is a saintly act to kill Rosas). Here he calls on the women of Buenos Aires, especially those willing to poison sharp sewing needles, to purge the mother country of Rosas: "Of all the women who Rosas insults and dishonors, and who penetrate his space, is there not one who in murdering him would like to make herself the heroine of our nation?"[27] Rivera Indarte then promises to erect a national monument in the potential female assassin's honor, proposing that she would be venerated almost religiously. Poets would never forget her, and orators speaking of national virtues would forever praise her.[28] Such patriotic musings did not bring to fore the type of female heroine imagined by Rivera Indarte. All the attempts on the lives of the Rosas family, ranging from poisonings to a time bomb disguised as a birthday gift for Manuelita, were promptly detected or detonated. The metaphoric space of the primer aimed to inspire unrest, imagining an end to the color-charged customs of Rosas and the Federalist family.

From very early on, the Argentine Confederation incorporated a civilian uniform into the rituals of daily life, encouraging allegiance to the regime's values. As evidenced in "The Slaughterhouse," strict dress codes mandated that all wear a crimson insignia regardless of gender, race, age, or social class. Without question, these codes exerted a great deal of influence over an individual's behavior and choices. The civilian uniform was in some sense the "homefront" of fashion, as it obscured the distinction made between plain clothes and the uniform. On February 3, 1832, a decree legalized crimson and declared it the national color of faith in the Federation.[29] The scarlet insignia served as a metonymical extension of the Federalist uniform for the "sons and daughters of the Confederation" and was strategically placed near the heart. Officials expelled professionals, like doctors and university professors, who did not place the insignia accordingly while performing their jobs. Even schoolchildren dared not remove their insignias.

The legalization of the uniform created a broad base of consumers that soon captured the attention of entrepreneurs. Although the insignia never underwent much alteration in design, updates to political slogans became a lucrative business. The insignia with the slogan "Confederation or Death!" became an almost obligatory purchase. Calvary guardsmen used emblems that pronounced "Long live the Fed-

Federal insignias from the last years of the Rosas regime. Each is 8 centimeters wide. Photograph by Felicitas Luna. Courtesy of Museo Histórico de Luján, Luján, Argentina.

erals! Death to the Savage Unitarians!" During the legalized period of mourning for the regime's first lady, one could easily find the addendum "Our illustrious Federal heroine Mrs. Encarnación Ezcurra de Rosas!"[30] Government authorities added similar slogans to official correspondence on pink paper: One can only imagine the eyebrows raised by mysterious splotches of blue ink such as those found on the papers housed in the Saavedra Museum.[31] Many pronouncements on insignias were quite similar to slogans recited by urban inhabitants throughout the day in schools, offices, and churches. Booksellers normally undertook the printing of the crimson ribbons that would grace most lapels, copying some slogans directly from the government documents they received for distribution. Like modern-day coolhunters, some booksellers appear to have been "on the lookout" for popular slogans celebrating Federal power. The writing of Benito Hortelano, a Spanish native living in Argentina, provides us with a unique insight into this enterprise and the increasingly fierce competition for customers. Shortly after the Confederation declared war against Brazil and a death sentence was issued for Unitarian General Justo José de Urquiza of Entre Ríos, popular refrains touted "Death to the crazy traitor, savage Unitarian Urquiza!" Hortelano rushed to create insignias for the celebrations that regime supporters were expected to organize in Buenos Aires.

> Having always had timely ideas, I read the new slogan and decided on a business venture. As always, I was an imbecile and let my partners participate. The idea was to print new insignias with *Die, Urquiza* on them that very night so that clients would rush to our store the next day. My partners, naturally, understood the importance of this idea and worked throughout the night—some taking to the printing plate, others to the advertising, and I left to buy all the ribbon that I could find in the dry goods store. At midnight I had compiled thousands of yards of ribbon and the press began to print these without pause.[32]

Although Rosas had not officially asked citizens to add this slogan to their insignias, the novelty sparked such interest that a long line of people waited impatiently outside Hortelano's bookstore the following day, determined to purchase their commemorative ribbons. Despite the popularity of new slogans, Hortelano's words also remind us of the fact that the materials needed to make these ribbons were not always readily available. This is partly because ribbon was a luxury item, as precious as silk, which made it all the more special when the regime began to distribute them through the provinces as special gifts from Rosas to the most faithful of the Confederation.[33]

The crimson insignia helped create a ready-made identity and, in a relatively brief period, projected a unifying ideology. In an attempt to thwart dissent, honorary civilian guards marched through streets and community plazas in crimson vests and with scarlet ribbons tied around their weapons. These patriots visually reminded the rest of the population of the importance of wearing the civilian uniform. At times support was so fervent that those guards unable to grow a full Confederate moustache pasted on fake ones.[34] The multiple wearers of the Federal uniform, with an array of slogans imprinted on their insignias, symbolically asserted and confirmed the power of government.[35] Rosas equated crimson garments and accessories with the push for consolidation of the Argentine Confederation, explaining: "This voice should resonate everywhere and at all times, because that is convenient for the consolidation of the system."[36] He strongly encouraged the use of crimson in regions overseen by other governors; its symbolism thereby gaining prominence throughout the country. This emphasis on the outward signs of dress was altogether a modern phenomenon, as the politics of dress in colonial times had been determined genealogically and did not allow for consensus-building practices among members of the population at large.

The Catholic Church and other religiously affiliated institutions assisted in this consolidation project when presenting a united Confederate family poised to defeat the solitary, disorderly Unitarian. At his inauguration, Rosas pronounced that he sought to conquer the "monsters . . . among us," a pronouncement reiterated in the words of a sermon depicted in the first paragraphs of "The Slaughterhouse." Echeverría quickly exposes the irony of such statements with his parallel representation of a young boy accidentally beheaded by a Federal butcher's whip, what is likely an allusion to the real death of the young child crushed by the coach of a Federal family making their way to Rosas's inauguration and who remains virtually forgotten by history.[37] In daily life, the Church venerated Rosas and the Federal family, mentioning them as part of the daily Catholic liturgy in Buenos Aires and the provinces. Their portraits became sacred "presences" in religious processions; in city churches, Rosas's image was placed to the side of the crucifix.[38] Draped in "federal vestments,"[39] priests encouraged parishioners to observe newly established customs. Bishop Mariano, a figure not unlike José Mármol's fictitious Padre Gaete in the foundational novel, *Amalia,* outlined a regimented dress code for the pious that he later presented to a colleague in 1837.

> There can be nothing more just than the Clergy whose opinions conform with those of the Superior Government. . . . Make [churchgoers] understand that men should wear their scarlet insignia on the left side, on the heart, and women on the head, on the same side, also warning them in advance that they must be sure to abolish the fashion that freemason Unitarians have introduced among their countrymen to starch clothing with indigo, so that the color that remains tends towards light blue, which is a completely evil act on the part of impious Unitarians.[40]

The bishop's words stressed the importance of regulating fashion and habits so as to avoid sin, which he viewed as the perdition of a national soul. Even the statues of saints and Jesus Christ were draped with scarlet vests and insignias. Changing fashions, such as the practice of starching of clothes with blue-tinted water, were deemed impure and suspect. Furthermore, uniforms in themselves were a form of instruction. The education system, overseen nationally by priest Saturnino Segurola, required all school-age members of the Confederation to wear scarlet emblems and their instructors to teach hymns honoring the Restorer of the Laws.[41] The charitable organization known as the Sociedad de Beneficencia (Beneficence Society) took on the responsibility of selecting insignias for young female orphans and even managed to convince officials in Buenos Aires to phase out a light blue school uniform and supply scarlet garments with matching hair adornments.[42] For all sectors of society, the mass processions during Holy Week became politically motivated processions. In 1848, French physician and travel writer Amédée Moure recalled observing an Easter march at which members of the public carried scarlet-robed and life-size figures of Judas alongside the likenesses of Federalist enemies like former president Bernardino Rivadavia, General Lavalle, the caudillos of the Banda Oriental, foreign dignitaries, King Louis Phillip, and Queen Victoria. The procession ended when participants burned these figures at a stake in the Plaza de la Victoria.[43] Consumed by flames, representations of Judas and members of the political opposition transformed the events of the public arena, namely the primary struggle between Federals and Unitarians, into a biblical morality play.

Regimented dress codes had a serious impact on the world of theater and opera, as actors and singers found themselves obliged to incorporate aspects of the civilian uniform into their costumes and the set. Prior to the production of any theatrical work, a committee consisting of the state budget director, the chief of police, a bishop-appointed judge, and two citizens reviewed all materials and issued its approval or recommendations.[44] Not surprisingly, many stage attractions represented allegorical struggles between Federals and Unitarians, such as Pedro Lacasa's predictable *El entierro del loco traidor, salvaje unitario Urquiza* (the burial of the crazy traitor and savage Unitarian Urquiza). Performances sometimes mobilized those in attendance; in the case of Lacasa's play, spectators took a doll representing Urquiza from the theater to Plaza de la Victoria, where it was burned the following day. Prior to the staging of a play, lead actors appeared on stage to shout, "Long live the Argentine Confederation! Death to Savage Unitarians!" Regardless of the historical period represented or the plot portrayed, opera singers utilized a scarlet insignia when on stage. Robert Elwes, a British travel writer, describes a sleepwalking Amina in the representation of Vincenzo Bellini's *La sonámbula* who, when entering the fantasy world of dreams, donned scarlet ribbons in her hair.[45] This disjointed commentary had the effect of fusing all cultural productions into one very long Federal history.[46]

Could one escape the visual power of Federalism? It seems unlikely, for even everyday material objects manifested partisan identities. Official portraits of Rosas and his family appeared on everything from gloves to fans, from plates to flower pots, from chairs to the borders of silk handkerchiefs.[47] William Henry Hudson recounts how the gaze of the portraits of Rosas and his family hanging in his childhood home in Argentina seriously modified the behavior of the household. In *Long Ago and Far Away,* he writes, "Why did those eyes, unless they moved, which they didn't, always look back into ours no matter in which part of the room we stood? —a perpetual puzzle to our childish uninformed brains."[48] As a way to enlist new supporters, government officials stamped images of the Federal family on sheets of paper and articles of clothing, which officers of the law subsequently gave away as prizes during holidays and at public gatherings.[49]

Perhaps the most famous image that circulated during the history of the regime is the portrait of Rosas's daughter Manuela that is housed in today's Argentine Museum of Fine Arts. Painted by renowned artist Prilidiano Pueyrredón, the image was reproduced and first distributed to 160 guests at a party in Manuela's honor in 1851. Unlike the official portrait described by Hudson, the graceful image of young Manuela did not stand vigil. Instead, with a cocked head, she leaned against a small table, as if inviting the onlooker to partake of her gaze and join other guests at the Rosas estate. Every item of the wardrobe and décor in the work pointed viewers to an omnipresent power, as if to grant them an imaginary place within Confederate society. María Sáenz Quesada directs our attention to the velvet-like waves of Manuela's red dress, the scarlet ribbons in her hair, and the explicit play with the vase of roses on a rosewood end table. Manuela's gaze, she imagines, must have solicited the attention of prospective admirers.[50] Distributed to invited guests of patriotic gatherings, this portrait likely gave the impression that the recipient had been extended a personal invitation to join the inner circle of the Confederate family.

Elizabeth Garrels explains that such cultural productions projected images of Rosas's presence. Even when he no longer appeared in a crimson coach at political celebrations, representation substituted for live presence. It was a shift that allowed Rosas to be in all places at once.[51] Visual and literary portraits of Rosas in uniform varied according to the context of the gathering. Official images depicted the Confederation's leader in military costume, often with a dark blue jacket and high collar, gold epaulets, crimson sash, and a sun-shaped medallion. When present for military campaigns, however, Rosas used essential parts of gaucho dress, those very items that persist today as symbols for national identity, like the indigenous poncho and the *chiripá* originally created by the Jesuits for indigenous peoples to cover themselves.[52] It is likely that Rosas also combined the poncho with

Prilidiano Pueyrredón, *Portrait of Manuelita Rosas*, 1851. Oil on canvas; 199 x 166 centimeters. Courtesy of Museo Nacional de Bellas Artes, Buenos Aires, Argentina.

European-style trousers, a hybrid style used by many Federalist superiors. In *The Voyage of the Beagle,* Charles Darwin described his encounter with Rosas dressed in full gaucho costume, as if to identify himself with soldier-brothers and not assert his role as their commander. For

Rosas, this visual uniformity was a strategy used to "gain a decisive influence" over popular sectors and, as he himself explained, "to control it and direct it; and I was determined to acquire this influence at all costs. I had to work at it relentlessly, sacrificing my comfort and fortune, in order to become a gaucho like them, to speak like them, to do everything they did."[53] From this statement, we see clearly that Rosas did "not necessarily seek to represent, or elevate, or save the gaucho."[54] He merely wished to identity with them in the official cultural register. It is known that Rosas always dressed like a gaucho when speaking to his foot soldiers. With this approach, he gained control over the main body of the military by theatrically rejecting the pomp and authority of other wartime leaders.[55] When mobilizing rural soldiers, Rosas prepared unifying discourses, positioning the appearance and valor of a gaucho in a poncho opposite a dandyish and cowardly Unitarian. Folklore preserves the notion of Rosas befriending the poor in a disguise of "humble status."[56] Rosas and other Federalist caudillos, Ariel de la Fuente adds, also attempted to turn "the social order upside down" during parades, as when Rosas paraded two buffoons dressed as a general and bishop in downtown Buenos Aires.[57] Selective shifts in uniform and dress, which the period referred to as *mudanzas de traje*, indeed helped sustain a wide range of support within the Federal camp. With official representations of uniform, one drew the psychological lines of battle and forced the opposition to slip and slide through contested terrain.[58]

In his personal correspondence to friends and editors, Rosas prepared tiny vignettes for dissemination to the public through Federalist print networks. From the onset, Rosas emphasized the role of the gaucho in maintaining public order. By this time, Rosas had united an "incongruous alliance of federalists, gauchos, delinquents, and Indians," Lynch writes.[59] Although Rosas's vignettes focused on the ideological battle at hand, his interests as a cattle baron creating more rural wealth through "territorial expansion and estancia formation"[60] made him an economic force to be reckoned with in the pampas. For those gauchos joining the Federalist cause, the motivations were often material: They expected to be provided with beef, clothing, and work in return for service.[61] The confiscation of property and the looting of Unitarian cadavers also allowed for the acquisition of goods not ordinarily accessible to most people. Perhaps for this reason, Rosas began one sketch with the declaration, "Long live the Father of the Poor and the Restorer of the Laws!" and then emphasized the unity of gauchos in keeping vigil over subversive forces undermining the Confederation:

> Countrymen! Those with jackets and ponchos, who together and under the orders of Sir Juan Manuel have sacrificed yourselves and faced danger for the restoration of laws, until the end of tyranny, must now live in a state of alert. A lodge has established itself with the object of overthrowing our general Rosas. Their objective is to trick you and capture you. Alert now, and prepare yourselves, for we have found them out and if you don't go out and hang two dozen freemasons, this country will produce new scenes of horror and blood.[62]

This particular piece aimed to strengthen rural political participation by calling on *paisanos de ponchos* (countrymen of the poncho) to rid the landscape of ill-disguised freemasons, a term that referred to Unitarian sympathizers. The hostile climate incited several to violence. The *British Packet* published reports of excessive Federalist force employed in the countryside, especially by groups of supporters who believed themselves capable of reading "Unitarian physiognomies." In one such case, twenty-three men robbed and threatened to kill a crimson-clad family as they made their way to Buenos Aires. Don Gallino, the head of the household, apparently was identified as having the facial features and hair color of a Unitarian.[63] One popular work professed that people had begun to widen their jackets to distinguish these from the elongated tails of European-style frockcoats that authorities often clipped, "because they are scared what others will say / Life's not fair, my dear."[64] Because Unitarian "difference" was difficult to read and sometimes looked "foreign," as when a Catalan merchant was killed for wearing blue stockings, some briefly entertained the proposal to brand the cheeks of foreigners and thus distinguish them more easily from Unitarians in disguise.[65]

While Rosas's militaristic texts acknowledged the heterogeneous nature of the population, his regime made a simultaneous push toward homogenization as he worked to consolidate the Confederation. Government-sponsored editors established compound print networks to link the publication houses of Buenos Aires with the people of the interior. Rosas encouraged friends living in the capital to send the

pamphlets and newspapers of Buenos Aires to the provinces in an attempt to encourage stronger cultural integration. His own writings
detail the standards for public and private discourse: "You know that
I don't like these kinds of things, but when it is necessary to unite the
country against anarchy, it is necessary to overcome mere trifles and
to realize that what sometimes seems insignificant means a whole hell
of a lot."[66] The language used on an individual basis and the images
of Rosas that circulated throughout the provinces were tailored to
ensure servitude to an emerging nation. And that nationhood, as Friar
Rodríguez wrote at the time, was a new muse who inspired divinely.

Under the guise of patriotic obligation, popular culture helped
initiate dialogue between the various regions represented by the Confederation. A uniformed society quickly delineated the Federalist from
the Unitarian and political poetry further disseminated these visions of
collective identity. The poetic representation of dress, especially when
it concerned a transgressing Unitarian, approached the hostility of a
declaration of war. This strategy emerged from poetic traditions dating
to the struggle for independence, when inhabitants of the River Plate
region conveyed heroic sentiments and narrated the deeds of war. From
the battlefield came the *cielito patriótico,* a simple and harmonic style of
poetry that inspired tired soldiers and relayed the news of important
battles to the civilian population. Gutiérrez linked this verse, its very
name reminiscent of the cerulean blue representing independence, to
the early creation of national identity. "The true popular poetry is
daughter of history transformed into legend by fantasy without culture, and we have not possessed her in all her character until we had
our own heroes and engendered national moments that flattered our
pride," he wrote.[67] Consisting of eight-syllable lines, the *cielo* could
easily be sung by soldiers to the tune of a guitar, as if it were a distant
dialect of the *seguidilla española,* thereby adding to its framing as a national literary form. Linked to the events of the public arena, the *cielito
patriótico* encouraged listeners to consider lengthy debates on issues
that concerned the newly established fatherland. Some of these poems
were sung during civic gatherings, and others circulated in pamphlet
form. Prior to the Rosas regime in 1822, President Rivadavia commissioned his Literary Society to compile poetry written and published
since 1810. The government later circulated this anthology under the

title of *La lira argentina* (The Argentine lyre), thereby documenting the beginnings of a national poetry.[68]

Recognizing the function of patriotic poetry in consensus building, the Rosas regime extended the use of the *cielo* to Federalist political goals.[69] Following independence, political literature had established the family as an allegorical presence through which to imagine unity among a fragmented collective. Sommer argues that the goals of political partisanship came into play with such familial relationships in the foundational novels of later decades. Fiction, she reveals, taught "people about their history, about their barely formulated customs, and about ideas and feelings that have been modified by still unsung political and social events."[70] Given the high illiteracy rates of the River Plate region, however, Rosas maintained that fictitious representations of members of the Federalist family were best represented in verse. In a private letter, he writes of the success of poetry chapbooks in creating a more fluid dialogue between the city and the countryside, between Federalist mothers and sons, between wives and their husbands.[71] Much of the transcribed dialogue in popular poetry leaflets thus took the form of letters between members of an imagined community that might not have convened otherwise, to borrow a concept from Benedict Anderson.[72] Public cantors sang serialized and tension-filled plots in the streets and, most likely, altered their contents at will. One can only wonder if "los locos de Rosas," a group of fools "made to learn Federal verses, speeches, and documents by heart and to tour the streets reciting them amidst a show of clowning, music and dancing"[73] would have integrated the theatrical perspectives of these conversation-style letters into their performances. The pleas contained in several of these letters responded directly to, and even hurled insults at, polemical arguments raised by competing newspapers and magazines. Some of these debates in verse became so popular that the printed versions apparently sold out quickly.[74]

Although portraying a variety of social bodies, the *cielito patriótico* maintained at its core the idea of the obedient Federal family in crimson uniform. In this regard, Josefina Ludmer reminds us that voice definitely mattered when writers inscribed oral culture to integrate the Other (the gaucho, in her analysis) into a system that required their service and integration into city life.[75] Only when "ungovernable hordes" found themselves placed in the context of a mass movement, Kathryn Lehman argues, did figures like the gaucho become patriots in the realm of cultural production.[76] The poetic voices of Federal poetry manipulated the terms of consensus by bringing together the members of an extremely diverse population in service of, and not necessarily in support of, the regime. Many poems judged an individual by his or her adherence to the power of uniform, as if this indicated support of or digression from the Confederate cause. Some helped drum up support among formerly disenfranchised groups, such as the gaucho and the African Argentine, who were lauded for being an integral part of the regime's military successes. Representations of a consolidated *patria* (fatherland) under the authority of the uniform served as a means of officially separating, and finally erasing, the Unitarian from the national family.

In the intricate genealogy of the Argentine Confederation, the compadre became one of the most prominent images of patriotic obligation circulated by the regime. Following independence, the gaucho had undergone a process of assimilation that increased his participation in city life. For the Rosas regime, this newly urban figure served as a link between Buenos Aires and the provinces of the interior, the customs of the city and the politics of rural life. A change in language paralleled the geographical shift: The compadre emerged from the gaucho and the city *compadrito,* Luis Soler Cañas explains.[77] No longer was he the gaucho who performed chores on estancias and roamed the pampas in solitude. He was a coachman, cattle dealer, butcher, a kind of "village gaucho," well versed in the dynamics of urban life. Two decades before Mármol took up the question of national consolidation in his allegorical *Amalia,* the voice of the compadre in poetry may have personified the desire to unite all urban and rural inhabitants under one nation. In Federal verses, a corresponding change in uniform marked this very cultural shift.

Pancho Lugares Contreras, the protagonist of a series of poems published in *El Gaucho,* was a popular character who fused countryside manners with the spectacle of urban experience. He represented the estancia peon who had become a Federal soldier, Julio Schvartzman explains.[78] *El Gaucho* and its counterpart, *La Gaucha,* published by the state printing office and edited by Luis Pérez, began as a series in

1830 and appeared regularly for several years. Graced by the slogan "Everyone for himself and God for everyone," both publications included on their frontispieces the representation of a compadre "in a studious attitude, with pen and paper in hand, and in full costume, his little hat and handkerchief placed upon a stile, on which he rests in a recumbent posture."[79] The generic nickname Pancho combined with the surnames Lugares Contreras toyed with the new political identity that Rosas had granted the village gaucho. This name clearly poked fun at the gaucho, who in the process of becoming an urban resident, found himself in amusing predicaments. As Pancho embraces his new urban lifestyle, he remains nostalgic for his previous life and especially the family he left behind.

Taking the form of personal correspondence, Pancho's voice explains how he came to Buenos Aires to serve Rosas as a *gacetero* (newspaper seller). Although the popular magazine dedicated most letters to Pancho's wife, or "my most beloved Chanonga," some were for Pancho's mother, Juana Contreras, and his milkman son Chanongolo. Just as Rosas desired, these fictitious long-distance relationships created the notion of a firm patriotic bond between the people of Buenos Aires and the residents of other provinces. Pancho details his urban experiences to help his wife Chanonga make a smoother transition to city life when joining him in Buenos Aires. In *La Gaucha*, Chanonga answers Pancho's letters, at one point asking her spouse to locate Rosas in the city and give him her regards. Several letters later, the residents of Buenos Aires force Unitarians to sweep the streets in preparation for Chanonga's arrival and embrace her with luxury and pomp.[80]

Although the disorderly state of the compadre's appearance and his diplomatic skills border on farce, this popular representation also implies that Pancho acquired substantial material benefits in exchange for his service. Finding himself out of his rural element, Pancho acquires a set of basic foreign expressions that he pronounces humorously, such as "Comanbu portebu, madama?" in French and "guan, tu, tri, for" in English. His elegant dress epitomizes the spectacle of excess prevalent in "civilized" Buenos Aires, where red bands adorned top hats and English merchants sold ponchos produced in Birmingham and Manchester.[81] Pancho sings:

Just bought some real strong boots
and a good fur hat.
I have an English-style *surtú;*
but I'm on the lookout for underwear.

With six shirt collars
and tie in place,
May the devil figure out
where it all got hidden.[82]

Pancho depicts Buenos Aires with good humor as a "center of civiliza-tion" in which the individual negotiated the materiality of culture. As Pancho prepares for Chanonga to join him in the city, he describes a newly found luxury that rural inhabitants would have believed exces-sive. This idea would have countered the doubts of Unitarian intel-lectuals who felt that members of the rural population were finan-cially and psychologically unable to consume goods under a system that "extinguished" European customs and tastes.[83] If England sought consumers in Argentina, Sarmiento quipped, what in the world could six hundred thousand poor gauchos consume?[84] On the other hand, the verses make it appear like city life "continued to attract immigrants and commercial interests" at the same time that "the cities of the interior progressively lost population and experienced economic decline."[85] Pancho and Chanonga's modern living arrangements would include a full-length mirror, English reading chairs, a piano, and a sheepskin rug.[86] Mark Szuchman confirms that the majority increasingly found European goods accessible, with "the possessions of humble families toward the 1850s and 1860s" including "such frills as bibelots on dressers and tables, framed mirrors on the walls, and white embroidered cloth contrasting with the surrounding wood surfaces."[87] Material goods had even begun to transform estancia culture, Lynch notes, where English clothing and wares now abounded. The frivolities of urban life pro-vided a convenient backdrop to the discussion of the compadre's rise in political consciousness. If Pancho was any indicator, the newly urban members of the Federal family consumed material goods because they could afford to do so, and this, in turn, allowed them to gain access to social rituals from which they had once been excluded.

As he prepares his Federalist wardrobe, Pancho gains the political expertise necessary for his evolution into a national patriot. Roaming the cityscape as he once did the pampas, he encounters several individuals who he feels compromise the goals of the regime by putting forth flawed appearances. This prompts Pancho to declare that, when conveying patriotic sentiments, the individual needs to regard his form as much as his actions.[88] When Pancho encounters two women wearing light blue belts at a civic march honoring Rosas, he quickly confronts them. While the two women explain that these colors commemorated independence from Spain, Pancho reminds them of the cerulean hues that also symbolized Unitarian interests and casts doubt on their affiliations. He recalls this situation in another letter to Chanonga, "I saw two women shout / *Long live the Confederation!* / And I warn that of a light blue hue / was the belt worn by the two." After Pancho brings this to their attention, the two women appear in public that same afternoon with the obligatory crimson insignia.[89]

As Pancho settles into the city, his poetic reflections take on an increasingly combative tone. He describes the decree legalizing the civilian uniform as an act of love that unites compatriots. In later issues of *El Gaucho,* his letters request that Chanonga incorporate aspects of the civilian uniform into the design of her next country dress. Sending along some pieces of luxurious red ribbon, he next explains that a matter of national security—top-secret information on the whereabouts of a Unitarian general—would take him away from his correspondence for the next several days. The fact that Pancho first explains the significance of Federal dress codes to Chanonga indicates an unwavering devotion to his spouse. His words also imply that the laws overseeing dress and adornment were as important to the Confederation as classified military details. Pancho concludes his letter by encouraging Chanonga to share the bits of ribbon with friends for the creation of other patriotic fashions. "You should place it / on your heart / because it is the insignia / of the Confederation," he sings while explaining that he now wears a rosette "and a ribbon on my chest / that the wind picks up." He professes feeling "strange" when in crimson uniform from head to toe, as if the subject of some ridicule. But in the end, he explains, it is best to have opinions that favor Rosas and roam city streets as a free man than spend a night in jail.[90]

When the poetic uniform did not help identify civic obligations, it projected a subjugated image of the chaotic Unitarian body. If not totally relegated to the margins of exile, Unitarian sympathizers hid their true affiliations and had long abandoned light blue and green garments. Despite such precautions, Federal loyalists subjected anyone suspected of political treachery to public humiliation and harassment. Patriotic verses reinforced the popularly held notion that Unitarians could be easily "found out" if citizen-soldiers just paid attention to appearance. Many even attempted to acquire such "reading skills" by means of farmer's almanacs, local newspapers, and government-sponsored chapbooks that circulated in the streets of Buenos Aires. In 1851, Rosas disseminated a portrait of Unitarian General Urquiza that played on such assumptions. Depicted as a beast of burden in uniform, the figure of Urquiza was decorated with anti-Christian medals and pulled by a three-headed dog. His head exposed two faces, one with a crooked nose and a serpent tongue, and on his back he carried several packages labeled "Masks," "Villainy," and "Despotism"—which he was undoubtedly threatening to deliver to the Confederation. This kind of propaganda encouraged citizens to search for enemies of the state in their midst and expose all Unitarian demons. The depiction of vaporous Unitarian bodies in official poetry further intensified these beliefs, with one anonymous poem portraying a ghostly creature incapable of connecting with the national soul: "Betrayal, intrigue and twists in the plot / he exercises with skill. / With his head filled with air, / he proclaims his own immortality; / And if he is decent he calls / The proper authorities."[91] The *Federalist Songbook* even implied that a Unitarian's vanity could be so intense that not even his own servant dared look at the images reflected in the mirror for fear of evil. Patriotic verses underscored a disobedient Unitarian body that never quite fit the masculine contours of the Federalist uniform.

Popular poetry made explicit the link between unruly Unitarian dress and the chaos that agonized the emerging nation. This association took on the characteristics of a simulated battle: First, the verses identified prospective Unitarian targets, and next, they referred to the methods of eliminating their bodies from public life. If clothes make the man, as one maxim reminds us, then the Unitarian depicted in Federal verse spoke of a potential unmaking. *De cada cosa un poquito* (A little bit of everything), a magazine in verse published by Luis Pérez, presents an image of a disorderly Unitarian uniform sewn up in haphazard fashion, an image that reminded readers of the publication's title. "Luggage List for the Engaged Unitarian," a poem in this same magazine, provides a detailed list of garments that had seen more glorious times. Deemed a social misfit by society at large, the Unitarian had packed his belongings as he contemplated the humiliation of either having to move in with his girlfriend or leave Buenos Aires. The poem takes the form of a first-person monologue that narrates his ill treatment by the masses. A chorus of street passersby repeatedly declare him an outcast. The Unitarian's miserable appearance renders him undesirable to those around him; his clothes are the scraps of poverty that are almost beyond words: "Because to say that they are broken / Is like saying nothing."[92] Riddled with holes, the Unitarian's frockcoat and vest have ripped seams and missing buttons. His feet apparently slide right through what is left of the socks and boots. Out of necessity, as if still declaring emphatically his elitism, he turns a white handkerchief into a cravat. He no longer wears one old pair of pants because they had split and crowds threatened to subjugate him. Even the contents of his suitcase are analyzed. In *De cada cosa un poquito,* the reader forcibly assumed the vigilant gaze of a Federal, viewing the Unitarian body as an entity easily dissected into parts.

Because the Unitarian encapsulated the "undesirable," it seems only logical that his amorous encounters should be doomed to failure. His personal life, like his uniform, was a series of mismatched and unpatriotic sequences. This is interesting in light of Sommer's argument that heterosexual unions often constituted prototypes for national consolidation, an analysis that she focuses exclusively on the novel of the post-Rosas period. Decades earlier, as we have already seen, the Rosas regime represented heterosexual unions of the Federal family in patriotic verse to create new alliances between the inhabitants of Buenos Aires and other provinces. The union of Pancho Lugares Contreras and Chanonga went on to produce a son, Chanongolo, whose rites of initiation into Argentine society would be chronicled in later poetry pamphlets. The difference at this point, however, is that the consolidation of Federal and Unitarian differences highlighted by Sommer in her reading of *Amalia,* was as of yet unimaginable.

Federal verse characterized the Unitarian marriage as an impossible relationship between a young, effeminate man and an elderly, delusional woman.[93] This pairing represented an unlikely union that would bear the nation no new offspring. In the pages of *El Gaucho,* Pancho receives a wedding invitation from an eighty-one-year-old woman planning to marry a sprightly Unitarian bachelor with an eclectic wardrobe. Federalist men, the elderly woman complains in an accompanying note, only desire young, beautiful women and overlook all other available partners: "But the Unitarians / are polite people / only interested in / old women and their ways. / Because young beauties / are not able to see them / and even detest them / like Lucifer."[94] Her letter provokes an interesting poetic response that berates the lack of compassion for the elderly in love, but over time, the plot unfolds with another revelation: It is not the woman's age, but her monstrous appearance that renders her undesirable to virile Federal men. She is, apparently, a cross-eyed pig whose vision allows her to see Unitarians in ways that others cannot. Her self-absorbed mate, on the other hand, seems surprisingly elegant and heavily perfumed. He is much too busy grooming himself to notice the insults hurled at this marriage of misfits. A chorus concludes, "God creates them and so they join." Fashion conscious to the point of losing his male identity, the Unitarian is an unworthy spouse and citizen in regime-sponsored hate literature. Even the archives reveal that authorities held "aberrant Unitarians" responsible for wreaking chaos on the Federal family.

Police arrest records confirm that the Unitarian body was subject to detailed inspection and punishment. One need only consider the list of possible transgressions to recognize the severity with which dress and appearance was judged:

MANUEL JORDÁN: Gossip against the Superior Government. He is a savage Unitarian and has removed his moustache.

MARTÍN LACARRA: He wears tails and is a staunch Unitarian.

JOSÉ JULIÁN JAIMES: He is one of those who trampled the insignia along with a portrait of His Excellency.

PABLO J. DÍAZ: He is a Unitarian with a frock coat who has also removed his moustache.[95]

Without question, the individual who deviated from Federalist dress codes was subjected to severe punishment. The absence of a moustache and full-bodied beard was often well documented: popular culture deemed it possible to judge a man by his facial hair alone.[96] Federalist popular poetry consistently drew similar metaphorical battle lines with contrasting descriptions of uniforms, thereby sealing the identities of citizens, soldiers, and enemies of the nation. Some early portrayals of Unitarians served as a pretense for debate on appropriate public conduct (prior to the late 1830s). Voices representing working-class sectors emphasized the destruction of dissent, educating the public on the vocabulary of color and the civilian uniform. Overall, popular culture reflected the hostilities of the police record, positioning a rebellious Unitarian body outside the limits of citizenship and Argentine cultural identity. Patriotic poetry engaged all the cultural terms of the dictatorial apparatus, identifying the status and position of the enemy, locating battle sites, narrating horror and punishment, and honoring Federal service.

Remember that the simulated battles represented in popular culture depended on an audience that had come to expect the performance of consensus. Perhaps this is why Echeverría cast his reader in the role of spectator.[97] Foucault's idea of the "publicity of punishment" is perhaps most useful to us here: "Posters, placards, signs, symbols must be distributed, so that everyone may learn their significations. The publicity of punishment must not have the physical effect of terror; it must open up a book to be read."[98] Such techniques were standard operation in the annals of Federal poetry. The popular "Violin Song" printed by the government depicted the decapitation of Unitarians: "And for the enemies / Of our nation, / Let's give them the bow / Violin and violate."[99] Whereas Federals were known to cut throats, Unitarians were reputed to castrate their victims. A group of concerned citizens in *El Gaucho* recommended that Federal soldiers beat the opposition with a club, a phallic symbol of superiority in a sexualized framework of punishment. "The beautiful Argentine sex / Has also suffered displeasure / Seeing that all these fags / Have profaned everything. / To conserve order / We have no greater remedy than the CLUB."[100] Official posters documented these tensions with publicity campaigns throughout Buenos Aires, reminding citizens of dates and actions favored by Rosas.[101]

Street performers transformed the terms of civil war into a the-

Portrait of Juan Manuel de Rosas surrounded by crimson insignias. Each insignia is 15 centimeters wide and states: "Long Live the Argentine Confederation! Death to the Savage, Abominable, and Foul Unitarians!" Photograph by Felicitas Luna. Courtesy of Museo Saavedra, Buenos Aires, Argentina.

atrical spectacle for plazas and streets. Judging from the presence of choruses in regime-endorsed patriotic verses, one wonders if the authors kept the possibility of street performance and mass participation in mind. "A rotten Unitarian," which appeared in *El Torito de los muchachos* in 1830, tells of a cook who had found a poem inside a rotten rhea egg. Disgusted by its contents, he had thrown it away, but the editors of the magazine then decided to resurrect the "garbage" to make their points. The contents of the found poem narrate the story of a Unitarian who criticizes the meaning of the Federalist uniform and accuses Rosas of appropriating its style from Spanish colonial powers and the indigenous peoples of the pampas. Throughout the poem, the Unitarian chides Federalists for not putting more thought into the implications of their ostentatious uniforms and declares their designs unpatriotic because they had abandoned the colors of independence. The poetic voice compares the exaggerated scarlet dressage of Federal horses with the second-rate beauty of women who wear a civilian uniform. All in all, this account does little but egg on an attack, especially when the Unitarian declares that another palette made up his insignia: "White and cerulean blue / In their union / Represent our rosette / Our true flag." As the Unitarian explains his position further, dueling footnotes prepare Federal loyalists for attack. Strategically speaking, this shifts the focus on the Unitarian as object rather than subject of poetic discourse in order to demasculinize him. Each response by Federals serves as a fear-inducing patriotic chorus that ultimately brings the Unitarian to trial. To the preceding strophe that associates the colors of independence with Unitarian ideals, the chorus replies: "You have put your invention / to an evil use / Do you know what patriotism is? / Shut up, Fag." Subsequent strophes attack him with equally violent words. Subjected to the patriarchal "potency" of the Federalist family, the Unitarian finds his poem tossed away once again.

Poetic warfare had on hand a series of metonyms that categorized Federal powers and weapons for domination: the voracious bull, the scarlet insignia, and the phallic ear of corn. Together with representations of patriotic moustaches and sideburns, these images led the reader to imaginary sites where Federalists punished Unitarians. A poem circulated in 1830 called on Federalists to stand up for their manly honor and quash those Unitarians who embraced effeminate styles:[102] "A countryman is worth more / With his ribbons / Than with those fags. / Hermaphrodites / Whose sleepless nights / Render little more than / some time to jerk off."[103] Living in fear, the Unitarians of popular poetry found their bodies exposed, put on display, and probed. *El Toro de Once* warned any Unitarian readers, "You're not safe at home when the BULL is in the plaza." *El Torito de los Muchachos* punished enemies of the regime by confining them to a vicious bullring where any hope of survival quickly faded: "All the Unitarians / To the sideburns. / I am sending you off, little Bull, / With this wartime flag. / They think they have hope / Of gaining power again: / Come on, Bull, / Start to gore the enemy!"[104] In cattle country, Schvartzman reminds us, the male reproducer was the sign of Federal strength.[105] This imagery took on such meaning that Lynch believes there was even "prejudice against unitarian livestock,"[106] an idea that also figures in "The Slaughterhouse." Sexualized images of cruelty reinforced the publicity of punishment and projected a fantasy of domination. Just four years after the publication of such militant poetry, the regime instituted the same haunting techniques of torture in everyday life.

The Popular Restoration Society, the secret police organization commonly known as the Mazorca and which acted on police reports, displayed ears of corn in a public terror campaign.[107] Because of the images of forcible sodomy that had appeared in popular poems, the public likely understood the meaning behind this symbol of Confederate power. The Mazorca became the regime's "eyes that see without being seen," to paraphrase Foucault, acting as an extension of the police force to ensure order and adherence to the Santa Federación. Notices of Mazorca punishment expressed activity levels of mythic proportions.[108] In reality, the organization began with forty regime supporters (mostly young men from the middle classes) and never surpassed two hundred members. Shrouded in secrecy, Mazorca members could not be distinguished from civilians, so the citizens of Buenos Aires initiated anti-Unitarian watch groups so their own neighborhoods would not fall victim to these homegrown terrorists.[109]

In postcolonial Argentina, to pronounce "Mazorca" created two significations: *mazorca* (ear of corn) or *más horca* (more hangings). Playing with the menacing duality of its namesake, the society brought violent images of torture and death to the public imaginary. In his correspondence, Gutiérrez described how the secret police humiliated their targets by forcibly introducing cobs of corn into their pants: "That society, which we commonly call the Mazorca, tries to introduce into the rear of the Unitarian enemy the delicious fruit from which it takes its name. So everyone who feels he is suspect has taken to using really tight pants, disguising in the name of fashion a preventative measure in line with order and reason."[110] It is likely that crowds convened to verbally humiliate the victim as he removed the ear of corn from his pants. Because Unitarian males had been represented as homosexuals in patriotic verses, the incorporation of sodomy into the punishment inflicted by the Mazorca fit the disturbing notion of crime advocated by the regime. Furthermore, the public display of this torture assured that the message got delivered to everyone.

Visual representations of corn painted on houses and public buildings became icons of Mazorca punishment. Citizens painted their houses crimson and incorporated groupings of roses for Rosas or other official decorations into the exterior design. Some homes boasted political inscriptions or poster-style manifestos attached to the sides facing the street. These public declarations must have registered in the minds of passersby, perhaps even eliciting the chant of some official slogan. Slogans, including ones written by Rivera Indarte before he joined the Unitarian cause, were routinely posted outside of the homes of Unitarian suspects. This poem appeared outside the home of a medical doctor:

> Long live the Mazorca!
> To the Unitarian brave enough to read this:
>
> That cob that you see
> Dressed in blond leaves
> Has sunk into the hell
> Of the Unitarian faction;
> And with great devotion
> You will tell your ass:
>
> Save me from this jam,
> Oh Holy Confederation!
> And you will be careful
> At the time of walking,
> For you never know
> When you're going to get it![111]

Stripped of a uniform and broken down into penetrable parts, the Unitarian's own body became the final battle site, an idea that readers would find replayed in the final paragraphs of Echeverría's political allegory.

Restrained by his Federalist aggressors, the Unitarian becomes a strip of meat in "The Slaughterhouse." "Behead me before stripping me, vile swine," the defiant Unitarian declares. The Mazorca hold down his body and inspect its parts, as if preparing for slaughter. Forced face down, with arms extended as if a victim of crucifixion, the Unitarian becomes the latest offering to the omnipotent Confederation. Foaming at the mouth, the Unitarian resists powerful hands that peel his uniform and prepare his torture. His solitary refrain of "Behead me before stripping me, vile swine" narrates a powerful struggle for survival. But before the Mazorca can finish its performance, the Unitarian suffers a fatal hemorrhage and the blood from his mouth and nose mixes with the fluids of "The Slaughterhouse" below, the same blood that stains the Federal uniform.[112] His sudden death, almost defiant in timing, stuns the onlookers, who are sure to have witnessed many other truculent, Federal rituals. Quickly, the Mazorca-like butchers lock the courthouse and abandon the site. The Unitarian, having willingly entered Federalist territory and deliberately defied its laws, dies with his body intact, a martyr for the Unitarian cause.

As the River Plate region struggled with the precepts of nationhood, narratives on uniform polarized Federals and Unitarians. Patriotic verses and other militaristic texts emerged during the armed conflict against Spanish colonizers and resonated the first nationalist sentiments. With details drawn almost down to the buttons, legalized dress codes prescribed ready-to-wear identities that sought to unify a fragmented collective. Although it would be virtually impossible to process mass fashion as a group phenomenon, the archival documents presented allow us to assess the ways in which the Confederation promoted a uniform culture. The repressive measures enacted by the Rosas regime to force consensus on the population at large, however, did not seek to unite opposing interests. Through contrasting descriptions of the military and civilian uniform, popular culture contrasted the prestige and masculine contours of Federalist costume with a disheveled and feminized Unitarian costume. Just as Echeverría represented in "The Slaughterhouse," Confederate soldiers sang declarations of war and supporters joined them in a familiar chorus that called for the elimination of the Unitarian from public life. As the opposition sought exile in neighboring territories, they turned away from the crimson uniform and the blood-drenched earth, looking up to a different flag, the sky, for the promise of freedom.

TWO   *Dressed to Kill*

THROUGH THE LENS OF DRESS, we can unravel some of the everyday transactions inflected with the burdens of the colonial order and the formation of citizen-subjects in the River Plate region. It can also bring us closer to "dreams full of history, of known unknown persons"[1] and enact a dialogue between the individual and the collective in the realm of the cultural imaginary. We have seen how the Rosas regime worked to create a consensus around Federalism, particularly through legalized dress codes and the display of masculinity that represented political legitimacy. Representations of uniform, in particular, forged a strong relationship between the soldier-citizen, the caudillo, and the Confederation. Because the regime feminized the Unitarian opposition to exclude its participation, the political agency of marginalized social groups and women presented a unique discursive challenge. How, then, to depict female supporters of the regime? This chapter analyzes representations of female bravery and beauty, sewing and embroidery, and other fashionable poses in the promotion of political vanity. The emphasis placed on their utility in mobilizing the population at large reveals an interesting shift in representation. When piecing together a flag the night before battle during independence, everyday acts like sewing became emblems of cultural and prenational identity. During the Rosas regime, a focus on recruitment and assembly extended the role of political actors to women as with all popular sectors—that is, on a discursive level. This was an altogether new phenomenon. Turning the mirror on the seams, this chapter uses dress to recover a diverse range of female voices—both real and imagined—and some of the creative forces that helped shape the postcolonial battlefront and home front.

Female complicity in war making has long been overlooked, argue Helen M. Cooper, Adrienne Auslander Munich, and Susan Merril Squier. "The paradigmatic narrative of 'men's wars' builds on the Western literary tradition celebrating 'arms and the man', to figure a culture in which men fight while women remain at home preserving the domestic front."[2] Those studies that do integrate women into the narrative of war tend to present a beautiful soul contributing to a just war or to challenge the "femininity" of the female soldier (beginning with the mythological Amazons). When studying the military history of postcolonial Argentina, one quickly notices that the images of the women viewed as instrumental in building loyalty and creating consensus have been rendered almost invisible. At the time, women's participation in the war effort (whether in uniform or during its construction) brought to mind sensations, continuities, and the dream of national happiness. During independence, many women contributed to the war effort. By the early years of the Rosas regime, networks remained in place and tensions at an all-time high. "All women need to band together," a popular magazine announced, "and, from our homes, tame the tempers of men once and for all."[3] Furthermore, its anonymous author threatened to tear off men's collars and put skirts over their heads if soldiers did not resolve the war quickly.[4] Meanwhile, the regime promoted images of women dressed to kill, as if vanity alone would advance the cause of alliances. The words of Shari Benstock and Suzanne Ferris thus ring true in this context: although popular poetry afforded women roles as political actors, violence lurked "just around the corner of those hidden grounds, the eye taking aim, sighting the subject."[5] Dressed to kill, women and other marginalized groups found themselves "prey to the Look"[6] and their images subject to manipulation. Beginning with independence war efforts and continuing to the first decades of the Rosas regime, this chapter traces the gender-specific assignment of political vanity in an altogether forgotten chapter of Argentine history.

In *Recuerdos del Buenos Ayres Virreynal* (Memories of Viceregal

Buenos Aires), Mariquita Sánchez de Thompson (1786–1868) depicts colonial Latin America in very gloomy terms, especially when it comes to the experiences of women. From religious customs to the economy, the Spanish dominated every aspect of life, and the inhabitants of the River Plate region felt compelled by their misery to band together. Women found themselves subject first to the Spanish, then to the Church, and finally to the whims of parents and husbands. For this reason, Sánchez wrote that many women felt sentenced to life imprisonment in their homes. She claimed that most would have chosen to enter the convent rather than face the shackles of matrimony if given the choice. For the women of this period, unions were an obligation, not the consequence of love; their dowries and material possessions often related to the social demands placed on them. The wardrobes of the majority of women were also limited to the bare necessities. According to Mark Szuchman, probates and other documents indicate that a woman "seldom owned more than a couple of shawls and blouses, perhaps as many as three skirts, and one pair of shoes or sandals."[7] Overall, it was not unusual for women's fashions of the colonial period to be subject to the critique of authorities and clergymen, who at times expressed frustration with exposure of the skin and eventually linked long petticoats to the tails of Lucifer.[8] Women's mobility also appears to have been a pressing issue, as if their presence alone cast doubt on the divisions between public and private domains, and racial and social categories.

It has been established that the brief but unsuccessful British invasions of Buenos Aires marked a shift in the way inhabitants perceived themselves and their relation to the Spanish Empire. In the context of Spanish America, Mariselle Meléndez recognizes that this shift had been taking place gradually as "Spanish fashion, hairstyle, eating habits, and diet, as well as the use of Spanish language, became cultural aspects which many marginalized groups utilized to their advantage to mislead the system and consequently improve their social life or survive difficult economic situations."[9] Although such relationships are impossible to ground empirically, scholarly interpretations suggest that colonial subjects increasingly resisted categorization by those deemed superior in the Spanish caste system. Strict codes governing dress and uniform had already begun to show wear; the representations of other empires as superior to the Spanish further called into question the status quo. When the British first stormed Buenos Aires in 1806, their tailored uniforms with sparkling accoutrements contrasted with the dull, piecemeal military costumes that Viceroy Sobremonte had ordered for native soldiers. The British also brought with them an assortment of high-quality goods, including tailored clothes, furniture, novel weapons, and other items that had not yet been made available to the colonized peoples of Spanish America. During this invasion, the inhabitants of Buenos Aires experienced the power of banding together in a war effort against a common enemy and emerging victorious, a process that brought to fore the patriotic sentiments that ultimately led to the war for independence. By May 25, 1810, following the news of the invasion of Spain by Napoleon Bonaparte and the suspension of Viceroy Baltasar Hidalgo de Cisneros, a group of male leaders established a junta in Buenos Aires that formally began the independence process. Given the marginal status of women in the colony, it is perhaps not surprising that the record remained silent on their contributions to the effort. By 1812, Belgrano revealed the sky blue and white flag that a group of women had confected for continuing military campaigns against the Spanish.

Few archival documents address the service of women during the British invasions and independence, although their participation appears to have been significant. From the balconies of their homes, the women of San Telmo (a section of Buenos Aires) dropped heated oil, a common ingredient stocked in most households, over the heads of British soldiers to defeat them. After killing an English soldier, Manuela Pedraza took up the soldier's rifle and continued in battle during the first British invasion. Viceroy Santiago de Liniers would later grant Pedraza the title of second lieutenant of the infantry, issuing her a salary to compensate her contributions in war.[10] Other women of this period assumed the male uniform in secret, cross-dressing to participate in battle. Not unlike Catalina de Erauso, the lieutenant nun who secretly stormed the Americas as a Spanish conquistador, Pancha Hernández and Pascuala (Pascual) Menéndez distinguished themselves in military service as males, their true gender unknown to their troops. During the struggle for independence, Susana Dillon notes that hundreds of nameless *cuarteleras* (women of the barracks) left their homes to assist male soldiers in the camps along the battlefront, a fact that military orders substantiated. These women tended to the injured, washed and mended uniforms, prepared meals, and organized dances and other events to divert thoughts from the horrors of battle.[11] Yet another select group of women earned military titles and stipends. Juana Azurduy, a native of today's Bolivia and perhaps South America's most legendary figure of the war, is still praised in song by the young children of the Southern Cone: "Juana Azurduy, / flor del Alto Perú, / no hay capitán / más alegre que tú" (Juana Azurduy, / the flower of High Peru; / There is no captain / any happier than you). This popular song grants Azurduy a unique place in military history, representing her as a dedicated mother, wife, and soldier who rose to the position of lieutenant colonel.

Dressed in male uniform, Josefa Tenorio, the slave of Doña Gregoria Aguilar, joined the war to fight oppression on multiple fronts. In a letter addressed to a high-ranking officer, she described her desire for freedom, believing that the ideals of liberty apply to all, not just men. Her words called into question the sexist rules that afforded liberty only to male slaves who had participated in battle.

> When the rumor spread that the enemy was trying to return to enslave the *patria* once again, I disguised myself as a man and ran to the trenches in order to take orders and a rifle.... General Las Heras entrusted me with a flag so that I might carry and defend it with honor. As a member of the corps under the command of General de Guerillas, Don Toribio Dávalos, I suffered the rigor of the campaign. My sex was not an impediment to being useful to the *patria*. If we recognize the value of men on the battlefield, then we cannot deny how extraordinary it is for a woman to have that same worth. I implore that Your Excellency examine what I present here under oath. And may it serve to declare my liberty, the only thing I crave.[12]

In her quest for emancipation, Tenorio addressed the fear of a return to Spanish rule and its practices of slavery. Believing herself to be equal to a man—if not even more extraordinary—Tenorio assumed the uniform in order to fight slavery and the limitations imposed on her gender. By placing her experiences within the framework of the military hierarchy that mirrored the racial and gender divides played out in real life, Tenorio helped wage war against institutionalized prejudice, both on the battlefield and with pen in hand, pressing for her status as an equal to men and for true *liberty for all* in the emerging Argentine nation. The public statement of Tenorio is an exceptional one for scholars; few first-person slave narratives exist in Latin America in general. It is likely that the experiences of Tenorio and other women dressed to kill, however, remained exceptions to the rule.

Women were generally spared persecution and death during the independence process, La Fuente writes, even as they assumed more significant roles in family businesses, political institutions, and personal relationships.[13] Representations of the female supporters of independence projected an image of women who occupied themselves with patriotic tasks undertaken in the domestic sphere, which served to control their interactions with the public at large. In the River Plate region, particularly in Buenos Aires, female supporters who bridged the political life of the household with the events on the battlefront were referred to as *patricias*. A play on words, the term feminized the republican ideal by representing female figures who worked within the safety of their communities and sacrificed time, wealth, and even themselves for the goal of independence. Led by groups of nuns, *patricias* of all social backgrounds helped sew military uniforms. Leaders used examples of female industriousness to lure patriots into service, as this article in *La Gazeta de Buenos Aires* indicates:

> What American does not feel his soul agitated by a multitude of great and valiant ideas, and does not feel his eyes swimming in tears of joy upon contemplating these amusing Argentine women, who taking time away from essential obligations in the home, dedicate themselves to sewing coarse linen for the champions of our nation![14]

Working with the coarse cotton and woolen fabrics often used in the confection of uniforms and everyday dress, the hands of the patriotic seamstress interpreted the "multitude of great and valiant ideas" and draped the soldier's body accordingly. Although it would be impossible to register how the seamstress meditated over uniform patterns, it cannot be doubted that her assessments and overall cartography of the garment were instrumental to the nation-building process. The intimate connection between the service of the seamstress and the soldier of independence apparently continued in death: A soldier whose life expired in battle received her utmost admiration, or so it was believed. The collaborative process that produced uniforms for battles against Spanish loyalists, as the editorial above points out, was the source of amusement but also respect. The fact that nuns ordinarily oversaw sewing circles emphasized the divine nature of these patriotic acts. With such a precedent, it is perhaps not surprising that representations of women outside the sewing circle often revealed a presence so spiritual that the female body practically vanished into thin air.[15] Glimpses of female beauty on the road to battle often compared to the miraculous apparitions of the Virgin Mary. The legend of the guardian angel of independence, often present in children's school textbooks, revealed an unworldly magnificence whose disappearances and reappearances helped guide soldiers across the treacherous Andes mountain range. Fatigued by starvation and the bitterly cold climate, even General San Martín was believed to have sighted a wind-swept woman pointing the way to the battlefields of Maipú and Chacabuco, immediately recognizing her as the female figure of Liberty.

The newspaper *La Gazeta de Buenos Aires,* in a move to enlist further the support of women interested in guiding the troops to victory, proposed to document symbolic presences on the battlefield. Encouraged by a women's commission organized by Sánchez, the newspaper printed names of women patriots and described their efforts. It was stated that many of these women had traded their jewels and heirlooms for weapons purchased from the United States. Several female sponsors had their names engraved on their purchases, arguing that such inscriptions granted them a unique way to enter the battlefield and ensure victory. Also, it was argued that if a soldier left behind his rifle, it would be easier to identify and reprimand him for abandoning the "beautiful sex." Some shrugged their duties, opting to send a slave or paid member of the lower classes in their place for military or police duty.[16] Desertions also became commonplace. Focusing on the glories of independence, Sánchez wrote that patriotic women would "crown the young man who had placed within their hands the instrument of victory, the proof of his glorious courage."[17] Such erotic presentation quickly caught the attention of the public at large. A letter to an official appeared in *La Gazeta Ministerial* in support of the women who desired to implement this idea on a larger scale.

When a joyous public cry brings news of victory to the bosom of one's family, these women will be able to say with passion, *I armed the arm of that courageous man who assured his glory and our liberty. . . .* Dominated by honorable ambition, our women subscribers have begged Your Excellency to mandate that their names be engraved on the rifles they have purchased. If love for the fatherland leaves a hole in the hearts of soldiers, the consideration of sex will provide a new stimulus in order to compel them to maintain their pledge of affection from the female compatriots whose honor and liberty they defend.[18]

When the love of *patria* no longer moved the tired soldier to battle, the article maintained, the novel promises of the *patricia* guided him. However problematic such representations might have been, it is interesting to note that women appeared to be united in their efforts, whereas male soldiers were easily swayed by seduction. Dressed to kill and "prey to the Look," images of the "beautiful sex" incited male warriors to emerge victorious in their struggles.

Following independence, declared on July 9, 1816, the region appears to have experienced a repositioning of some gender roles, particularly the one attributed to women in raising young, upstanding patriots. The ideal of Republican motherhood became central to the debates for women's education, positing a learning son—dependent on his mother—before the political goals of the nation. Without question, such goals targeted the predominantly urban and Creole elite, whose children would be expected to maintain racial hierarchies and neocolonial values.[19] Children of the working classes, some of whom served as apprentices in fashion enterprises, committed their lives to service as "debt peons."[20] Targeting its elite readership, *La Gazeta de Buenos Aires* published advice "To American Women of the South" that presented a more nurturing role for women in the early formation of patriots while it maintained their status as alluring objects.

One of the ways to introduce customs and to promote enlightenment in all branches and, over all else, to stimulate and to propagate patriotism, is for American women to make the firm and virtuous decision not to appreciate nor to distinguish anyone but the moral, enlightened young man whose beliefs are utilitarian and who, most importantly, is a patriot, a faithful lover of LIBERTY, and an irreconcilable enemy of tyrants. If mothers and wives studied in order to inspire their sons, husbands and their servants with these noble sentiments; and if in their attractiveness they should be recognized by young men, and should use their empire of beauty and natural artifice in order to conquer unnatural men and to electrify those who are not, . . . what progress could our system not make?[21]

Calling on women to use their looks as weapons in the "conquest" of disenfranchised men, prevailing discourse froze women into limited, often sexualized, roles. The vocabulary of empire could not have been more disconcerting. Although the future Argentine nation rested on republican ideals, Halperín Donghi argues that the colonial past was still a heavy burden on the social and cultural life of the new nations in Spanish America.[22] The premise of Republican motherhood appears to have rested on a political agenda that continued to maintain elite visions of dominance and male power.

The idea that a nation's future rested on the efforts of individual women received much comment in subsequent letters to the editor. In an attempt to substitute beauty with substance, one reader came up with amusing results by mocking the "liberating" principles of independence that seemingly afforded women two distinct roles: angels of the home or sirens for misguided men.

> At first, I reacted with indignation upon considering the miserable state of America, given that its natives require the influence of women in order to become patriots. I foresee that this patriotism can last only as long as one appreciates his object of desire. Because women are fickle by nature, this all might lead to the annihilation of patriotism or at least to a frequent variation in its quality.
>
> Next, I burst my seams laughing, realizing how ludicrous it would be for the women of this country to carry out these proposed desires. The author might better have exhorted fathers to leave their daughters in full possession of the liberty that duly belongs to them. In this way, they might lavish their caresses on young men more easily. Without a father's permission, it is useless for any woman to exert herself in any endeavor.[23]

While such discussions were presented anonymously, writers like this one presented themselves as the defenders of male parental authority. This framing projected a sense of order and harmony in an otherwise volatile public sphere that debated the status of women in independence. "The absence of consensus in political rule," argues Szuchman forcefully, "necessitated a societally valued tradition of authority that could overcome the inability of early republican forms to forge stable communal links."[24] The figure of the caudillo fit the notions of hierarchy established by the *patria potestad* (laws of parental authority) of colonial times. In this context, it appears that beautiful roles for women that involved their potential as citizen-subjects threatened existing social structures. Women could assemble with their husbands and children for parades and hangings alike,[25] but their presences continued to be manipulated and their voices ultimately silenced by authorities.

Contestations over women's role in society and the ideals of independence continued to play themselves out during the Rosas period. A few women responded to the patriarchal notions that assigned them the role of political vanity, believing that this somehow overlooked the solid political decisions they had based on logic alone. An anonymous woman declared in *La Argentina,* "I recognize that the majority of my country supports Federalism and I wish to belong to the Confederation."[26] Political vanity, the same magazine also insisted, differed little from the pride attributed to male soldiers and leaders. During this period of regional instability, material culture reflected women's alliances and the cult of male leadership. Women of the elite Federal class commissioned special porcelain tableware with Rosas's portrait stamped on each piece. A few had neck scarves and gloves with the images of the caudillo confected in Spain.[27] Fashionable homes revealed crimson décor. The gossip of fashion magazines identified apolitical women as Unitarians.[28] Rosas, who clearly understood the symbolic significance of material culture during his regime, personally selected the dresses his daughter wore to social events.[29] Crimson was the Federal color and "so she had to be dressed in it,"[30] with her cherry-colored merino wool garments making their way to the pages of Mármol's *Amalia.*[31] The regime even implemented the ideal for women to govern their homes when it advertised in 1834 the *Manual de la criada económica y de las madres de la familia* (Manual for the thrifty servant and housewives) that included secret recipes, sewing, and garment washing tips. Such gender-specific and thematically inspired approaches to material culture represented the absolute power that guided all interactions and

Juan Camaña, *Soldados de Rosas jugando a los naipes* (Rosas's soldiers playing cards), 1852 (detail). Oil on canvas; 82 x 99 centimeters. The wool garments of the woman are crimson and white. Courtesy of Museo Histórico Nacional, Buenos Aires, Argentina.

further underscored the kinds of domestic and beautiful roles required of women.

La Cotorra, a satirical magazine dating to this period, reprimanded those male leaders whose vanity maintained the hierarchies of their Spanish predecessors and did nothing to resolve the tensions between the sexes. The magazine's title could be translated into English as *The Female Parrot* or *The Chatterbox* (in the sense of the *parlanchina*, a woman who gossips indiscreetly). Its authors mocked the actions of men, who as members of what they called "the ugly sex" had relegated women to the domains of the home even as their pronouncements seduced the public with words such as *liberty, equality, citizenship, social rights,* and *constitutional unity.* "All tyrannical dominations have their last hour, and this hour has sounded for the male sex," an article on the constitutional rights of skirt citizens read.[32] With a cackling voice, *La Cotorra* appropriated many of the words circulating in postcolonial society and transformed them through cynical games into a series of nonsensical concepts. Inevitably, the original meanings of the vocabulary of independence were lost. And so *la política* (politics) became as much *Paco* as *polka: óptica, palco, lícito, Paco, pica, taco, copa, alto, cito, palo, topa, ato, toca, pito, polca, plato, Hipólito, Pilato, tío, tipo, ola, pato.*

Inverting many of the narrative strategies that had called on women to use their beauty to electrify men to build a nation, *La Cotorra* asked women to turn their beauty *against* men. Women thereby found that their fashion accessories and natural grace could be easily transformed into an arsenal and a political strategy. A poem written by Petra Pía Pito de Carriquirri y Sepúlveda, likely a pseudonym, asked men to renounce their power and avert a women's revolt. Scholars will find this poem unfamiliar; it therefore bears reproducing here.

> How well we know those tyrants
> Who belittle the female sex
> What have they done with the destiny
> of the universe in all this time?
> Do they not see that their plans are in vain
> and that to follow them is a mistake?
> Renounce your wicked power now
> Or women will revolt.
>
> Let us revolt already: It's easy to change
> the commonplace parasol into a cruel sabre,
> the frivolous distaff into a sharp lance,
> the *mantilla* into a steel helmet.
> We're not made of marzipan or butter:
> Should a knee fold before these men,
> it will not show a humble request
> but instead will form the first row of the firing line . . .
>
> Ugly sex, respond: What great
> sin did we commit to cause you

to deny us a post in the State
as if we didn't have a brain?
Without representation in the Senate,
without representation in the Congress,
We see that you are messing up the world by yourselves
Without listening to us as we cackle and fly about.

You'll hear us nonetheless: women who,
united together with strong bonds,
have views that are not useless,
and which words and deeds will prove.
From this day forward their duties
entail the final conquest of their rights.
While men kick up a row,
others will pick up *The Parrot*.[33]

The march of the skirted citizen, then, belonged to the woman whose desire to participate in the public arena far outweighed her interest in prevailing notions of beauty, fashion, and social obligation. Fashion was about progress, juxtaposing the body at rest with its movement through public spaces. As male leaders set out to arrange the political hierarchies of the state, they found their very spaces obstructed by the presence of fashionable women. Increasingly these women wore mutton sleeves and enlarged hair combs that endowed them with the status of unavoidable public participants. Self-fashioning served to challenge the discriminatory system that excluded women's participation in political life.

Despite the visual force of these emerging trends, women continued to carry out traditional roles that the regime emphasized to preserve the authority of Rosas. In this sense, their evolving social position was still subject to the requirements of war. Serving soldiers, especially through sewing, remained a patriotic act. Illustrations of military uniform established a standard for distinction and provided important visual details for construction. Even children wore military attire; some served and the few who broke the law were punished and even executed wearing these garments.[34] Rosas's Ministry of War dispensed material to volunteers who followed the specifications established by military authorities and performed these duties free of charge.³⁵ Advertisements that appealed directly to a female readership indicate that women also purchased the accessories needed to finish the male uniform. Between reviews on new schools for dance and the meteorological almanac, *La Gazeta Mercantil* announced newly arrived women's dresses alongside lists of available military accessories.³⁶ *El Progreso de Entre Ríos* included police advisories for men who did not pick up their finished uniforms.³⁷

Urged on by the regime, private schools for girls presented sewing as a path to female heroism. Annual sewing competitions sponsored by organizations like the Sociedad de Beneficencia granted prizes to female students for extraordinary achievements. Newspapers in Buenos Aires and other provinces published the names of the youngest members of sewing circles. An all-female sewing class that met at the Argentine School founded by Pedro de Angelis, Rosas's own "minister of propaganda" who began working for *La Gazeta Mercantil* in 1829, received special mention in that newspaper for the caliber of its creations. The school had apparently put on display handkerchiefs, dresses, and other fine embroidered items that compared in quality to those fashioned in Paris: "In spite of the young age of the artists, these works are in our opinion most superior to those made for the May celebrations and for this reason have been granted the Beneficence Society's prize."³⁸ *El Progreso de Entre Ríos* announced the distribution of special prizes for sewing and embroidery in girl's schools alongside ads for clothing and tailoring services.³⁹ For young girls, sewing and other contributions to the republic were utilitarian goals that fomented national pride, not beautiful roles, a fact underscored by popular culture. The daughter of Chingolo, the archetype of the compadre, who had appeared previously in *El Gaucho,* was praised for knowing how to milk cows and sow wheat for the republic but was criticized when she left it all to acquire French and the vocabulary of fashion in Buenos Aires.⁴⁰ The work of a disabled girl from Córdoba, on the other hand, provided readers with a chronology so inspiring that the *British Packet* granted the story front-page coverage. Born without arms, young Merceditas Roberez demonstrated her support for the Argentine Confederation when she stitched an elaborately embroidered towel for Rosas's birthday. With her mother's assistance, Roberez wrote Manuelita Rosas with the request that she kindly accept this gift on her father's behalf.

The towel, in which the initials of His Excellency's name, J. M. R., are worked in red silk, is stated to be of the most exquisite needle-work. The mother says that [were it not] for the unfavourable state of her circumstances she would bring her daughter to this city. H. E. the Governor has ordered said letters and towel to be deposited in the Museum in this city.[41]

Having surpassed extreme obstacles, Roberez presented Rosas and the city of Buenos Aires with a national treasure that reflected the courage, perseverance, and love of Argentina's youth. The "public ritual of judg-ment and observation"[42] of children's performances emphasized the "state's nominal concern"[43] for the education of future patriots and, in the process, delineated the roles that young girls would assume and that mothers had overseen.

It is likely that sewing circles attracted a diversity of social groups, although each appears to have been represented as markedly sepa-rate. The politics of Federalism had elevated the status of popular sec-tors, although this acknowledgment of the region's heterogeneity did not at all prove liberating for the marginalized.[44] A fear of mixture among castes still predominated daily life. Although women of the postcolonial period had access to the same styles, it is clear that dis-tinctions were still made according to the quality of materials used in their confection. If servants did not inherit the hand-me-downs of the people for whom they worked, visual documents from the River Plate region indicate that they wore replicas of the styles worn by their families in another, perhaps more economical, fabric. The sewing columns of newspapers sought to constitute a space for the discussion on women's role in the formation of national customs. *El Progreso de Entre Ríos,* for instance, stated that women's issues deserved coverage in the columns of their newspaper, as their choices ultimately shaped the very national fabric.

> Undoubtedly our readership will be surprised by this title that would seem a stranger to politics, commerce, agriculture and those items that men normally find in the pages of our newspaper. It is so: because this article is specifically destined to our ladies. They, too, are crucial to our society's progress, adding impulse and brilliant light with their elegance, their culture and their virtues.[45]

Arthur Onslow, *Winter Dresses*, ca. 1830. Lithograph on paper; 19.5 x 17.1
centimeters. Private collection, Buenos Aires. This work can also be found in
the archives of Museo de Arte Hispanoamericano "Isaac Fernández Blanco,"
Buenos Aires, Argentina.

Addressed at first to the male head of household, this introduction
presented women's issues within the parameters of existing power relations. More specifically, prescriptive highlights maintained a distinct
hierarchy that preserved the divisions of the antiquated caste system,
dictating the appearance of women, girls, and black female slaves.
Slaves and servants alike wore formal dress when in the company of
their mistress. It was customary for a woman of the upper and middle
classes to go to church in her *saya de iglesia,* a dress ordinarily of black

fabric, as a male or female servant trailed her every step and carried the mat on which she would sit.[46] Runaway slaves, as evidenced by the images and descriptions published in the classified advertisement sections of some newspapers, were often identified by the clothing they carried with them: In 1848, *El Federal Entreriano* described the clothing a thirteen-year-old slave girl would have layered or bundled and the half ounce of gold that her master, Mariano Montaña, now offered for her return. Petrona, the young girl, carried with her what would have been a sizable wardrobe for the period: a brand-new checked dress, a special crimson dress, a dress of North American fabric, a white dress with a black apron, a green shawl of cotton cloth, and a handkerchief.[47] The same newspaper repeatedly used an image of a female African Argentine carrying a bundle of clothes when reporting missing slaves. In other contexts, fashion lithographs depicted emotionless servants behind or to the side of the Creole elite, thereby elevating the perceived status of the upper class whose luxurious pursuits included theater outings, shared *mate* tea drinking, and evening soirees. *La Argentina* described the amount of lace needed to adorn a female slave's dress to denote status in public while distinguishing the presence of the mistress with an elaborate headdress.[48] As William Katra reminds us, "Racial hierarchies, surviving from colonial society, favored White European descendants, who held that racial purity constituted a prerequisite for elite status."[49]

Alberto Julián Pérez argues that the cultural politics of the Rosas regime created the illusion of dialogue among sectors when the regime in fact perceived members of marginalized groups as "possessions" to be dominated by the estancia economy.[50] Although the slave trade had been abolished on April 9 and on May 14, 1812 (when blacks and mulattos made up 29 percent of the population) and totally suppressed legally in 1825, an illegal slave trade still functioned throughout the region.[51] At the same time that Rosas courted the vote of the lower classes, especially mestizos, pardos, and blacks, he revived the slave trade from 1831 to 1838. Rosas himself owned up to 34 slaves, one of whom was branded on the forehead and for all of whom he preferred flogging to preserve order.[52] John Lynch explains, "Upper-class families held slaves; domestic slaves added to social prestige, and in a time of extreme labour shortage even a few slaves could make a difference on the land."[53]

"Women of Buenos Aires—in the Morning." Fashion lithograph from Bacle's *Trajes y costumbres de la provincia de Buenos Aires* (Buenos Aires: Bacle y Compañía, 1833). Courtesy of Biblioteca Nacional, Buenos Aires, Argentina.

Fashion lithographs reflected racial inequality by depicting young slaves who served as the "accessories" of the well-to-do mistress. Black and mestiza women, recognizing that "living conditions worsened for the black when he obtained his freedom,"[54] continued their servitude when not able to find work as seamstresses, washerwomen, or street vendors. Despite the fact that Rosas had forged alliances with several indigenous tribes, any idea of their agency "disappeared" altogether when official culture referred to their existence in the past tense. The regime certainly did not recognize those indigenous militants who had refused the terms of colonialism, limiting their representation instead to the role of "cruel attackers of peaceful white settlers."[55] Federalist demonstrations paraded Indians deemed friendly by the regime as if to imply their conversion at the same time that posters in the Plaza of Montserrat proclaimed, "Indians are worth more than a Unitarian."[56] Rosas may have depended on the support of popular sectors, but the repressive measures and strict laws sponsored by his regime, including the limitation of citizenship to free men over the age of twenty,[57] restricted the terms of representation.

In spite of such contradictions, poetry chapbooks and songbooks sponsored by the Confederation projected an elevated status for the African Argentine. If African Argentine women had found themselves censored in sewing circles, their potential role in public life was lauded in the realm of Federalist popular culture. The first decade of the regime paralleled the "high point in demographic history of black Buenos Aires," Oscar Chamosa writes, with some fifteen thousand African Argentines representing a quarter of the city's population.[58] From the patriotic songs of washerwomen to the call to young African Argentine males made by fictitious female characters in popular poetry, the regime appropriated the voices of marginalized women to mobilize disenfranchised groups seeking representation in the new nation. To the dismay of many Unitarian intellectuals, the power of Rosas seemed to rest on a majority that they perceived as "biologically unfit for modern civilization."[59] Sarmiento, for instance, argued that the "racial stock of . . . mestizo and indigenous peoples acted as an impediment to [the country's] material and social development."[60] Racist explanations of the inferiority of gauchos, African Argentines, and indigenous peoples only helped fuel the tension between Unitarians and Federalists. La Fuente writes that in La Rioja, this tension "lent itself to interpretations that likened the conflict to a caste war,"[61] with Unitarians represented as white and the Federals as people of color. In Buenos Aires, African societies offered donations for weapons and members of the *negrada federal,* a term applied to African Argentine militias in crimson shirts.[62] "Rosas's success with the black population," George Reid Andrews explains, "owed more to his systematic murdering and repression of the liberal opposition than to any concessions or benefits that he offered Afro-Argentines."[63] At the same time, depictions of the African Argentine's growing power and material wealth in popular poetry implied that those joining the mobilization for Federalism enjoyed improved status, clothing, and work. The regime, however, was not promising an extension of civil rights for African Argentines and instead placed "demands on the black population to fight the civil, foreign and Indian wars" that in turn "disrupted black family and community life."[64]

Recognizing the role of oral culture in the nation-building process, the regime astutely integrated manifestations of African culture into official programs aimed at garnering popular support. Artistic works such as the *Cancionero Negro* (Black Songbook), appealed to the traditions of the *candombe,* African associations of which more than fifty existed in Buenos Aires. Chamosa notes that these African nations "were neither modern nations nor what scholars recognize as pre-colonial African ethnic groups."[65] These associations, he argues, preserved the memory of African ancestry while allowing members to integrate themselves more effectively into postcolonial culture. The Congo Society, for example, linked its members to seven different nations through its burial practices, mutual aid assistance, and social gatherings for song and dance.[66] In previous years, the Rivadavia government had assigned members to public works whenever they were caught dancing,[67] so the celebration of African traditions in an official songbook was a bold new step. In the "Hymn to Manuela Rosas Sung by Black Women on Her Birthday," Congo nationhood placed Confederate political life at its center and ultimately selected Rosas's own daughter as its queen with this song: "You embellish, Madam, / The Confederation, / Throwing into the Abyss / The Diabolical Union . . . / If not enough Black women / Can sing for you today, / The nymphs of the Congo / Will come to praise you."[68] Celebrated as the spiritual guide of African Argentines, Manuela Rosas represented an ethereal political figure that respected the ethnic diversity of her followers. *El Nacional,* the Uruguayan periodical staffed by exiled Unitarians, sharply criticized Manuela Rosas for her presence at *candombes*. Andrews writes that *La Gazeta Mercantil* responded in kind, stating that she was meeting with respected, hard-working *mulatos, pardos,* and *morenos.*[69] Appropriating the terms of Greek mythology, however, the hymn reproduced the social boundaries of Federalist affiliation by characterizing African Argentine supporters as forces of nature in service of the divine patriarch.

The visual arts, like songbooks, romanticized the subservient roles assigned to African Argentine women when documenting the rhythms of celebration and everyday life under the regime. At the same time, a close look at these problematic representations of complicity and labor reveals forgotten fragments of postcolonial material culture. Renowned painter Martín Boneo remembered a *candombe* from his childhood at which Rosas and his family presided over a group of African Argentine dancers and musicians whose performance honored the Confederation at a humble ranch.[70] In this context, amulets and the poorly printed cloth of styles intended for more popular consumption would have linked the cosmology of ancestors to the political hierarchies of the regime. As a distinguished guest, Rosas appeared solemnly represented in uniform alongside family members and government authorities. Carlos Morel, on the other hand, focused his urban vision of daily life on the black laundresses who carried heavy bundles of clothes on top of their heads and on their shoulders before unloading them at the shore of the River Plate for washing. During the work day, as a lithograph by César Hipólito Bacle indicates, many laundresses smoked pipes marketed by local stores as "pipes for blacks" and which are believed to have been used almost exclusively by African Argentine women.[71] Morel's series on urban customs included a domestic scene in which colors immediately politicized the scene. Clad in an elegantly tailored crimson dress, a female member of the Federalist elite smugly returns the viewer's gaze as she holds a book with one hand and brings *mate* to her mouth with the other. We find her sitting room's divan draped with light blue and gold trim, reminiscent of the colors of independence. In contrast, the servant wears a blue apron and faded yellow uniform; her crossed arms in this room of national colors call into question the sense of belonging to a single political community. Although such depictions brought into play the tensions of everyday life, the constancy of representation in the arts circulated messages of a prevailing social order.

When popular song appropriated the female African Argentine voice to mobilize urban communities, their messages often attributed political shortcomings to the Unitarian opposition. If most people possessed very little in the first half of the nineteenth century, popular verses made it look like Unitarians hoarded their belongings at the expense of others. The character Franchica Cambundá, the voice of

Carlos Morel, *Manners and Customs of the River Plate* (detail). Published by Litografia de las Artes, Buenos Aires, 1845. Courtesy of Biblioteca Nacional, Buenos Aires, Argentina.

conscience, represented the intense suffering experienced by slaves and their descendants when at the mercy of corrupt Unitarians. Writing to Pancho Lugares Contreras of *El Gaucho,* Cambundá described how Unitarians had tied her up on poles, whipped her, and left her for dead. Demanding an end to racial harassment, she then criticized Rosas for not confiscating more Unitarian property and lowering rents for city dwellers in need.[72] The current system, she claimed, allowed the political opposition to monopolize the heart of the city while Federalist supporters were forced to travel long distances between their homes and work. Hoping to alleviate crisis through some form of civic action, Cambundá called on Pancho's expertise to distribute resources more fairly among the inhabitants of Buenos Aires. Since readers were well acquainted with Pancho's rise from gaucho to compadre, this advice and Cambundá's persistence gave the impression that Federal authorities would bring about change and material wealth by defeating the Unitarians in their midst.

Because the regime had successfully mobilized the black male population, many women took charge of the household, community endeavors, and the African associations.[73] In another song, a *mulata* laundress named Catalina asked Pancho for his perspective on current events. Describing herself as a *negra bosalona,* a term often applied to African Argentines who did not speak standardized Spanish,[74] she described a procession of soldiers returning from battle. Together with Rosas, their faces revealed the deep red hues of sunburn acquired after long days on the battlefield. Her verses inspired the celebration of the black female patriot in newspaper descriptions of those who welcomed their soldiers home: "Vamos a juntá, moreno, / Y vamonos a bailá; / Que hoy es día de candombe / y no es día de lavá" (Let's get together, black man, / And let's dance; / For today is for the *candombe* / and not for the wash).[75] Similar songs were likely heard when laundresses marched at the end of their workday to Rosas's Palermo estate; articles describe the participants waving crimson flags to the beat of a *candombe.* Songs also gave listeners a sense of what had transpired on the battlefield; many found out from songs that Unitarian leaders like General Paz had been taken prisoners of war. The image of unity among African Argentine communities in popular verse emphasized the fact that urban "militias gave the black population the possibility of a prestigious career and space for male sociability."[76] The regime, in turn, projected an empowered role for black female patriots who would assist their spouses, relatives, and fellow community members in preparing for war.

The protagonist of *La Negrita,* Juana Peña, became the African Argentine version of popular authority figure Pancho Lugares Contreras some two years later. Published on July 21, 1833, under the title of *¡Viva la patria!,* the leaflet was published by Luis Pérez and lasted but two issues.[77] Its short run is impossible to explain because the first issue sold out immediately and the second apparently fared very well. Characterized as a "Black Girl of Buenos Aires," Juana takes a humble yet allegiant stance when first positioned as a newspaper seller like her Federalist brother-in-law, Pancho.[78] Having recently assumed an official government post in Buenos Aires, Juana detailed the rising status of the African Argentine under the regime with a list of benefits she had earned: a long list of noble suitors, exuberant accessories, and confidence in her future. "I'm a true Federalist black girl," she explains in the first verse, for her character distinguished her political vanity, a wealth that she deems patriotic in nature, from the egotistical expressions of those who did not commit themselves to civic service even when benefiting from the system. "Because of the *patria* we are free / And this heroic gratitude / we must assert our saintly duty / To give the country our lives and health."[79] The poems create the image of human chests forming a mural to defend the nation from Unitarian attack. As a young, single woman, Juana concludes with words addressed to the Black Defenders of Rosas, certain that their efforts will never let her down—or the rest of the Argentine Confederation, for that matter. Following earlier traditions that urged patriots to battle, Juana enlists soldiers as they reply in chorus: "Give me the orders, General." We will never know what effect songs like this one in *La Negrita* had on building support among members of the African Argentine community, but it appears that the regime assigned a significant role to the creation, dissemination, and performance of propaganda featuring female African Argentine voices. At the very least, figures like Juana Peña demonstrate that the regime encouraged and counted on the support of popular sectors in the quest for political domination. Furthermore, it appears that oral culture promoted the possibility of a national political space in the minds of listeners and participants.[80] The delegation of political vanity and focus on subservience to the Federal family, however, manipulated these voices for political gain and did not even come close to pressing for equal rights for all.

During the struggle for power during independence, most women found themselves carrying out patriotic obligations within the domains of the home front. As the unseen and unheard agents of military history, their identities in independence remained concealed as their products remained in view. With the rare exception of Josefa Tenorio, dressed in male costume on the battlefront during the struggle for liberty, most women must have felt like little had changed for the patriotic sewing circles that maintained the strict hierarchies of colonial times. As tensions escalated between Unitarians and Federals, the Rosas regime swiftly appropriated female voices from popular sectors to mobilize supporters against the Unitarian elite. Although the songs of characters like Franchica Cambundá and Juana Peña certainly encouraged women to participate in public life, their voices represented the manipulations of a comprehensive propaganda campaign calling for the violent elimination of the political opposition. Perhaps their voices were not unlike the gaucho's, in that one found the songs of the *candombe* manipulated to integrate the African Argentine further into the national army, literary culture, and finally "civilized" law.[81] Perhaps the motivations of those mobilized were material, as La Fuente has argued in a similar context; militias would have expected beef, clothing, and work in exchange for their service.[82] The potential links between military complicity, the female patriot, manipulations, motivations, and the reproduction of colonial structures in postcolonial Argentina beg us to continue culling the archives so that we might more accurately represent the road to cultural independence.

The designation of "beautiful roles" during the struggle for liberation from Spain continued to limit women's participation in postcolonial society. As civil wars between local caudillos ravaged the countryside, women focused their sights on the cityscape, paying close attention to the acquisition of material goods and the politics of exclusion. Although the appearance of strong female poetic voices had signaled a shift in the representation of marginalized groups in popular culture, this unfortunately did not parallel any new legal status. Final abolition for the African Argentine did not come until 1853, when Unitarian leaders sponsored legislation one year after Rosas's defeat. Responding to the problematic role of political vanity that women had been assigned, the editor of *La Argentina* wrote, "If we are to have influence, we must start to practice." As seen in the next chapter, women of all backgrounds asserted their own independence when they shattered expectations in public with a three-foot-square comb. Their participation in political life simply could not be avoided. The final chapters show the columns of newspapers and magazines that helped women break through the mirror-dress that had for so long glorified male participation and relegated them to the margins. Despite finding themselves "prey to the Look," women began to record their individual and collective experiences and weave alternative narratives into the fabric of public life.

THREE   *Fashion as Presence*

A S A PROFOUNDLY SOCIAL PROCESS, fashion invites individual
and collective bodies to assume certain identities and, at times,
to transgress their limits. At a moment when the obligatory
scarlet insignia ordered and unified all under the pledge of Federal
power, variances in style helped solidify the politics and position of the
wearer. The official literature of the period often intensified distinctions in male costume, delineating the patriotic subject and implicat-
ing the Unitarian in a drama of national betrayal. Dress codes seem
to have enabled authors and bystanders to "read" a person or group
in the same way one might read the "suits" on Wall Street. Unique
styles still reveal the tensions of political transition, as if to indicate that
the workings of culture, citizenship, and social change are inextricably
linked to dress. This chapter traces the emergence and decline of a
postcolonial comb, the *peinetón,* used by politically inspired women.
The immense popularity of this exuberant accessory that crowned the
female inhabitants of the River Plate region for almost two decades
eventually became the source of great concern and cultural debate.
With their fashion presence, women of the postcolonial period became unavoidable public participants, a fact few could overlook.

As we have already seen, Federalists could be identified by their scarlet vests, insignias, and hair ribbons, if not by their fervor alone. Anonymous letters to the editor in the major newspapers often reflected
this fact, employing patriotic metonyms rather than signatures. Hence,

one could sign patriotic messages as "Patillas" or "Los Patilludos," alluding to popular Federal characteristics (in this case, "men with sideburns") rather than formal names. Aristocratic Unitarians, on the other hand, showed a predilection for high French fashions and soon risked their lives with U-shaped beards or green and light blue hues. The mere public mention of the word *celeste* (light blue) no longer evoked the days of Independence, but represented an outlawed political position. Patriotic presence increasingly relied on the vocabulary of uniform and fashion, with particular styles solidifying hierarchies that posited Federalists as Argentines and Unitarians as marginalized *afrancesados* (Francophiles).[1]

As male leaders set out to arrange political hierarchies, they found their very spaces obstructed by groups of women wearing elaborate headdresses. The fad for audacious combs had begun in the 1820s, when women of the region began to discard Spanish customs for other styles. The hybrid *peinetón* soon represented a gendered link to the creation of customs in a newly independent region. Derived from *peine* (comb) and, later, *peineta* (convex comb worn in hair), the *peinetón* might translate into English as something more elaborate than a "grandiose comb." Unlikely to be found in dictionaries of Spanish, the Argentine word is pronounced as if to proclaim a statement. The accent on its final syllable demands the listener's most undivided attention. At the cusp of its popularity, the *peinetón* measured one yard in height and width.

The *peinetón* has often appeared in twentieth-century historical and literary works as a mere anecdote, a testimony to an earlier, more distinct Argentine aesthetic. Numerous travelogues from the post-colonial period featured prominently this unique accessory, with reactions ranging from graceful praise to dumbfounded marvel, "the ponderous yet not inelegant comb giving to their little heads a great deal of importance."[2] French traveler Alcides D'Orvigny likened the combs to large convex fans that followed *porteñas,* or the port-dwelling female residents of Buenos Aires, throughout the city; with dramatic tension, fellow traveler Arsène Isabelle equated the *peinetón* to an elaborate building or fortress in the air.[3] In New York, words did not suffice. The *British Packet* reports that New Yorkers admired the beauty, while contemplating the oddity, of an Argentine comb on exhibit.[4] Many writers made associations between the *peinetón* and growing nationalist sentiment. The expressive styles of young Argentine women, so it was believed, distinguished them aesthetically from their peers in other countries, a declaration still made today in prominent designer circles or on the nationally televised Roberto Giordano fashion show.[5]

Fashion lithograph from Bacle's *Trajes y costumbres de la provincia de Buenos Aires.* Courtesy of Biblioteca Nacional, Buenos Aires, Argentina.

Despite the significance of the *peinetón* in postcolonial culture and its numerous mentions in nineteenth-century poetry, travelogues, and news reports, scholars have tended to overlook this aspect of material culture and its relation to debates on the status of women and citizenship. As the countryside struggled with the anguish of civil war, the headdress represented an urban and gendered response to the quest for public space. In the postcolonial context, the *peinetón* became synonymous with the female public participant whose presence could no longer be overlooked. Spurred by negative press targeting the Argentine headdress, this fashion became the subject of satirical caricatures and depicted women as unstable forces in the cityscape. Regardless of such criticism, fashionable women continued to wear their combs at social events, during theatrical performances,[6] and at public meetings, until the Rosas regime made the final push for its demise. Redefining the ideals of independence, women of postcolonial Argentina wore the *peinetón* fashionably and yet defiantly to assert their presence in the public sphere.

The evolution of the European-made hair comb into an elaborate and enlarged Argentine *peinetón* must be traced to the push for independence from Spain. The first hair combs in Argentina, brought by Spanish colonists, date to the early part of the eighteenth century. Over a century later, most Argentines looked to the fashions of France in an attempt to distance themselves from the customs they shared with Spain.[7] The Romantic rebellion in Europe had brought about several changes in fashion, affecting women's hairstyles most markedly. The intricately woven hair designs of courtly Versailles, having reached dramatic heights, evolved with revolution into more free-flowing styles. By 1820, perhaps as a nostalgic revisit of monarchical times, the *chignon* appeared in French fashion plates. Tortoiseshell combs secured ornately woven hair atop a woman's head, the extended height leading to its humorous portrayal as giraffe fashion. Although some fashion historians believe it possible for the Argentine *peinetón* to have evolved from the *chignon,* it is more likely that a cross of influences ultimately formed this unique hair fashion.

According to the writings of British ship captain E. E. Vidal, River Plate dress was remarkably hybrid in the 1820s, especially in the case of women's clothing. Given the collapse of the colonial market, Vidal registered the customs and material needs of the population, as competition now existed with goods made in England and in provinces like Cordoba and Santiago del Estero, known for their woolen cloth and ponchos.[8] Although it is difficult to assess the exact size of the fashion industry in Buenos Aires during this period, Vidal would have encountered "numerous urban establishments for the manufacture of clothing, uniforms, leatherware, shoes, hats, silverware, vehicles, furniture and building materials."[9] Because foreign imports had already saturated the marketplace, Vidal writes that the more privileged women of Buenos Aires "adopted a style of dress between the English and French," while retaining the Spanish *mantilla,* a kind of shawl often made of silk.[10] On their heads, they placed headdresses "consisting either of a handkerchief of gold gauze with braids of diamonds, or of chains of gold, twisted in and out of their shining black hair."[11] Independence no longer enforced the sumptuary distinctions of the colonial caste system, but women of lesser means still used the *rebozo,* an embroidered scarf, to cover their heads and shoulders. Although identical in appearance to the *mantilla,* the *rebozo* was considerably more ornate because it was often the most elegant piece of clothing a woman possessed. By 1823, the limited *peineta* began its decade-long transformation into the lofty and commonly used *peinetón.* By 1830, the word *peinetón* appeared in the advertising section of *La Gazeta Mercantil,* and women of all social backgrounds wore the fashion.[12]

With her corseted waist, Elizabethan collar, mutton sleeves, and *peinetón,* the fashionable woman of Buenos Aires looked like a walking hourglass. One early fashion lithograph reveals a model with hair dressed in glamorous crimson and rose embellishments to convey support for Rosas (which means "roses" in Spanish). To carry the immense comb, which could have from six to fourteen teeth and weigh about 1.65 pounds (750 grams), women sometimes wove their hair into a French-style *chignon,* using concoctions of honey and hemp seed oil, or similar ingredients, to maintain their style. The French comb used for the *chignon* style, however, would have been shaped of several coordinating and interwoven strips of tortoiseshell. Although these certainly existed in Buenos Aires, Claudia López and Horacio Botalla diagram three other basic shapes. The two shapes that allowed for more narrative designs, the oval and inverted bell shape, usually sported animal and flower motifs. Most women apparently aspired to wear the fourth, trapeze-like style, or so the fashion lithographers would like us to believe.

Responsive to popular requests, artisans amplified the comb (traditionally crafted from African or Caribbean tortoiseshell, and sometimes from imitation tortoiseshell made from a composite of cow horns), in a laborious process. After boiling the material in saltwater to soften it, the artisan overlapped sections and then shaped and cut them manually. After additional processes helped shape the comb further, the artisan dried and polished the final piece. The horizontal shape of some combs allowed the artisan and client to work together to create elaborate motifs, such as natural and patriotic scenes, for the comb. When detailed with precious metals, a *peinetón* became a costly status symbol and part of a bride's dowry.

Although the variety of styles were easily discerned, reporters from the period still admitted to being at a loss for words. The *British Packet* recounted:

> How shall we describe the immense comb, which now forms so prominent a part of the head-dress of the fashionable fair of Buenos Ayres, its fretwork with ornaments, and the graceful mode in which it is arranged in the hair—truly we might exclaim with the "noble Poet," 'I can't describe it, though so much it strike, Nor liken it,— I never saw the like.'[13]

This male reporter's endeavor to capture the essence of the immense comb attempted to open an honest discussion of the novel fashions circulating in the cityscape. The most outstanding characteristics of this trend, however, became the immediate object of critique in other newspapers. The fashion chronicles of *El Monitor* describe the comb as "an exaggeration so exaggerated that it exceeds the limits of the exaggerated; and if women believe that the enormity of the combs favors them, they are mistaken."[14] The newspaper found no practical use for the *peinetón,* only to quip that a woman with such a monstrous head could best serve her family as a walking parasol.[15]

As foreign travelers and reporters sought to classify uniquely Argentine customs, the eye-catching comb represented a gendered link to the nation-building process. When comparing European style to an

Argentine aesthetic, accounts invariably focused on the highly original style and stunning hourglass figure of the fashionable *porteña*. The Argentine woman and her "signature comb" stood out from Europe and the rest of Latin America. Unlike the men and women of England, one British reporter remarked, Argentines were not at all susceptible to "perpetually undergoing tasteless variations by following the fashions of a neighbouring nation."[16] In the reporter's native England, as Aileen Ribeiro has shown, women wore elaborately decorated bonnets, sleeves shaped like air balloons, and wide skirts; their presence in the press was already suspect. Despite the initial admiration for the feminine styles of Argentine independence, the *British Packet* later criticized women for their lack of rational choice in hair accessories.

> The most prejudiced persons acknowledge that the ladies here have infinite taste in dress,—there is scarcely but one opinion in this respect. They do not copy from France, England, or any other nation; neither are they the slaves of mantua-makers and milliners. We should be glad, however, if they would discard the outrageously large comb, and the superfluity of artificial flowers, which now disfigure their pretty heads."[17]

If reports had admired fashionable Argentine women for their unique styles on one hand, their independence appeared limited by the critique of their excess on the other. The rest of this chapter exposes the very tensions that surrounded the *peinetón,* situating this emblem of fashion presence in the evolution of public space in postcolonial Argentina. As the *British Packet* had already reported, a woman could use her *peinetón* to communicate her difference quite powerfully. By rupturing sartorial norms, it appears that comb-wearing women challenged the consensus of their time by insisting on their complete integration into public spaces and the nation-building process.

With great artistic license, contemporary author Eduardo Gudiño Kieffer tantalizes us with the idea that the *peinetón* is as Argentine as the pampas, the comb's exaggerated size perhaps inspired by the horizon of geographic expanse. He writes,

> I think, with the fantasy afforded me as a writer, that the vastness of the horizons of the pampas transformed the Spanish *peineta* into a *peinetón*. Why not think that a river-ocean, that a land apparently

without limits, would enlarge not only ideas but also the simplest of "things"?[18]

The seemingly limitless national boundaries—from the River Plate to the Patagonia—contributes to a feeling of promise and infinite space. The panoramic paintings of the countryside by nineteenth-century artist Prilidiano Pueyrredón certainly evoke this sense of boundless pastures and unrestrained sky. The vast Argentine landscape, Gudiño Kieffer suggests, engenders ideas and transforms everyday objects into larger than life allusions to national pride.

Following the thread of this creative proposal, one might consider the design of a *peinetón* as a reflection on the demarcation of national boundaries under the new Argentine flag. Indeed, the comb emerged alongside the quest for independence and during the development of unique, national customs. Argentina of the 1820s, however, was anything but united. The tumultuous evolution of the United Provinces of the River Plate into the Argentine Confederation had seen its share of power-driven personalities, contradictory political poses, and territorial disputes (both internal and international).[19] Tensions escalated between arrogant leaders in Buenos Aires and caudillos of the interior who viewed themselves as independent from political decisions made in the city. Despite the ebbs and flows of the civil war that ensued, the move to forge the underpinnings of an Argentine national identity carried on during Rosas's regime. And it was indeed during the years of the Confederation, and not independence, that the native comb finally grew into the outlandish *peinetón*.

Postcolonial Argentina had experienced a temporary repositioning of gender roles, due in part to the domestic role attributed to women in raising young, upstanding patriots, and to a shift in the representation of the sexes.[20] As Francine Masiello writes,

> The emphasis on nuclear family life, childbearing, and female participation in civil society was subject to shifting interpretations and uses, and the feeble separation of spheres of activity—in which the masculine domain was identified with the public sphere and the feminine with the private—already showed signs of wear. Indeed, the cultural documents of the period indicate a less stable set of gender assignments than one might have expected.[21]

In this uncharted moment in the public sphere, women stood to gain a more pronounced access, despite numerous obstacles and male anti-sentiments regarding their political participation. The Association of the Young Argentine Generation, a literary society comprised mostly of Unitarian males (see chapter 4), would certainly capitalize on these gender shifts and spatial transformations in their literary work. When voicing resistance to Federalist power, these writers assumed women's pseudonyms and the rhetoric of fashion writing, thereby initiating "the possibility of feminine discourse as a way to structure the space of the imagination."[22] With this possibility of feminine discourse and the spatial flux underway in the public sphere, a woman and her *peinetón* represented a subversive possibility.[23]

At the core of head dressing lay the quest for coexistence in the public arena. When worn in public, the seemingly frivolous and exuberant *peinetón* commanded from all observers the special acknowledgment of its wearer. Despite the fact that a woman faced several obstacles, among them legal limitations imposed on her because of her gender, the *peinetón* endowed a woman with the status of a conceivable, almost unavoidable, public participant. Although the period's documents suggest that the comb caused headaches and hair loss,[24] women still sought this particular fashion accessory when claiming public space of their own. Undoubtedly, the *peinetón* served as a symbolic gesture, a visual demonstration of what was on a woman's mind.

Although portraits have tended to immortalize elite women with their jewel-encrusted combs, there is much evidence to suggest that women of all social classes enjoyed this fashion. As Saulquin reminds us, there were already few differences in the styles used by distinctive social classes by the mid-1820s.[25] The merchant class certainly helped make certain fashions prominent, but that did not mean that others could not partake in such pursuits. An early lithograph by Bacle depicts an African Argentine woman wearing a *peinetón* as she makes her way by the corner *pulpería*, a popular marketplace. The female protagonists of *La Gaucha,* the gazette by Pérez that circulated widely throughout the River Plate region, discuss in verse the pride felt in making patriotic statements through dress in the same way one might advertise a politically inspired t-shirt. But even when fashioned with homegrown materials, such as bovine horns, the comb still remained inaccessible to a great many. *La Gaucha* documented the sentiments of an impoverished and spirited female street vendor whose sales of chickens, ducks, and pastries on a hot day would help her buy a *peinetón* and dress in patriotic colors for an upcoming Independence Day.[26] Despite the fact that Buenos Aires was considered by most to be an expensive city, an official wrote that its streets appeared to have become inundated with *peinetones*.[27] The *peinetón* also began to appear in Montevideo, where artisan Tomás Escudero opened a shop, and in Asunción, Paraguay.

Women who aspired to wear the *peinetón* received much comment in the press, provoking several unfavorable comments even though the regime initially linked the accessory to the image of the "decent Federal woman." Many men complained about the aesthetic of the comb in letters to the editor, denouncing what they saw as the ghastliest proportions ever concocted, the monstrous height of the comb contrasting too sharply with women's delicate attributes. One "Young Man of Healthy Taste" wrote *La Gazeta Mercantil* to protest, claiming that the *peinetón* inspired in him no desire for its female wearers.

> The use of combs or baskets is dishonest and ugly. The women from around here have fallen to a tedious distraction and one does not know when this will end. They have completely forgotten the importance of proportion and measurement. Seen from behind, a girl with a veil might look like a jug if it were not for her size; but she ends up looking like a mortar with feet. Beautiful figure with which to captivate a young man![28]

Believing that women merely adorned the streets of Buenos Aires for his own satisfaction, this male reader felt threatened by the prospect of a woman dressing for the sake of her own self-recognition rather than solely to attract a man. This sexist logic was obviously at odds with the significance of women's fashions—which were evidently not impressive to the men witnessing them. For this reason, the subscriber found their mere existence "dishonest" in that they occupied public spaces designed for men. The anonymous writers of *La Argentina*, who professed to experience on a daily basis the prevailing attitudes that discredited women, soon advised their female readers to proceed with caution in public spaces. They believed that male egotistical behavior had become fashionable, and subscribers might need to carry needles for their own protection.[29]

In the struggle to arrange the public arena, men found themselves obstructed by the very presence of women. Clearly, they were not usually perceived as objects on which to fix the gaze; on the contrary, their presence evoked the spirit of Medusa. With the comb, women shifted the directions of men uncomfortably, and in a few noted cases, ran them off the street. The *British Packet* portrayed the woman and her comb as a military paratrooper, her potentially explosive *peinetón* endowing her with a "grenadier-like appearance."[30] *El Oficial,* who sent a series of provocative letters to the editors of *La Argentina* about the *peinetón,* likened the enormous superstructures in women's hair to a national landmark: "All of you women are walking around so weighed down that you have lost a lot of your natural grace, for each of you wears the tower of the School on her head."[31] Referring to today's Colegio Nacional de Buenos Aires, the official envisioned with horror the weight of an all-male institution flaunted atop women's heads. Given that several journalists of the period believed the editorship of *La Argentina* to be female,[32] the official's strong words pinpointed the "little female friend" whose very magazine had decided to publish his complaints.

> Let us defend ourselves from these female tyrants, because their despotism is intolerable and they will always obtain all that they want through infinite ways . . .
>
> Let us not fool ourselves, my little female friend. You all need one huge reform, for you are very spoiled. It is time that you get used to fulfilling exactly your obligations, the single woman leaving luxury and flirtatiousness behind, so that you can learn useful things and not run around putting on silly airs in the street.[33]

With allusions to battle and a volatile public sphere in the wake of invading females, *El Oficial* implored women to desert their combs and regroup within a more appropriate domain, namely the home. To some degree, the official's words reflected contemporary concerns about the mobility of citizens. Wandering in the streets of Buenos Aires was strictly suspect at this time, Szuchman writes, with entrants to the city presenting passports in exchange for local documentation, and workers circulating with *libretas de conchabo,* books recording employ-ment, that authorities consulted regularly.[34] Already there were strict fines for children "moving into, out of, or within the city without permission and valid documentation"; flying a kite was even prohib-ited.[35] And "public space was reserved for those men—and for certain types of women, most belonging to the lower classes—whose trades required them to be manifest,"[36] which helps explain why women out for a leisurely stroll would have raised eyebrows. Even Sarmiento felt it necessary to equate the combs with frigates coming in at full sail from the wrong direction.[37] As fashionable women asserted their presences *en vogue* and *en masse,* the simultaneous push toward private quarters made the pursuit of space look like an even stronger challenge to the authority of male leaders.

La Argentina immediately called into question the jaded character-ization of women and the cultural tendency to promote male superi-ority. In one satirical response to *El Oficial,* the magazine declared that women had long sacrificed their own needs for the benefit of society. The time had come to configure new forms of cultural expression in order to disrupt the civil war underway.

> You men insist on our society becoming a valley of tears. Man has always inherited error and weakness. In vain he feigns great knowl-edge and strength. The very little good that men accomplish they owe to determination of a woman, but then again, you are not around to philosophize all day.[38]

If women stood accused of falling for endless fashion cycles, then men needed to take a good look at the chaos they had spawned. *La Argentina* further countered prominent stereotypes by refuting popular images of fashionable women as undependable, irrational, and competitive. Finally, the writers asked, who most represented erratic change if not men themselves?

Assuming a didactic tone, the editors of *El Iris* published a series dedicated to resolving these differences, appealing to the fortitude of the female character by asking women to choose family prosperity over luxurious excess. Given that tortoiseshell was being imported from the Caribbean and Africa at the costly rate of 95 pesos a pound in 1831, roughly the cost of two healthy cows, the final cost of the *peinetón* had the potential to leave most families on the verge of financial ruin. Botalla explains that prices for tortoiseshell rose sharply as the demand for it increased, up from the 18 to 24 pesos a pound in 1824.[39] Although alternative materials existed for the same designs, such as the malleable and locally produced bovine horn, these seemingly carried with them the stigma of fakes. In today's terms, we might make the parallel between the Louis Vuitton handbag advertised to the luxury market for a few thousand dollars and the knock-off made from materials of lesser quality and sold on city streets. For a real tortoiseshell comb, it appears that one had to trade the equivalent of two weeks of a blacksmith's salary, making the real tortoiseshell combs inaccessible to most. The *British Packet* explained "*the heart-ache, and the thousand natural shocks,* which tender mamas and husbands must feel in the present hard times, when importuned to purchase such expensive articles, and the poutings which a refusal oftentimes generates."[40]

El Iris placed the *peinetón* within the framework of materialism that threatened hard-earned riches and compromised a family's livelihood. "To Fashions" reminded women of the need to hold their moral ground and not give in to costly fashions. It might be necessary for styles to vary every now and then, the male poetic voice explained authoritatively, but luxurious consumption could have potentially serious consequences.

> How will a poor old
> working man like it
> if his wife wastes
> the ranch for a comb,
> pawning the premises
> for fashion's sake?
> What will he do
> when in a short while
> the fashion changes
> with some new fretwork
> or if they alter the shell
> in height and width?

Recognizing that the comb had become a "must do" accessory, the poetic voice exposed the woes of a loving husband whose marriage crumbles because his wife has succumbed to the lure of luxurious goods.

The real subject matter of the poem, however, was the future marital happiness of young women. The poetic voice therefore focused its praise on the virtuous woman who did not give in to the whims of luxury, "because you are more firm / than the hardest marble."[41] *El Investigador,* a revolutionary periodical printed in Montevideo, presented a similar topic: Blinded by vanity and foregoing her obligations, a woman leaves her starving children alone at home to "plant her *peinetón* without delay" at the comb maker's store.[42] In this case, however, the culprit of domestic instability could be attributed to the scarcity of material wealth in the Confederation. Regardless of the motivations, to surrender the *peinetón* meant to take on symbolically the financial stability and well-being of the Argentine family.

As "Argentine" as the *peinetón* may have appeared, a dose of irony resided in the fact that many of the more popular designs were fashioned by Manuel Masculino, one of several Spanish artisans living in Buenos Aires. When one heard word of new designs in progress, it was promptly reported in the press: "It's best not to say anything about the next combs Masculino is creating because we have to focus on how we will compose ourselves."[43] Masculino had opened shop in Buenos Aires in 1825, two years after his arrival from Spain. Fellow entrepreneurs Custodio Peis, Martín Suárez, and Salvador Videla soon followed suit. The fact that a Spanish artisan was creating a typical *porteña* fashion provoked the critics of the *peinetón,* especially those who disregarded the fashion as antithetical to Argentine family values and believed it necessary to discard these icons of vanity. To protect regional markets, the regime had already imposed tariffs of up to 35 percent for clothing and shoes, a move that favored the provinces but not the residents of Buenos Aires.[44] The sale of foreign ponchos, which were on the average 30 to 40 percent less expensive than ones from the provinces, was also prohibited.[45] Despite such "provincial federalism," Masculino's business appears to have thrived in a depressed market in which consumers ordinarily purchased the least expensive clothing and footwear.[46] As a result, he even registered some one hundred native employees, almost all African Argentine (both male and female) and child apprentices.[47] A few fashion columns pointed out that the creativity of current styles appealed to the majority of the population. Otherwise, as appeared in *La Argentina,* why did so many men insist on buying women these novelties as gifts? The numerous contradictions were just too rich to ignore.

A lively debate in print involved the fictitious and, yes, malicious correspondence between an Argentine lady and Don Cid, a man of Spanish descent who had begun to market combs of his own design.[48] From the lady's pen came a title that would have had no trouble commanding the reader's attention, "Down with the Spanish!" The contents appeared to be more conflicted, though, because the Spanish designer was at once responsible for women's dreams and their miseries. The reader could probably not help but remember the times "when we were slaves," or when Spain imposed its customs on the people of Argentina. Don Cid, a figure that apparently few had met in person, seemed responsible for reviving the legacy of Spanish economic despotism as he subjected women to great discomfort by fashioning the costly *peinetón*. Although initial verses indicated that women were somehow unhappy with the styles currently sold, an idea conveyed by the lines "It is not possible / for there to be / a man so cruel / with the beautiful sex," the truth was that women's unhappiness resulted from their lack of agency in a society that recognized only male struggles and accomplishments. If there existed some Spanish conspiracy to impose designs and seize again the earnings of River Plate inhabitants, it could only mean that the Creole male population currently profited from the very items they claimed to abhor. And their control of the political economy had done little to expand the roles of women in postcolonial society. The verses openly lamented such impositions and suggested that women could legitimize only the "resolute project" of landing a husband.

> Jesus, what craziness!
> Jesus, what blockheads!
> To desire at whim
> to limit our sex,
>
> when by disgrace
> they hold us down.
> Only to the latest fashions
> do we have rights
>
> because from fashion
> man derives profit

and it helps the arts
progress immensely.

In spite of the song
in the tone of a maestro
and the advice
a missionary would give us

to not use combs
that make hair fall out,
thinking that this will
impose fear on us

so that we will abandon
the resolute project
to which all women
have subscribed.

Male authorities could make all the attempts they needed to force
women to relinquish their combs, but it was still up to the individual
to decide what to wear and how to behave in public. The poem in-
sinuated that women would band together respectably, but without
any concern for what others deemed attractive. During one spiteful
correspondence, the Argentine lady evoked the image of an Easter
procession at which the body of the Spanish designer was consumed,
erroneously, by the flames meant for a dummy of Judas.

In the midst of such heat, Don Cid could only offer a cheerless
reply. "The Defender of *Peinetones*" humbly apologized for provoking
the wrath of this Argentine client. Because of the comb's popularity,
his business schedule had become far too hectic for his taste, toiling
long hours and experiencing financial setbacks whenever he failed to
meet his customer's expectations. An apology appears to have been
all that was needed. The Argentine lady begged for his forgiveness,
showing concern for the unintended consequences of acidic barbs that
had jeopardized his business, and conveyed her understanding of cultural differences by proposing marriage. "Argentina greets you / and
awaits you in her arms," she writes. In the case that he did not bow
to her, however, she threatened to expose him for the Spanish tyrant
that he might be in disguise. In another bizarre twist along the lines
of the foundational fictions that helped shaped a nation, the Spanish

designer became the "adored belonging" of the Argentine lady and, together, the two would serve the Republic.[49] Once the designer had left Spain in the dust, or so the verses reveal, his Argentine bride could shed her comb confidently.[50] Reconciled in marital bliss, the struggle between the Argentine lady and Don Cid ended peacefully, with the *peinetón* providing the impetus with which to discuss and resolve political differences.

The press also capitalized on the fact that women could use their imposing presences to shift forcibly the direction of men. In the streets of Buenos Aires, it was believed that women could force pedestrians off the streets with a flick of the comb. In response to the perceived onslaught of traffic jams by *peinetón,* the city adopted a set of social codes that required men to pass comb-wearing women on the left. In a letter to *La Gazeta Mercantil,* "Men with Sideburns" responded to what they viewed as an unjust distribution of space. These Rosas supporters insisted that women discard their immense combs and puffed-up sleeves for a more graceful appearance, as their current fashion accessories had them monopolizing city sidewalks.[51] A group of mothers responded in agreement with such male critiques, arguing that the *peinetón* symbolized the modern-day demise of family values when its fashionable wearer deprived her family of food in order to flaunt an expensive comb. Las Madres de Familia, or the so-called Pro-Family Mothers, further reprimanded *peinetón*-wearing women for invading spaces off limits to them. "Our friendly countrywomen can not be happy when they assume the fashionable *peinetón* and the ambition of men," they wrote.[52] Moved by the high volume of responses, the editor of *La Gazeta Mercantil* "cut the matter short, (all Editors being arbitrary) and declared the affair to have been sufficiently discussed," yet another indicator that the *peinetón* seemed to take up much too much space.[53]

With so much attention focused on the fashionable crowns, one "Poor Christian" called for the ecclesiastical order to mandate their removal from women's heads. In the wake of one solemn sermon, an entire congregation had apparently witnessed with alarm a man who crossed himself when some women—and their large combs—passed his pew. If women focused instead on the realm of the unseen and the devout virtues inherent to their sex, Poor Christian explained, then

"*Peinetones* in the Street." Satirical caricature from Bacle's *Trajes y costumbres de la provincia de Buenos Aires.* Courtesy of Biblioteca Nacional, Buenos Aires, Argentina.

men might dedicate their thoughts to matters of spirit and not the futility of human vanity. In a letter to *El Lucero,* he denounced the female invasion of the Church. The *British Packet* did not hesitate to translate into English this summons for prompt clerical action:

> *To those who can remedy it:*—Is there any ecclesiastical or secular authority in the Capital of the United Provinces of the River Plate, who will unsheathe a sword of fire against the want of reverence to the house of God? If there be, they out to put forth a ray of their authority against those who are forgetful of that sacred place. What great irreverence can there be, in a people the most Catholic and religious of the Christian world, than to see a crowd of females enter the temple of God with castles and towers upon their heads, horrifying even the least religious among us? Some of these females, in addition to their large combs, have high *banderas* [flags] on each side, so that when they enter by the door they appear as if wishing to

dispute the homage due to the God of Majesty. Is it not horrible to the Catholic possessing the least piety, to see a female who, not being able to enter the narrow passage to these temples passes through the Sacristy with these imperial crowns, and by the High Altar, to take her place in the church? Is it not painful to the pious Christian to be a spectator of these things occurring as they do every moment? . . .

What a pity it is that they are permitted to assume the *giralda de Sevilla,*[54] or a windmill, in order to promenade, to go to the theatre, or wherever they please! . . .

This multitude of devout ladies coming to the house of God, all crowned, and disputing about the height of the castles which they carry on their heads! Yet all this is passed by as a matter of little import: scarcely any one raises his voice against it. The females come with diadems of such an enormous height, that the religion of Jesus Christ imperiously demands a reform or a prohibition against their entering the Church.[55]

Because the crown awaits us in heaven, the author implied, it must not be flaunted here on Earth. Such a religious standpoint certainly holds true for those who subscribe to Christian principles. Yet the presence of women, and the "distractive" qualities of their fashion obsessions, competed with more than higher ground. The Poor Christian's letter insisted that voguish women wreaked havoc with the hierarchy of religious ceremony on earth. Because of the large size of the *peinetón,* women sidestepped the narrow passageways they had used traditionally and barged through those entrances reserved for clergyman. In the eyes of the congregation, women appeared to have invaded the Sacristy, when in reality the sermon had not yet begun. With this change in movement and spatial allocation, it appeared that women could go wherever they pleased, a sacrilegious act in the eyes of many. If not stopped, the *peinetón* threatened to besiege all vestiges of power with its demands for space, both physically and symbolically.

As the struggle between Unitarians and Federalists intensified, the *peinetón* became a kind of political billboard that women carried when making a public show of support of the Rosas regime. One advertisement in the daily newspapers announced the sale of combs engraved with a miniature portrait of Rosas.[56] Nineteenth-century artist Carlos Pellegrini incorporated the *peinetón* in several of his portraits to identify the most noteworthy women of the epoch, the cherished possession placed neatly atop each subject's head. While the *peinetón* became synonymous with the richness of Federalist fervor, in part from its use by first lady Encarnación Ezcurra, might a seemingly neutral comb design have announced Unitarian leanings? The archives are certainly silent in this regard; any outright display of support would have been censored by the early 1830s. As political tensions grew, however, so did the *peinetón*. When combs finally measured one square yard, they made an ample span for lengthy patriotic slogans. In 1833, the very year that Rosas was granted dictatorial powers, some combs proclaimed "Federación o Muerte" (Confederation or Death) and "¡Viva la Confederación Argentina!" (Long live the Argentine Confederation!).

In due time, the *peinetón* became an ambiguous term and, subsequently, underwent a catachresis. Speakers began to misapply the word in a consistent fashion, clearly identifying the comb that women wore in public but also implying other connotations. For most speakers, a *peinetón* appeared to represent a woman whose aspirations combined domestic obligations with political action. The pages of *La Argentina* portrayed its version of the archetype of the *peinetón* in issue after issue, pairing the unfolding plot of civil war with descriptions of the woman of fashion (*always* complete with her signature comb). Furthermore, *La Argentina* argued that women who cared about their appearance evidently possessed the self-confidence necessary to pacify the barbarous tendencies that war had uprooted in men. The idea evidently caused chagrin to those who believed that women should not meddle in affairs of the state, let alone occupy themselves with the responsibility of a newspaper.

In news accounts and popular poetry, the *peinetón* soon became a shorthand term reserved for third-person accounts that described the public presence of women. To clarify the phenomenon for its English readers, the *British Packet* issued an editorial statement regarding the *peinetón*. Reporting the appearance of four hundred large combs at a political gathering, one journalist prepared the ground for future readings with a special note. From that point on, the newspaper would view the *peinetón* as "a new figure of speech to designate the ladies."[57] The politics of metonymy appear to have relied on two prominent factors in the transformation of public space in postcolonial Argentina

(identified previously in this study): a negotiation of gender assign-
ments and the changing perception of women's role in public life.
As an early nationalist response to foreign monarchical rule, head-
dressing reflected the desire to distance oneself from the customs of
Spain. Following independence, male leaders recognized that women
should undertake a participatory role in the nation-building process.
The *peinetón* helped visualize this very goal, commanding public recognition through creative agency.

Playing with the indisputable associations of gender, fashion, and
politics, popular literature and satirical caricatures transformed the
metonymy of female presence into a "public woman." Ridiculing
women's potential subjectivity so as to better serve male political interests, artistic pretense turned the comb into a malicious code word
for the prostitute. Poetic gestures encouraged this particular catachresis
by representing the need for male protectionism and the return of
women to a domestic lifestyle. In her study of *Sex and Danger in Buenos
Aires,* Donna J. Guy maintains that a national discourse on prostitution has served as a means of social control in Argentina at numerous
historical junctures. The designation of strict gender roles became a
method with which to force women out of the public sphere and
into the home. "If women's social and economic roles linked family
and nation, then women who existed outside traditional family structures threatened the nation."[58] Some premises regarding the public
woman argued that a psychosexual impulse for fashionable clothing
and expensive jewelry helped lead to her demise.[59] The link between a
woman and fashion revealed a most difficult paradox: While expected
to follow the fashions of the day, a woman also ran the risk of others
speculating undesirably about her moral character.

In the annals of popular literature, a unique poetic discourse developed in response to the completely desirable yet utterly despised
peinetón. By appealing to widespread sexist attitudes and poking fun
at the new roles women had assumed, disdainful depictions of "the
beautiful sex" delineated new parameters of public and artistic representation. A series of verses published in the 1830s by the government-
sponsored Imprenta del Comercio illustrates this point. "Lo que cuesta
un peinetón" (What a *peinetón* costs), which, as a result of catachresis,
might have read as "What a *woman* costs," detailed the precarious lives

of men who found themselves at the whims of female fashion dicta-
tors.[60] The poem's title, repeated throughout the poem for rhythmic
and almost humorous effect, serves as an anaphora. As a result of this
effect, the reader quickly recognizes the value of the *peinetón* and the
men who seek her presence.

The anonymous text follows the style of a *cielito,* the Latin American
poetic form generally reserved for patriotic themes. "What a *peinetón*
costs" responds with irony to the upcoming celebration of a national
holiday, a time when great men should occupy themselves with profound meditation on their civic duties. The women of Buenos Aires,
however, drive a competing agenda that diverts men's attention away
from their immediate obligations. Elaborate schemes they have devised
include the entrapment of fathers, husbands, and strangers to purchase
the largest combs that money can buy. In fact, women stop at nothing
to please a potential buyer.[61] A wife dutifully fawns over her husband
and rubs his back nightly, hoping that this will benefit her material
desires. Unmarried women are represented in more compromising
positions: A young woman acquiesces to her lover's needs. A widow
sells her late husband's possessions to purchase a lavish comb. And local
prostitutes set out to earn their combs.

> For those women who in the end
> Are not single nor married,
> The *peinetón* costs them
> Sighs and late nights.[62]

Grouped together by sexual innuendo, women heed to the insatiable
desires of men in order to reach their goals. Men, in turn, are unable
to ignore how much a *peinetón* will cost them both personally and
financially.

"What a *peinetón* costs" dedicates a stanza to each man whose
pocketbook may have been affected by its existence.[63] First, it lists the
male members of a family and then goes on to typecast several profes-
sions that make up the all-male workforce: the baker, the doctor, the
soldier, the businessman, the judge, the policeman, and so on.

> The priest who cures no soul,
> Even if not able to remedy pain,
> Must know by force
> What a *peinetón* costs.[64]

The prototypes of more established men contrast with the poor beggar, who on this occasion suffers greatly from the lack of compassion his situation generates. As women now struggle to gather money for their prizes, they forget altogether about the beggars once fed by their generosity.

In the wake of a national holiday, one might expect the poem to ask men to contribute more wisely to the wealth of the country. However, a woman's comb also puts on display the affluence and ideology of men. This, in turn, leads to its subsequent incorporation as a marker of class as well as political affiliation. With swift logic, the poem showcases the Federalist patriot while playing down the inferior Unitarian.

> The Unitarian does not ignore
> the truth that, in his faction,
> No one has the funds necessary
> To buy a *peinetón*.
>
> Every black bull knows
> That red and scarlet
> Are signs that one surely has
> What it takes to buy the *peinetón*.[65]

Only a Federalist man, as the poetic voice implies, has the financial standing to purchase a *peinetón*. With civil war having bankrupted his remaining assets, the undesirable Unitarian suffers great financial duress. As the public eye evaluates who buys what for whom, the poem calls on guards, the mayor, and the police commissioner to use the *peinetón* as a device to separate Federalists, those who have retained their purchasing power, from Unitarians, who have not.

A complementary poem, "El que paga el peinetón" (He who pays for the *peinetón*), furthers this premise of Unitarian desperation.[66] If Unitarians do not possess the funds necessary to please a woman's tastes, as "What a *peinetón* costs" maintains, then prospective mates resort to immoral acts to satisfy their vice for luxurious goods. "He who pays for the *peinetón*" also maintains strict consonant rhyme and eight-syllable lines. Its stanzas, however, consist of clusters of ten (and not four) lines, allowing for the development of more heated diatribes. The poem's ambiguous title and its use of the *peinetón* can also be read as a catachresis, allowing for a most provocative reading on partisan politics and the construction of gender. "He who pays the peinetón" categorically identifies women as prostitutes and adulterers who cheat on their lovers to obtain combs, the ultimate prize of sexual conquest. Most importantly, women are classified as sympathetic with Unitarian views, a tactic that symbolically reproaches the *peinetón* while also serving as propaganda against the state's most pronounced political enemy.

The poetic voice evokes the color green, the color of the Unitarian uniform, in a denigrating fashion. In Spanish, to describe something as inherently "green" is to regard the object as potentially perverse and overtly sexual. When the poetic voice paints a section of Buenos Aires "green," it weaves the reader through the windows and alleys where desperate Unitarian women linger, awaiting their prospective buyers. The omniscient narrator observes Buenos Aires street life with a careful eye, noting the city's open spaces and describing the interaction between the sexes. Strangely enough, the poem does little to describe the presence of the men who pay for the *peinetón*. Instead, the reader takes on the male gaze, observing silently the women who have strayed from their homes into the domain of public circulation.

Glimpses into the sad appearance and lives of individual women reinforce the perverse context of the poem. Beautiful, ugly, young, and old—in the spectacle of the public sphere, women parade themselves before men as if prized cattle in a show, the onlookers evaluating each of their poses and contemplating the investment. A young beauty initiates the game of illusion and deceit. Engaged in a starvation diet, she configures her body to appeal to the man who will make her *peinetón* payments.[67] Another girl fakes tears to evoke her beau's pity and, should she be so successful, a marriage proposal. Marriage, however, seems the last of her desires; the poem implies that she desires a lavish comb for an engagement gift.[68] Each of these young women appears at the crossroads between a virtuous life and irredeemable behavior. The penchant for fashion pushes them into the first stages of a dishonest lifestyle, with the obsession for the comb providing the final transformation.

Every woman risks being "read" by others in a potentially unbecoming fashion, not unlike the way in which a *piropo,* a flirtatious remark made by males, might address the clothing or body parts of a female passerby. Even if a woman is married, she is not shielded from others who regard her public character with suspicion. The extravagant *peinetón* does not necessarily represent the wealth of a woman's husband, the poem suggests. It can also serve as a kind of public revelation, alluding to the possibility that the wife is engaged in a clandestine affair. In one stanza, a mulatto woman deceives her Unitarian husband every time she rushes to the arms of a young boy who can afford to buy her the lavish comb.

> That young mulatto woman
> Taller than a campanile
> Is the wife of a Unitarian
> Who pawns even his shirt.
> Her husband beats her
> With reason and cause.
> And because she allows him
> To care for her this way;
> He must know that a young lad
> Is the one who buys the *peinetón.*[69]

At another point, a prostitute brags that another woman's husband has favored her with a new headdress.[70] The poem presents a chain of gossip that, while calling into question the motives of the *peinetón,* also hopes to catch a glimpse of the man who might have paid her way.

The public spaces of "He who pays for the *peinetón*" become the setting of a makeshift morality play, a place where the reader can explore the outrageous defects of Unitarian life and the prostituted body that predominates the cityscape. The poem forces the reader to assume the Federalist gaze and, in the process, to view negatively the position of the Unitarian in postcolonial society. Identified as a Unitarian by her light blue dress, one woman desperately searches the neighborhood for a suitor who will pity her impoverished state and reward her with a *peinetón.* Because she is a Unitarian, everyone avoids her like the plague, fearing that she might carry a transmittable disease.

> That fiery beast of a girl
> Wearing a light blue dress,
> All fear she may be infected
> And so she finds no one to love her:
> But the poor girl is going mad
> Trying to find the occasion
> When someone might be moved to compassion;

> And for all that she has searched,
> That she's a Unitarian makes it a challenge to find
> Someone to buy the *peinetón*.[71]

Another woman's physiognomy identifies her as the wife of a Unitarian, an argument consistent with popular beliefs during this period. Because of her willingness to compromise, she accepts the advances of a more affluent suitor.[72] A different scene depicts a mature prostitute who served as the concubine of a Unitarian soldier during her youth. To pay for her comb, she now walks the streets in the company of a promiscuous rake.[73] Through metonymy, the *peinetón* represents the object of lust as well as its embodiment. By relegating fashionable women to the political margins of Unitarian politics, government propaganda pushed its own ideas on the redistribution of space and power in postcolonial society.

A glimmer of hope appears in the final stanza of "He who pays the *peinetón*." Over the bustling street scene, a young woman stares out the second-story window of her family home, daydreaming of the prince who will buy her a *peinetón*.[74] Though she desires so desperately to join in the freedoms below, her family has protected her from the ensuing clash of the sexes. During the fleeting moment at which the poetic voice focuses on the young female, her image evokes neither pity nor fear, which separates her from the multiple, degraded visions of the *peinetón*.

> At last, that wench over there
> Who sticks her head out the window,
> About to fly like a bird:
> She has no one who empathizes
> With her sad situation.
> Forced into seclusion,
> Not allowed to leave,
> She has no one to tell her
> "I'll buy you the peinetón."

Having situated the *peinetón* within the framework of female prostitution and partisan discourse, government-sponsored propaganda established new boundaries of representation. Popular poetry advocated a more pronounced separation between the public and private spheres, while also mandating the elimination of women from political life.

The wordplay inherent to the *peinetón,* or the public woman, sought to undermine the value of women in the political development of the nation. Having assigned the *peinetón* and Unitarians alike to fixed, undesirable positions within the public sphere, poetic discourse hinted at the desired alternative. The government could force women to return to the less politicized and more traditional spaces of the home front.

Although barely touched by the binary opposition of Federalist and Unitarian struggle, the visual arts foreshadowed the change in gender roles and the redistribution of public space. In fact, one could argue that the visual arts helped plot the fall of the oversize *peinetón.* Alejo González Garaño specifically credits Bacle for a change in the visual representation of women, a transformation that ultimately led to the comb's disappearance.[75] Bacle had moved to Argentina from France with the intention of publishing a joint European and Latin American fashion newspaper, *Diario de la Moda.* This project never materialized, and Bacle turned to fashion lithography instead. His highly acclaimed *Trajes y costumbres de Buenos Aires* (Dress and customs of Buenos Aires) depicts numerous customs of the early nineteenth century, from the pipe-smoking washerwoman to the fashionably corseted *porteña* with her signature *peinetón.* Bacle holds an important place in Argentine history, as the nation's founding lithographer and as the director of the government-sponsored Imprenta del Comercio.[76] The press, which González Garaño dates to January of 1835, published government bulletins, Federal ribbons, official portraits of Rosas, as well as the two anonymous poems discussed previously.[77]

Just as Spanish author and costumbrista Mariano José de Larra documented the customs and rapid growth of modern Spain, Bacle sought to capture the aesthetic of an emerging fashionable class as well as to record the sentiment of daily life. In his early lithographs, the poses of fashionable women imitate the static mannerisms characteristic of European fashion plates. Because Bacle surrounds his human subjects with little or no background, the viewer relies on the gestures and poses of each character to place their status and surroundings in context. The washerwoman's carefree stride, for example, contrasts with the rigid subservience of the servant who obligingly carries the overcoat of a fashionable lady. Below each print, a brief title provides a narrative thread that enables the viewer to frame the scene. These acute observations of national character, dress, and manners brought a unique visual vocabulary to the printing arts of Argentina.

Bacle combined his interest in fashion observation with an emerging scientific discourse on women's clothing and health. *El Recopilador* (The Compiler), a magazine of universal scope edited by Bacle, published a treatise on the importance of visual and literary portrayals of fashion to the management of women's well-being. Writing to denounce the metal-cage corset, Bacle argued that unhealthy dress warranted even the most distasteful criticism. When putting women and her fashions under the microscope, Bacle found an ailing female figure. He believed that science could help direct women away from danger and toward a healthier life style. Grace and beauty, he argued, only existed if women did not fall slaves to fashion. Even the *peinetón,* or so it appears, limited women's bodily movements because the wearer balanced her expensive, breakable comb ever so carefully. Bacle's didactic approach forced women to educate themselves about the havoc they wreaked with their corsets and other fashions that limited their performance of domestic chores.

> It is not such a great disgrace if one fashion or another is ridiculous and leads to some form of discreet or humorous satire. It is a disgrace, and a very serious one, when a fashion mandates like the tyrant it can be. Some uses can lead to the darkest consequences. In such a case, it is imperative to attack it without respite, to expose the ills it occasions and not view it with indifference.[78]

Clearly, Bacle believed that fashion writing could function as the impetus for change. Such action helped ease the mental anguish of those who loved fashion victims. Continuing critiques appeared to work, which could not have made Bacle happier. In 1836, some two years before Rosas imprisoned Bacle for depicting hanging corpses and thereby exposing human rights violations of the regime, the lithographer sighted smaller combs in theater balconies and declared, "Happily, we have buried the *peinetón!* . . . Let us return to the living!"[79]

We have already noted the limited, if not contradictory, terms of female representation in postcolonial society. Those who disregarded the *peinetón* out of national concern also emphasized the ultimate cost to the financial stability of the Argentine family. As a symbol of female persuasion, the headdress was capable of—quite literally—shifting the direction of men. The female editor of *La Argentina* proposed that women use their combs to usher men back into the home and away from the war-torn countryside. Under the title of *Extravagancias de 1834* (Extravagances of 1834), Bacle distorted this intense vision of powerful women and portrayed them instead as destabilizing forces in the public domain. Titles listed under each lithograph in the series allowed for a playfully ambiguous notion of the infamous *peinetón*, complete with allusions to the revolutionary breakdown of space in the streets of Buenos Aires.

The series begins with a woman who emerges from her home elaborately dressed for a walk in the street. "*Peinetón* at Home" depicts a woman who desperately seeks to leave the house, her immense comb and enlarged mutton sleeves preventing an easy exit. Here, the central female figure makes a statement as she enters the public sphere. She

"*Peinetón* at Home." Satirical caricature from Bacle's *Trajes y costumbres de la provincia de Buenos Aires.* **Courtesy of Biblioteca Nacional, Buenos Aires, Argentina.**

becomes a "home wrecker," who has hired a day laborer to unhinge the front doors and dismantle with a pickaxe the façade of her family's house. In a burst of energetic activity, the laborer inadvertently splits the comb of another female passerby, who drops her fan in surprise. "Still more, my lady?" the laborer asks. Uninterested in the disaster she sows, the stubborn *peinetón* urges him to finish the task at all costs.

"The Meeting of the *Peinetones*" and "Strolling *Peinetones*," also lithographs in the series, imply that women carried on unpredictably when convening in public. The first depicts two women who force one another to the ground when the horns of their combs interlock. Refusing to drop their fans and save the fall, they contend for the preeminent position they see as rightfully theirs, "Jesus, get out of the way!" and "Give me space, by God!" In a merciless competition for space, neither acquiesces to the other's right of passage. Across the street, one woman screams, "Oh, she's breaking my comb!" as the *peinetón* cracks in two, one side having hooked itself onto the heavy package that a young laborer carries on his head. In the far left corner, a couple somberly witnesses the spectacle before them. The man watches passively, clutching a thin umbrella in one hand as he courageously balances his wife and her overextended *peinetón* on the other. In the second, winds sweep through the port of Buenos Aires, and the *mantillas* wrapping their lofty combs lift the women of the city off into flight. Braving the powerful gusts, men rush to the aid of one soaring female. Knocked to the ground, a husband holds his wife's feet as she dangles above him; he shouts, "Help: the strong wind has taken my wife!" Floating helplessly in the air, swaying female bodies are caught between the men who wish to ground them and the headdresses that propel them.

By carefully selecting the words that describe the women who find themselves swept away by changing currents, Bacle highlights the vocabulary of the female compulsive shopper. The cry of the helpless husband in "Strolling *Peinetones*" refers to a *ventarón,* not a *ventarrón,* seizing his wife. Although the visuals play with the idea of wind *(ventarrón),* Bacle opts for a subtle change in spelling and thereby alludes to an all-out clearance sale *(ventarón).* Furthermore, the verb *arrebatarse,* which implies that the wife got "carried away," alludes to other period vocabulary from the marketplace, the *arrebata peinetas* (comb snatcher).

In 1830, *La Argentina* warned its readers of this new delinquent who quite literally ripped the combs from a woman's head and resold them for 100 to 200 pesos on the black market. The *arrebata peinetas* lurked in the shadows, spying on women secretly and waiting for the opportune moment to make off with their precious possessions. Given the comb's high resale value, women could often not afford to buy back their combs if they ran across them in the marketplace. Some accounts describe women who, having located their combs for sale once again, attempted to make a trade. This practice led one alarmed *porteña* to write the editor of *La Argentina,* with descriptions of the fear and sorrow experienced when combs were knocked from their heads and into the hands of a complete stranger.

> You know how our husbands scold us when they have to hand over one or two hundred pesos for a treasure that is so necessary for a lady's adornment. You see this when we run away in fear from these officious men. Is there not a solution to this problem? One occurs to me.
>
> May the first man to commit such a sin and be detained find himself handed over to the victims so that they may judge him. I assure you, Argentina, that the example we will have made with the one who should have the misfortune of falling into our hands, would be enough to curtail this abuse for good.[80]

To help women hold onto their prized possessions, the *porteña* offers a jury of women for the trials of delinquent comb snatchers, assuring that a tough stance on crime will ensure safer streets and benefit all. The magazine issued appeals to women to avoid the black market and instead try to secure the pity—and a good deal—at the comb maker's shop.

In "Pérdida y hallazgo de una peineta" (Loss and discovery of a comb), *La Argentina* cautions women against publicizing bountiful rewards for the recovery of lost combs. Charting the fictitious history of a missing *peinetón,* the poem follows Juanita, a lone bather in the River Plate, whose comb left behind on the shore disappears mysteriously. Worried about the potential loss in status that will follow, Juanita advertises two thousand kisses for the man who recovers her comb. As she laments her loss, the thief returns for the promised moments of passion. Although horrified by the situation, Juanita lives up to her promises.

What happened afterwards?
The story does not say,
but our imagination
easily helps us understand.

Juanita, Juanita:
Live your life attentively
and when you bathe,
do watch your comb.
Should misfortune
make you lose it,
do not make such an offer
in order to find it.

Perhaps discovery,
once the bill is squared away,
will cost you more
than twenty combs.[81]

Forced into a compromising situation of her own making, Juanita pays dearly to retrieve her comb. *La Argentina* reminded its female readers to hold firm and not be pressured into making promises they could not keep.

Whereas most columns emphasized what female victims could do to protect themselves from comb-snatching delinquents, the *Extravagancias de 1834* series emphasized the domination of men by comb-wearing women. "Dancing *Peinetones*" presents men swerving to the unpredictable movements of flamboyant combs rather than to the tempo of the music. At the center of this caricature, an embarrassed gentleman rushes to recover his toupee, unleashed from his head by the rhythmic swing of a *peinetón*. In "*Peinetones* at the Theater," the men who kindly accompany fashionable ladies to their theater balconies humbly remove their top hats and are reduced to figures who must squint through the tiny, decorative holes of the women's combs.[82] Based on their European-style clothing and lack of a crimson insignia, the women may have associated themselves with Unitarian men, a visual cue that surely would have added tension to this public spectacle and referred to their weakness. Although some men have brought along opera glasses and spectacles, the devices are rendered useless. The combs impose upon their views; they will be forced to piece together the fragments of their evening. On the floor of the theater, in contrast, a comfortable and sexually segregated crowd of men stand proudly with their top hats in place; they await the upcoming spectacle with lively conversation.

Like the warriors before her, the *peinetón*-wearing woman was "dressed to kill" and "prey to the Look." Her towering comb linked the "sight of something" to the terror of castration, with effects not unlike those produced by the snakes on Medusa's head.[83] As women's combs take to downtown Buenos Aires in the final lithograph of the series (see "*Peinetones* in the Street" figure) a man would swear out of the desperation, "Damn the *peinetones!*" His exclamation responds to the exaggerated proportions and oblique angles of the headdress that invades city sidewalks. Having successfully generated her own expanse in the public arena, one woman parades down the middle of the street and right through two men. She injures one in the groin and permanently maims the other, who cries, "Ouch, for she has gouged my

"*Peinetones* in the Theater." Satirical caricature from Bacle's *Trajes y costumbres de la provincia de Buenos Aires.* Courtesy of Biblioteca Nacional, Buenos Aires, Argentina.

eye!" The enlarged crests of women overpower the top hats of men. With a confident stride, the woman at center responds in a demanding tone, "Disperse yourselves, gentlemen!"

In early nineteenth-century Argentina, the notion of a female-dominated public arena remained an option suitable only for satirical caricatures and burlesque commentary. While women's fashions like the *peinetón* had once been emphasized for their unique and patriotic character, the tensions over women's roles in the political realm and the negative representations prominent in the press and the visual arts ultimately led to the demise of this intriguing chapter in Argentine material culture. Without an understanding of the historical context from which it emerged, it would otherwise be difficult to conceptualize how an object representing political solidarity with the independence movement and, later, the Federalist cause at the time of Rosas, could have been discontinued so abruptly. Yet women had been assigned the problematic role of vanity, and this limited their participation spatially and politically. Authors and artists alike used the ambiguity of the *peinetón,* which equated a woman's comb with public participation, to reflect on the breakdown of rigid gender roles and the transformation of public spaces. Shattering expectations, the emblematic *peinetón* called into question the exclusivity of male participation in the public sphere by allowing women to improvise their citizenship individually and collaboratively. Engaging fashion as presence, women took their vision of independence to the streets of Buenos Aires. They were promptly reminded, however, that their fashionable crowns granted them reign over domestic obligations and not over the streets of Buenos Aires.

FOUR *Fashion Writing*

C LOTHING HAS FUNCTIONS SO APPARENT that they become easily dismissed, trivialized, or forgotten. But the same coat that
keeps out the elements can also distinguish one's social class and
political affinities. In postcolonial Argentina, several influential writers used the apparent triviality of fashion, or what seemed to be innocuous descriptions of clothing and fashion, to import revolutionary
ideals. Going far beyond the reporting of innovations in the fashion
industry and the detailing of new articles of clothing, these writers
imbued everything from pantaloons to petticoats with radical significance in the spectacle of an emerging public sphere.

Icons of Federalist power so permeated the etiquette of daily living that simple gestures, such as the type of fan, vest, or dinner plates
used, served as indicators of partisanship, indifference, or rebellious ani-
mosity. Women's gloves that revealed crimson-hued portraits of Rosas,
for instance, allowed a lady to direct an admirer to kiss her extended
hand *and* the Confederate leader's face. Some men positioned political
allegories inside their top hats so that, when bowing to make a formal greeting, they might display the underside of their hats and their
thoughts on government. In an effort to procure order in a period of
civil strife, the Rosas regime implemented a series of dress and conduct codes vested with compromising ideological postures. Previous
chapters analyze various pledges of allegiance to the Federation, ex-
ploring how popular narratives helped legalize Federalist customs and

prioritize the power of uniform. Because this canonization of taste occurred alongside the rise of feelings of nationhood, many intellectuals stressed the importance of assigning customs a pivotal role in the development of an Argentine republic.

With great ease, the writers and statesmen of the Rosas period linked the creation of uniquely Argentine customs to the goals and ideals of an emerging republic. Although some argued that the collective regulation of cultural identity would ensure national stability and industrial progress, others maintained that the development of customs would elevate and renovate the character of the nation. Some even discussed the necessity of creating a fashionable order comprised of young intellectual males. The virtuous dress of this elite, argued the editors of *El Mártir o Libre* (The Martyr or the Free Man), would serve all Argentines as an archetype of moral fortitude and righteousness. Narratives on customs and the morality of dress were to play an important role in the configuration of a national subject.

At the same time, the rhetoric of fashion served as a means to defy censors and challenge the traditional and tyrannical practices of the period. Because government censors often thwarted open political discussion, fashion emerged as a metaphor for political change and renovation. This chapter demonstrates how intellectuals of the opposition depended on a protocol of unveiling to introduce topics that, presented in any other forum, would have been censored. Using the concept of fashion writing as a guiding thread, we explore how fashion writing served as a viable means of political protest. *La Moda* (Fashion) of Buenos Aires disguised its ideological leanings and patterns for national reform in the descriptions of appearance and dress. *El Iniciador* (The Initiator), a magazine published in Montevideo, carried on this tradition when *La Moda* was closed down. To press their status as citizens and push for education reform immediately following the fall of Rosas and into the late nineteenth century, women writers co-opted the vocabulary of fashion previously used by their male predecessors. The female editors of *La Camelia* (The Camellia), for instance, embarked on an ambitious path to restructure and democratize society of the post-Rosas period, resorting to fashion description to make some of their most vital points.

In *The Empire of Fashion,* Gilles Lipovetsky pursues the evolution of modern democracy through the history of dress. He traces the rise of nationalist sentiments to the creation of national forms of dress in Europe of the Middle Ages. Fashion, he argues, reinforced the "awareness" of one's individual and collective identity. He writes, "As a collective constraint, fashion actually left individuals with relative autonomy in matters of appearance; it instituted an unprecedented relation between individuals and the rule of society." [1] Although emerging customs seemed to grant sovereignty to the individual, they also required that the citizen relate him or herself to society at large. Lipovetsky thus argues that this shift in responsibility to the individual made it possible to configure a civil and political identity for the national subject.

Following independence in Latin America, the rhetoric of fashion would contribute to the creation of a national identity and the formation of a model political body. The establishment of new customs in the realm of literature, it might be argued, served as a means to liberate symbolically a prenational subject from Spanish domination. In his article "Fashioning Cuba," Norman Holland has demonstrated how nineteenth-century fashion narratives played a role in constructing aesthetic and political identities in pre-independence Cuba. Drawing from the rich descriptions of dress found in Cirilo Villaverde's *Cecilia Valdés,* Holland illustrates how portrayals of national style organized a host of characters within a framework of ethnic pride. He writes, "Though Cuba's stratified, colonial society hardly seems to resemble the Enlightenment democracy of the European bourgeoisie, the novel's preoccupation with fashion constructs an inclusive social contract in which all participants are invited to dress and dance." [2] Although Villaverde's novel does not revolutionize the status quo of colonial Cuba, it does bind each character to specific codes of behavior and a network of national consumption, offering a presage of a national subject for postcolonial Cuba.

Other regions of Latin America made similar calls to dress and dance, and many narratives explored the makeup of the imagined political community that was to dominate after Spanish rule. [3] Long after independence, a newspaper published in Montevideo, Uruguay, titled *El Corsario* (The Corsair) summoned its Latin American readership to establish national customs and paint layers of distinction in a sea of confusion. When expressing its vision of young America, its editors

Carlos Morel, *Manners and Customs of the River Plate* (detail). Published by Litografía de las Artes, 1845. This dance celebrates cultural independence from Spain. Courtesy of Biblioteca Nacional, Buenos Aires, Argentina.

appropriated a corporeal metaphor. In one instance, a young, independent man emerging from battle against Spanish domination came to personify a new, yet sadly underdeveloped, republic. "Unfortunate days," the Montevideo newspaper proclaimed, "but so natural in the life of all young societies!"[4] *El Corsario* would characterize the continent as an unformed, if not malformed, body. Dispossessed of its past cultural identity, a country was not to run on military glory alone.

> Literature, the arts, customs are all elements that still do not figure into this body that we call society. One might say that the social body does not live but in an incomplete and mutilated state, for all its members have worked on developing one part alone: the arm. This life of action is physical and tempestuous by nature; the life of intelligence, beautiful and tranquil, may be discovered only in the distance.[5]

Society, the editors argued, could lead its warriors to a peaceful existence by instituting a series of changes that aimed to decorate the body politic not with weapons but with the ornaments of progress and virtue. Such an argument no doubt also addressed the struggles of the Rosas period. Later issues of *El Corsario* extended this analysis to the emerging Argentine nation, wrought with civil strife and stagnated by lack of direction. In a series of satirical portrayals of the Rosas regime, leading government figures appear in disheveled clothes and join the burlesque rituals of carnival. Such representations certainly suggested that contemporary leaders were apt to mobilize the popular classes for their own political gain rather than channel energies to create a more "civilized" national body.

Organic metaphors have often served in literature and art to outline collective identities, but the French Revolution may have established the strongest connection between dress and democratic values. The shifts in representation that it brought about certainly inspired the young Argentine intellectuals writing about fashion and politics, especially as they assigned pivotal roles to liberty and social interaction in the nation-building process. Nicholas Mirzoeff reveals that a regenerated body politic prominent in the French visual arts represented the dramatic transformations brought about by that nation's revolutionary period.[6] A shift from the traditional representation of the state, symbolized by allusions to the monarch, to allegorical representations depicting insurgent men and women and metaphors derived from sexual reproduction projected the rise of a popular constituency. He argues, "The constant calls for unity which permeated the political scene were matched by an artistic effort to resolve the contradictions of the nation into one durable image."[7] The terms of reception also became a significant question for consideration; the visual arts now disseminated new meanings of citizenship in a field of political struggle. Spectators assumed the status of actors in "radical constructions of the state"[8] and of participants in an ever-transforming body politic, Mirzoeff explains, further emphasizing that the body politic could now be sustained by consensus.[9]

When considering the register of dress, however, one quickly realizes that representations of radical democracy were hardly consensual. Richard Wrigley argues that the visual arts "drew on divergent referential ingredients, exemplifying the contestatory nature of such imagery, and the multi-layered symbolic power of dress."[10] The ancien régime satirized the *sans-culotte* (men of the people) with red caps, short jackets, and loose trousers when mocking this new political constituency.[11] With the onset of the Revolution, the disruption of fashion practices embodied displays of collective pride that quickly gained positive meaning. In neighboring European countries, fear of revolution led to the ban of "proletarian" styles, such as the light-colored and tight-fitting buff pants for men that imitated a nude look.[12] Even textiles became associated with democratic values, with silk as a symbol of "aristocratic indolence," and wool, linens, and cottons used in the creation of accessible garments representing the "less luxurious tastes of the true republicans."[13] Responses to the anarchistic styles of working-class clothing led French and English contemporaries to link the Revolution to "a general decline in manners and standards of dress." By the 1830s, men's fashions had given way to sober hues and conformist styles, as if emphasizing the nobility's loss of power.[14] Representations of the feminine disappeared altogether in the public sphere, as the republic signified an order of simplicity and rigor based on the precepts of equality and fraternity.[15] Amidst shouts of liberty, the shift in representation ultimately affiliated male citizens with the interests, customs, and manners of the French Republic.

During the formation of the United Provinces of the River Plate, the Phrygian cap of the French Revolution appeared temporarily alongside the white and light blue national badge representing independence from Spain.[16] Although social columns put similar representations of the French Revolution in dialogue with homegrown ideas, the desire for democratic institutions—to be achieved through social interaction and intellectual independence[17]—was apparently as strong as the disdain for aspects of popular and rural culture. Many of the newspapers and magazines published by the Creole elite poked fun at the "diaperlike pants" of regime supporters,[18] and highlighted the need to create new customs that would allow future citizens to exude a more "upright" cultural identity. Marzena Grzegorczyk argues that some intellectuals, such as Sarmiento, conveniently overlooked the use of crimson as a symbol of resistance to despotism as it had prevailed during the French Revolution, as if the strategy were to resemanticize the political tensions haunting the landscape of the River Plate.[19] While some Unitarians believed that Rosas ruled legitimately because the masses supported him, these same voices continued to emphasize the urgency of improving the region's moral state. According to *El Mártir o Libre,* the status of nations would rest on the respectability and decorum of its domestic subjects and not on any resonances attributed to the French Revolution. "Many times customs are beyond the control of a legislator, its existence owed to domestic education. If citizens are unpleasant, establishing laws for them is in vain," one author professed.[20] *El Mártir o Libre* instead asked readers to embrace the ways of the fashionable American ideal highlighted in its pages. Like the premise of fashion itself, this design promised to initiate a chain-style reaction that would lead the nation to greatness.

> If customs are reformed with good example, everything will have changed: this metamorphosis is the prodigious work of the heads of household and the leaders of Nations, founded in the axiom of a wise politician who says that all that one wishes to establish and to destroy must be initiated by the example of those who govern . . .
>
> A Republic that is born into the political orbit, that begins to form its customs and its tastes, must measure the extent of its spending within the limits of its resources; dress and the decoration of rooms are external indicators of the qualities of the people who possess them, and therefore it is all the more respectable when its dwellers display their magnificence.[21]

Vesting one's possessions with ideological meaning served to bring together the citizens of the emerging republic into national forms of dress and dance. The consumption of seemingly frivolous details was significant when associated with American magnificence rather than the charged vestiges of Spanish imperial or French revolutionary culture. Such descriptions of fashion provided the individual and society at large with a set of more "organic" prescriptions, making known the needs of the "civilized" subject and Republican cultural ideals of decorum and decency.

For many, the promise for national greatness depended on the moral stance upheld and disseminated by the country's leaders. Luis Saavedra, the editor of *El Grito de los Pueblos* (The cry of nations), argued that happiness and order would prevail in Argentina if patriotic citizens fully realized their role in organizing the political foundations of the country. To achieve this fully, one had to fictionalize somehow the secret to Confederate power.[22] Caricatures depicting Rosas as a barbarian in farmer's wear busily dissecting Unitarian bodies or making unethical pacts with demonic figures cast a dark shadow on the traditions to which most residents of the River Plate region aspired following independence. Proposing an alternative model for the nation, Saavedra explained, "Good morals and honest customs are the solid foundations upon which the happiness and prosperity of a nation rests. Consequently, the governing bodies of a nation must devote themselves to the reform of vices and the domestic customs of the citizens they represent."[23] Even when negotiating contradictory views on race and class, it was expected that this body politic represent *all* citizens through the institution of a set of civil codes that would exude integrity and goodness. In this manner, the national subject would embody a new spiritual ideal. It was still made quite clear, however, that such a view advocated representation *for* the people rather than *by* the people.[24]

What effect, then, could the moral qualities of an individual constituent have on the overall political image of the country? Early on, the editors of *La Mariposa,* a society weekly published in Montevideo, maintained that the defining tastes of the individual revealed a great deal about the stage of a country's development. Prescriptions made to the individual in a fashion magazine were thus designed to serve society at large.

> The customs of a nation are nothing more than the expression of its people's character and moral condition. Since the moral condition of individuals can vary according to the impressions they have received . . . it follows that each Nation possesses its own particular customs and that each of these indicate the level of progress at which they find themselves.[25]

One might correct national flaws more efficiently, the editors contended, if citizens adopted a set of preferences that defined them and their ideals. Government representatives could also use their power to institute and enforce certain virtues, thereby metamorphosing a host of individuals into serving patriots.

Calling on the power of narrative to help configure the national subject, *La Mariposa* offered such meditations on customs and etiquette to the consensus of nation-building. A political agenda promising to transform a flawed community into a virtuous nation fueled the essays, with the belief that governments would be shaped by customs and that individual customs from all segments of society would ultimately be informed by literature. "Literature is the only medium that can indicate an improvement in customs and one that can improve these customs without foregoing their purity," an article on the subject explained. "This is the best way to propagate knowledge and to disseminate moral and divine precepts."[26] A literary work had the power to shape the customs of a nation, ascertaining strengths and exposing moral flaws. G. P., the anonymous author whose initials signed the article "Customs," argued that literature had been attributed functions not unlike those of a handheld mirror. The reader, assuming the role of spectator, could thoughtfully gaze on his or her own reflection and form a judgment on the nation represented. Because the mirror was so powerful, the onlooker would inevitably find characteristics, customs, and styles that he or she would want to embellish or conceal. According to G. P., this literary mirror would allow "everyone to observe clearly what is ridiculous and harmful, to correct the image in the mirror and in so doing, to improve on customs."[27] Writers, like statesmen, would therefore plot the direction of the future country, manifesting the ideals and adornments for the nation's social body in their narratives.[28]

Given the antithesis of civilization and the barbarism so prevalent in Romantic Argentine literature, articulations of ideological tension can help unravel the distinctions made between Federals and Unitarians. Viñas looks to the linguistic nuances of Mármol's *Amalia* when uncovering the fluid political identities and gender constructions of its characters.[29] The adjectives used to denote physiognomy and permutations of dress of characters produce a kind of "halo effect" with which to adorn the novel's Unitarian protagonists. The cloaks of Federalist leaders, on the other hand, emerge from the blood, ignorance, and divisions following three centuries of Spanish rule. Mármol, a Unitarian intellectual who would eventually seek exile in Brazil, often employed creatively the tensions between the ideal (represented as Unitarian rule) and the real (Federalist power following the legacy of colonialism) when representing his characters or poetic voices. Viñas contrasts the dark shadows and labyrinthine layout of Rosas's ranch house with the narrow confines and ornamental grace of Amalia's fashionable Unitarian boudoir, complete with hues of light blue, white, and green. In Mármol's poetry written in exile, green resonates as the new color of freedom, or "the green hope of your life!," as mothers lift their sons up to the golden sun, a symbol of American independence.[30] These astute fictive representations sway the reader back and forth between civilization, represented by a most ethereal group of Unitarians, and the emblems of barbarism, manifested by the carnality of the Confederation.

Without question, many Latin American intellectuals of the nineteenth century attributed political significance to narratives on customs and etiquette. The rhetoric of fashion, having initially served as a means to configure a national subject, evolved into a device used by ideologues to plot the nation's course and to disseminate progressive political agendas. In their attempt to inspire individuals to collective action, some relied on metaphors appropriated from the realm of fashion. Fashion writing seemed tailor-made for political discourse, a concept that might seem foreign to the twenty-first-century reader accustomed to paging through *Vanity Fair* and *Vogue* only on an airplane or in a waiting room.

In *The Fashion System,* Roland Barthes reminds us that fashion writing does not simply re-create some already existing garment, arguing that "the function of the description of fashion is not only to propose a model which is a copy of reality but also and especially to circulate Fashion broadly as a meaning."[31] Its primary function is "to immobilize perception at a certain level of intelligibility," that is, to filter out the static innumerable but less suitable interpretations.[32] But description, as we are quite well aware, does not only limit possibilities. Language can relay information about color and spatial dimensions that a drawing or photograph simply cannot capture. Fashion writing can emphasize specific features—whether a collar or a hemline—and thus allow the garment to unfold in a calculated manner according to its own logic. The ideology of the fashion group, as we have already seen, emerges through the act of naming and assigning function.[33] The writer constructs his or her own garment when assigning function and value to the otherwise neutral article. It is here that we can see that fashion itself is a carefully constructed language.

Vested with the structure and authority of language, the written garment becomes a site of rhetorical connotation. Fashion exhibits nebulous qualities that go beyond grammatical coherence to the core of a latent signified. To unveil the characteristics of this rhetorical guise inherent to the ideology of fashion, we must remember that

> Connotation generally consists of masking the signification under a "natural" appearance, it never presents itself under the species of a system free of signification; thus, phenomenologically speaking, it does not call for a declared operation of reading; to consume a connotative system (in this case the rhetorical system of Fashion) is not to consume signs, but only reasons, goals, images.[34]

Because the rhetorical connotations inherent to fashion writing are neither implicit nor explicit in nature, fashion writing thus constitutes a genre that rests on a unique, if not paradoxical, axis. Its messages are altogether hidden, not unlike the political unconscious.[35] For Barthes, the meaning of a fashion narrative is not read. It is received.[36] Such an explanation helps us understand how textual descriptions of color, adornment, garments, and other aspects of material culture helped constitute and make manifest political positions. Next we see how descriptions of the most ordinary objects revealed sources of postcolonial political tension in Argentina's first fashion periodical.

In May 1837, a literary society to be known as the Association of the Young Argentine Generation was founded by Esteban Echeverría. Meeting in a Buenos Aires bookstore, this group of young intellectuals, later named the May Association, sought to explain and criticize their country's past and present failures. With their faith placed firmly in ideas of progress, these enlightened Argentines began to devise a program for the modern nation as "theirs was a generation of writers who apparently felt that progress lay in the right words, the right beliefs, and the right constitution."[37] Shumway points to a biblical verse, more specifically the words of Saint Paul in Romans 13:12 (KJV), that the generation used to elucidate their strategy for consensus: "Let us therefore cast off the works of darkness, and let us put on the armor of light." This metaphor granted ideas the status of weapons and expelled from the national body any unenlightened practices or beliefs. The generation portrayed the openness to new ideas as analogous to national strength and many believed that a democratic spirit was like a strong armor withstanding the impotence of tyranny. "By the right words," Shumway writes, "Argentina would be saved."[38]

In hopes of importing the European enlightenment to Argentina, these intellectuals founded *La Moda,* an imitation of *La Mode,* the French periodical that later became a force of violent opposition in Paris. Published in Buenos Aires during the Rosas regime, the weekly magazine had a life of twenty-three issues (November 1837 to April 1838). In an effort to secure the publication of the magazine, *La Moda* listed its editor as Rafael Jorge Corvalán, the son of Rosas's aide-de-camp. The real editor of the magazine was Juan Bautista Alberdi. Alberdi was an independent thinker who was perhaps more interested in affiliating himself with the intellectual underpinnings of the Romantic movement than with countering the ideals of the Rosas regime.[39] Perhaps this was due to a personal conviction that cultural identity served to inspire intellectual independence and precede nationality.[40] Whatever the case may have been for Alberdi, he and other members of this generation certainly agreed in their rejection of the colonial legacy, which they perceived as having had devastating consequences on the future of Republican customs and institutional life.[41] Such discussions continued to take place at the *Argentina* bookstore owned by Marcos Sastre,[42] an Uruguayan who moved to Buenos Aires a few years earlier and was well known for his support of women's rights and popular education.

Under the banner headline of "¡Viva la Federación!" *La Moda* identified itself as the "Weekly Gazette of Music, Poetry, Literature and Customs." Without a doubt, the Federalist slogan at the top would have appealed to government censors. When most volumes were bound, however, the slogan at the top was easily cropped and cast aside. If, as Valerie Steele suggests in *Fashion and Eroticism,*[43] changes in fashion precede rather than follow great historical events, then surely the men of *La Moda* were setting the scene for an end to the tyrannical reign of Rosas. Because an avowedly political journal would have been censored, and because few would associate fashion with politics, what better medium was there to import enlightened European ideas than to, quite literally, cloak them in a fashion magazine? The prospectus would reflect upon the state of fashion in Europe and Argentina, elaborating on the social value of each so long as it was one of the

intelligent, "simple and healthy notions of democratic and noble politeness."[44] To help its readers adopt such manners for their own, the
magazine proposed ways in which the Argentine man could appropriate the trends for more practical needs. The adoption of foreign styles,
however, was only a path to enlightenment and not an end in itself.[45]

There is even evidence to suggest that members of the Generation
of 1837 also took their own dress very seriously, as if to envisage the
Unitarian ideals proposed in their writing. Katra writes that Echeverría,
the leader of the literary salon, conscientiously projected a "self-image
of refinement" during an early period when the regime appeared to
ease repressive measures. Wearing luxurious suits from Paris in downtown Buenos Aires, Echeverría was known for lifting periodically "a
gold-rimmed monocle to the eye in order to recognize a passerby
on the street."[46] It is not clear if he performed such gestures when
frequenting popular stores or strumming his guitar alongside the gauchos in the countryside, both activities that he engaged in and enjoyed
frequently. Touting French designs, Echeverría strongly believed that
the people of the River Plate should embrace the values of the French
Revolution to address the need for material welfare and industrial
infrastructure in Argentina.[47] The sartorial pursuits of other members of the generation do not appear to have been as extravagant as
Echeverria's but their predilection for French styles is unquestionable.

The first issue of *La Moda* began by detailing the latest French
fashion from the pages of *Petit Courrier des Dames* and *Gazette des Salons,*
without including any readily apparent social commentary. However,
it still initiated a subtle play between the political nature of color and
history that would have been received in a very particular way at the
time. When presenting the latest in French home decoration, one
fashion column highlights the crimson and green tones, which given
the political climate, would no doubt have been a daring interplay
of the colors that represented Federal power and Unitarian opposition.[48] The author guides the reader from Paris to the homes of Buenos
Aires, asking for a reconsideration of the old-fashioned armchairs that
once belonged to the country's Spanish grandfathers. If one exhausts
all the fashion possibilities, he argues, there can be no recourse but to
return to ancient customs (even if they date to the Middle Ages) and
initiate another cycle of trends. In this context, the classic armchair

of Buenos Aires, described as a mass of crimson cloth attached to the frame by rusty nails, made a powerful allusion to the expired qualities of the seats of power held in Buenos Aires. Thus, the pages of *La Moda* recorded the fashion dictates of the day, providing a forum for change while commenting on the need to restore and, ultimately, to replace the old.

Under the heading "Fashions of Buenos Aires," the editors defined the new Argentine male as one who patterned himself after Europe and altered accessories so as to dress in step with national style. "Our fashions are, as we all know, nothing more than alterations of European style," the column read. "However, this modification is one that is executed artistically by intelligent men. In these pages we will present their testimonies, highlighting the latest modifications of this elegant crowd."[49] In light of later issues, the article demonstrates the double focus of *La Moda*'s discourse: to demonstrate the significance of implementing European customs modified for the particular social dynamics of the region, especially as responses to the persistence of Federalist values, and to reveal that such practices could only be enacted if public spaces were secure. Masiello explains,

> On the one hand, elegance of style symbolized European civilization and represented a dramatic break with the unsavory crassness of Rosas' regime, suggesting that if fashion could be imported acceptably from England and France, then ideas about liberal reform could also cross the Atlantic. On the other hand, fashion discussions drew attention to appearance and frivolity, to the faulty design of the garments chosen to cover the national body. In a country lacking dominant ideas or customs, fashion came to signal a weakness of the cultural imagination.[50]

Just as Unitarian intellectuals could alter Parisian fashion for an Argentine climate, so too could they tailor French and English liberal ideals for Argentine consumption. Artistic modification was taking place at the level of discourse, allowing for an increasingly political reading of most fashion writing.

The first images of women's hairstyles provide an intriguing example of the nuances of fashion during this period. "Women's Fashions—Hairstyles" began with a discussion on the importance of democratic ideals in all areas of national culture, including grooming habits. Criticizing the lack of dominant ideas, fashions, and customs, the author directed the reader's attention to the values of progressive democracy in the United States rather than focusing on the incredibly provocative hair accessories worn by the women of Buenos Aires. To distance themselves from the styles of colonial times, fashionable women in Buenos Aires had taken to wearing enlarged *peinetones* to mark their presence in the public sphere. This article reinforced the belief that one's gaze did not rest on the styles or crimson ribbons adorning a Federalist head. Instead, it redirected one's gaze to the virtues of democracy inherent to simple hair fashions with lines down the middle. The writer then engaged a much more provocative style, "the lighthouse, or let us just call it that, on which we must rest our eyes in order to escape the chaos of antithesis that envelops us—in legislation, morality, education, science, art, as well as Fashion—is democracy."[51] Encouraging reflection on political constitutions, this time North American rather than French styles prevailed in their ability to put ideas into sartorial dialogue.

> Democracy stands out there as much in dress and manners as it does in the political constitution of the United States. Placed on an identical route, we might observe the same laws. A fashion, like any custom or institution, will be all the more beautiful for us the more restrained, the more simple, the more modest it be, and the less it has armed itself with insulting pomp against the honorable average citizen.[52]

In the midst of political repression, the emulation of fashions from revolutionary France and the United States allowed for interesting political alternatives. Interestingly, the regime struggled at this time to convince the Federalist women of Buenos Aires to discard extreme hair fashions—even those containing images of Rosas and Federalist slogans—for more sober styles. Might such a reading have provided further symbolic ammunition against the regime?

Just in case, *La Moda* carefully voiced support for Federalist policies in the article that immediately followed. "Political Fashions," a report on the symbolic uses and display of Federalist crimson, bordered on full-fledged patriotic support for Rosas. Although the author acknowledged that the color disgusted some Argentines, he also concluded that the repulsed should still wear it, as the popular majority had chosen this style. "Political Fashions" complimented Federalist politics to such an extent that, according to José A. Oría, the presented information could have done little else to please Federal censors.[53]

> When a political ideal adopts a color as its emblem and this ideal reigns triumphant, the color used symbolically quickly becomes voguish in the eyes of the public. All individuals wish to flaunt on their garments the color that expresses the thoughts and interests of the majority. In this way, it achieves the double success of gaining both public approval and fashionability, which is another form of public sanction. This is the case with the color scarlet, emblem of federalist ideals; at once it is a political and voguish color. With confidence, the population wears this color on its clothing and on the national flag, thus depending on a double authority which it would be ridiculous to ignore.[54]

For the editors of *La Moda,* the might of popular accord determined the dictates of fashion. Yet the scarlet insignias and vests were still a mere reflection of the times, part of a larger cultural process underway. From the standpoint of a fashion magazine, this seemingly celebratory article easily gave way to a particularly critical reading of the same regime and its immutable Federal uniform. If popular decree espoused a given "fashion," then it would logically follow that one trend could easily be deposed by another, more cultivated, alternative.

In the midst of absolute stagnation, fashion writing promised change and progress. *La Moda* dedicated its fourteenth issue to the concept of movement and flow. The cover story made *flow* synonymous with *customs,* and attributed varying gradations of flow to different countries of the world. Within this paradigm, Argentina contrasted with its Spanish ancestors in that it exhibited the characteristics of a vital flow, a concept that promised a civilized future for all its citizens.

> He who dares to lose himself in the labyrinth of customs and manners of nations, or the popular, indigenous and domestic uses of fashion, will be reminded of the sheer numbers of those who weigh on the Earth. He will find that those who blindly obey the course paved for them are not unlike the water of a river that gently flows

Red cotton scarf with image of Juan Manuel de Rosas. In each corner is a saying that affirms Rosas's power over various festivities held throughout the region. Under his portrait is the slogan "The Federation Affirms Rosas." Courtesy of Museo Histórico Nacional, Buenos Aires, Argentina.

because a stream propels it. That is why the Englishman has mercantile flow; the Frenchman, scientific flow; the Turk, sensual flow; the Spaniard, listless flow; and we, who make such an effort to move ahead, progressive flow.[55]

If Argentina did not answer the call for national reorganization, the article suggested that citizens would bear the responsibility for halting the natural rhythm of progress. By contrasting a youthful Argentina with an apathetic Spain, *La Moda* asked readers to consider the cultural ramifications of their actions and work to transform the power relations at hand.

Using the pseudonym of Figarillo, Alberdi combined humor with a didactic approach when cultivating an intellectual forum for democratic ideals in Buenos Aires. His weekly column berated the lack of interest in new ideas. Such apathy rendered the mission of the fashion magazine as utterly hopeless, he wrote, as if the words articulated had compiled a sermon for a desert. How could *La Moda* instruct the nation in the fine art of elegance, he asked, when its citizens ran from change and progress in a way that sheep, long sheltered from the elements, run from the open spaces of the pampas? Alberdi believed that the inattention to ideas and national customs could only stem from the lack of a proper education and the sheer volume of regime propaganda.

In comical form, Figarillo engaged the reader in a series of dialogues that posited the popular voices that supported Rosas in a civilized setting. Each column carefully observed the speech and mannerisms of the stereotypical characters of society and issued judgments that aimed to "civilize" them. "If in Buenos Aires ridicule exists, then there also exists a critic who destroys this ridiculousness," Figarillo quips.[56] And so he would teach the city-dwelling gaucho, well versed in the easy rhymes of popular song, about the cadences of the minuet. He would talk to his wife who, instead of attending an elegant ball in proper attire and with distinguished guests, brought along her country relatives and hired help. Doña Rita Material, the first character to make her appearance in Figarillo's column, gossips about the disguised wealth of the butcher's daughter and then "says *replubic* for republic and *threate* for theatre."[57] As if throwing his hands in the air, Figarillo says, "I do not know if this will be progressive, for I know not what progress is."[58] Sarmiento would issue similarly negative responses to the flawed speech of Doña Josefa Puntiaguda in his newspaper of regional interest, *El Zonda de San Juan*. A later column in *La Moda* outlined more clearly the elements of style and good taste with an ABC directory, further underscoring the didactic intent of some of the fashion writing of the period.

One reader who claimed to represent the interests of the people called into question the virtues of the formal dress and etiquette advocated by the series in a letter to the editor. Signing his letter as "One of the People," his condemning words appeared on the cover of the fifteenth issue. "Politeness, far from being a virtue, is the most contemptible of the vices. I would desire courtesy for my enemies, for my slaves, but never for my compatriots," he writes.[59] He further disputed the positive qualities of civilized customs by maintaining that these feminized men of might.

> The strong youth is the beautiful youth. Little does it matter to know how to remove one's hat when one knows how to die for liberty on the battlefield.
> . . . The cream of society, that luxury of Argentine youth, is a group of young people who are industrial, patriotic and warrior-like. This segment of society makes up its heroism, its strength and its glory. Public temples shine with the flags stolen from enemies of the nation with strong arms, not elegant ones.[60]

For this reader, national glory emanated from the aesthetics of war and not from the elegance of civilized customs. He deemed the postcolonial battlefield as more beautiful than a flower and a warrior more important than a gentleman. Similar beliefs apparently created turmoil in real life when Federalist Simón Pereyra was mistaken for sympathizing with Unitarians after discarding the warrior-like *chiripás* worn by soldiers for European-style dress.

Figarillo reminded readers that the idea was not to *be* a gentleman. One only had to look like one. His comical bulletin presented a novel approach to image politics, suggesting that fluid identities were necessary under a system that had not been designed to take this opportunism into account. In any case, he wrote, "Even if you have all the courage in the world, no one will think you are handsome if you do not wear a large sword, fierce expression, an enormous moustache, insulting glares."[61] One need only remember Daniel Bello, the noble Unitarian who disguised himself as a high-ranking Federal in the bestselling nineteenth-century Argentine novel *Amalia*. Appropriating the dress and behaviors of the ruling powers, the novel's protagonist gains acceptance and power from the Federalist regime and then serves those Unitarians who need his assistance to escape Rosas's cruelty. *La Moda* reminded its subscribers of that same power, asking them to bear in mind that God alone could expose the core identity of a given individual. Clothing might serve as an indicator of the powers governing the nation, but it would never determine the ideals of the heart.

Through the lighthearted prose of Figarillo, Alberdi provoked the residents of Buenos Aires to evaluate and subsequently improve their unenlightened traditions. Though one might trace the lack of etiquette to the days of Spanish colonialism, this left no room for excuses when analyzing the current state of affairs. Writing as Figarillo, Alberdi jokingly referred to himself as a pygmy with a colossal name. "Figarillo" was a diminutive form of "Fígaro," also the pen name of Spanish Romantic author Larra. In "My Name and My Plan," Alberdi further undermined the seriousness of his column on national culture. As a "son of a Spaniard," he claimed that he would always be an imitation and therefore prone to recycle the barbs of his namesake. He reminded his public to receive his latest words with nonchalance, "I do not occupy myself with anything but frivolities, with things that nobody cares about, like fashions, styles, their uses, again and once again ideas, the letters, customs, and so forth, thing to which serious spirits should not heed attention."[62] In granting room for laughter and self-reflection, Figarillo countered the grave voices of authority. Masquerading editorial and political stance under the guise of frivolity and entertainment, Unitarian ideals thus entered into the realm of public discourse. "If frivolity was their public pose," however, "in private the members were deadly serious."[63] One anonymous author proclaimed that liberty was not to be achieved by perfume alone.[64] In expressing the desire for progress and more perfect institutions, members of the Young Argentine Generation had daringly challenged the current regime and embarked on an ambitious path, but one from which there was no return.

By March 17, 1838, the editorial staff issued a warning to its subscribers and critics. Such a signal could only mean the editors were under fire with the regime and felt it all the more urgent to bring forth honest opinions. As the archives reveal, the warning responded to those who viewed *La Moda* as a vehicle for espousing damaging ideas and values:

> *La Moda* is not a hostile plan countering the customs of present-day Buenos Aires, as some have ventured to believe. Daughter herself of

porteña ideas, she does not leave the pages open to all attacks, but instead focuses on the old age and tendencies of those fashions that are unworthy to belong to Buenos Aires anymore. Young Buenos Aires has lifted herself over the old Buenos Aires. All the editors, editing, ideas, and observations belong to our country: Why, then, are you offended by its shots? We are all the same people we criticize. It is not a foreigner. It is our society criticizing itself.[65]

The revolutionary tone of this article exposed readers to the strategies *La Moda* had employed to make way for liberal, independent thought. The magazine, its editors state, "has followed and will continue to follow similar forms. It is a disgrace required by the still immature condition of our society."[66] Strangely absent was discussion of the French Blockade that had brought about rampant inflation and job loss, which would have only added further fuel to the fire. At this time of public uncertainty, the regime began to censor heavily and pushed for an increase in torture, killing, and looting by the Mazorca. By 1841, the majority of the generation was living in exile in Chile and Uruguay. In his autobiography, Alberdi recalled removing his scarlet insignia a mile from the shore of Buenos Aires as he made his way to neighboring Montevideo.

In Uruguay, many of the members of the Young Argentine Generation who had written for *La Moda* settled into the ranks of other magazines and newspapers. "Our dear Figarillo," welcomed one issue of *El Iniciador*, "how did you end up here?"[67] Andrés Lamas and Miguel Cané, the Uruguayan and Argentine editors of *El Iniciador*, respectively, opened the doors to Alberdi and other newly arrived exiles of the young generation, believing that their participation in the magazine would revitalize the philosophical climate of the region. *El Iniciador*, published from April 15, 1838, to January 1, 1839, had a short but productive run. In the push to initiate a path to progress and enlightenment, editorial pens became swift metaphorical swords directed against the residues of Spanish colonialism and the tyranny of Rosas.

In this climate, fashion writing remained the genre of choice for intellectuals of the generation, despite the fact that its writers no longer suffered under the arm of Federal censorship. Through the rhetoric of fashion, the writer could put into question the role of the individual in the context of democratic change. As Lipovetsky points out, the

emergence of fashion is as much an indication of the rise of nationalist sentiments as it is a reflection on the possibility for movement and
change in a given society.[68] In the pages of *El Iniciador,* Alberdi wrote
that emerging nations should prioritize the education of their citizens and the formation of customs best suited to the consensus of the
young generation. "Liberty as well as despotism lives in our customs,"
he writes in "Sociability." "Whoever says customs, means ideas, beliefs, habits, uses."[69] For Alberdi, customs served national interests only
when serving the community at large with the values of democratic
equality.

Others further theorized that the creation of national customs
would counteract the tendency among emerging nations to adhere to
the traditions left by Spain. Manuel de Irigoyen reminded the readers
of *El Iniciador* that the struggle for independence had been only one
part of a larger chain of events leading to national sovereignty. Great
nations, he believed, did not depend culturally on others, but instead
rested on the laurels of their own customs and ideas. He reminded
readers of the precarious history of ideas in the region in a review of a
play shown in Buenos Aires, *Carlos o el infortunio.* Irigoyen writes, "We
placed the cap of freedom on top of a freed slave head, enslaved not
by chains anymore, but enslaved by ideas, manners, of learned customs
that are inherently slave-like."[70] For Irigoyen, new republics needed to
represent the reality of American experience by implementing new
colors, proportions, and forms. Such a task, as all could imagine, posed
a great challenge. In "War, the Gallows and the Dagger," Carlos Tejedor
proposes that men should continue to battle for an end to the despotic
remnants of colonialism; Federal power was a direct result of these
earlier conflicts, as it appeared to possess the "threads of imperial costume."[71] Furthermore, Tejedor explains, "Ideas are not the wardrobe
of humanity if they are shed without pain."[72] This clothing metaphor
resounded in other articles published in *El Iniciador.* If one disrobed the
body politic across the River Plate, it could be reconstituted with the
shield of democratic virtue.

Editor Cané incorporated fashion as a metaphor in his writings to
reflect both on the current state and the future of the region. Referring
to the antiquated dress and manners of colonial times as "cruel monu-
ments," he sought to eliminate the relics of Spanish domination from

the continent. In a manner similar to *La Moda,* Cané and others at the Uruguayan periodical evaluated the history of cultural stagnation. Because Spanish imperial culture had permeated all aspects of daily life, one felt the force of the effects even if not registering them visually. Cané explains,

> Two chains connected us to Spain. One chain was physical, visible, and ominous. The other chain was no less ominous and no less weighted. It was invisible and intangible, like those incomprehensible gases that subtly penetrate everything. It appeared in our legislation, our letters, our customs, our manners, and it imprinted on everything the seal of slavery, which in turn denied our absolute emancipation. . . .
>
> The same goes for those ridiculous, exotic customs that we conserve with the respectful devotion of an antiquarian who guards his useless trinkets. Let us try to show the antiquarian this embarrassing anachronism: American society, intelligent, republican, plebeian, religious, can not be the old, rude, slavish, fanatical society of the days of the colonies.[73]

The challenge of a young republic lie in creating fashionable manners and ideas that would always represent a particular order of constituent values, while providing a constant source of dynamic and innovative change. In this process, Rosas and his followers were like "poor parrots" busily mimicking the laws of Spain almost two decades after independence.[74] New fashions had the ability to capture cultural attitudes and "the movement of spirit in the same way that one judges the level of culture of a man by looking at his state of dress."[75] As Cané soon realized, "Fashion is the most flexible side of society, and because of this, it is perfected daily."[76] Although his essay certainly spoke to all Latin American republics, it primarily targeted the Rosas government by rendering it obsolete. "What will it take for us to *not* be what we are?" Cané asks, and to which he replies, "To march with the times, with fashion," a comment that also restated the premise of *La Moda,* which had been published a few months earlier in Buenos Aires.[77] For Cané, a society could be timely and mindful of progress only by opening itself to the forces of change.

To expand on these ideas linking fashion to nation-building, Cané published a treatise in *El Iniciador* titled "Fashions." This treatise also engaged fashion in a metaphorical sense when conveying political and philosophical currents that would help tailor the modern nation. "Our century is a dressmaker because it is a century of creating movement, novelties, progress," Cané proposes.[78] In this presentation, the excess of luxury was not unlike the excess of liberty: Could one really have too much, especially if one contrasted these options with the excess of misery and tyranny? With fashionable clothes and ideas, the emerging nations of the River Plate region would open themselves to the forces of philosophical enlightenment, distancing Americans from the darkness of ignorance that had pervaded under Spanish domination. A fatherland would elevate itself, he concludes, when the citizens of a new republic assert themselves and institute the fashionable precepts of a democratic political system. In terms of content, this treatise might have seemed quite similar to articles that had appeared in earlier issues of *La Moda*. The novelty of the treatise, however, lay in the fact that Cané advocated a kind of political dressmaking—a process of fashioning the body politic that would not necessarily involve the appropriation or an exact copy of European models.

From the margins of exile, prominent members of the Young Argentine Generation continued to express their fashionable ideas and political goals for the emerging nations of the region. Through the unlikely medium of fashion writing, intellectuals such as Alberdi and Cané generated new philosophical currents that addressed national sovereignty and the ongoing renovation of the political arena. In the process, Cané decided that fashion was the most active of all agents of progress, writing, "There are no retrograde fashions, because all fashion is a learning process, a new edition, always more and more perfect, even if it is the same one thing.[79] With the genre of fashion writing, Cané deposed the vestiges of Spanish colonialism and pondered the despotic tendencies of Federalist rule. If fashion and revolutionary politics were at the heart of the nation-building process, then one might expect to assume a proactive role in renewing nationalist sentiments and remaining open to the winds of change.

In April 1852, two months after the Unitarian opposition finally defeated Rosas, a newly formed Buenos Aires newspaper produced an unusually audacious banner; it read "Liberty, no licentiousness; equality between both sexes." Just below, between the two refrains "Being a flower—one can live without odor" and "Being a woman—one cannot live without love," there appeared an engraving of the cloaked and blinded female figure of Justice. The newspaper was *La Camelia,* dedicated to the issues concerning the "beautiful sex," and would have a life of thirteen issues (from April 11, 1852 to June 20, 1852). Though its editors remained anonymous throughout publication, Janet Greenberg identifies them as Rosa Guerra and Juana Manso de Noronha.[80] Through fashion writing, the female editors of *La Camelia* pressed their status as women, and more important, as citizens of the new republic. The magazine touched subjects as diverse as the art of editing a magazine, education reform, and most important, the interrelationship between fashion and politics.

In the premiere issue, the editors greet their readers and colleagues in a way that places them on equal footing with their male colleagues who edited fashion magazines.

> What a bold enterprise it is when one throws herself into writing in a city that is so enlightened and when so many talents dedicate their pens to newspaper editing. Confident in the gallantry of our colleagues, we dare to present ourselves among them. We regret, however, that modesty inhibits us from extending to them a firm hug and the kiss of peace. Even though one famous woman writer says that *Genius has no sex,* we who lack their ability do not wish to overstep the limits that genius imposes on us. Instead, we extend to our male colleagues a strong, friendly, and fraternal handshake.
>
> The weakness of our sex allows us to take refuge in the shadow of the *strong,* and so without any more preambles, we beg of our colleagues that they view our work with added indulgence.[81]

By characterizing their endeavor as a fearful and audacious enterprise in an already enlightened city, the editors compliment their male colleagues while paving the way for an alternative, but equally significant, point of view. Although "genius had no sex," *La Camelia's* editors would not go beyond the limits established by their contemporaries. Such a modest introduction to their readership, like a peace treaty amidst a potential storm, managed to open a forum for the discussion of issues that affected these women of Buenos Aires.

By entering a male-dominated public sphere, the editors became public owners of their discourse and thus were able to challenge existing institutional structures that had barred women from the Argentine cultural consciousness. Such actions and the role of fashion writing seem to validate the theories that Rita Felski has posited in other historical contexts, most significantly that the feminist counter-sphere, made up of those marginalized by society, must be read as a process that engenders "processes of discursive argumentation and critique which seek to contest the basis of existing norms and values by raising alternative validity claims."[82] Through the channels of the fashion column and magazine, women's values and ideas of morality were being disseminated to the public. The idea that the editors of *La Camelia* created an oppositional discursive space might seem to contradict their initial outline of intentions. However, they did contest existing norms and values in the way they chose to define—or not to define—their editorial participants.

La Camelia's three anonymous editors carefully disguised their identities in writing, defining themselves only through negation: "Being neither girls nor pretty, we are neither old nor ugly." One might hypothesize that such camouflage served as a means of protecting their private lives, now before the public eye. By defining themselves through negation, the editors created an opening in a society that otherwise would have placed limitations on their political involvement. Covered in the shroud of anonymity, women writers seemed especially able to assert themselves as authoritative sources of information and challenge contemporary political attitudes. "In refusing to specify physical attributes, the editors excluded themselves from circulating discourses on fashion, in which beauty and youth determined individual merits and condemned women to the judgment of others," Masiello writes.[83] Without a name to judge, the reading public could take issue only with the validity of the newspaper's claims, and could not base any opinions on the reputation or the appearance of affiliated women writers.

The editors were fully aware of the freedoms and pitfalls that accompanied anonymity, in part because of the controversy that had surrounded the use of female pseudonyms in fashion magazines like *La Moda*. Several of the male members of the Young Argentine Generation had assumed female pseudonyms as a protective measure when mixing fashion and politics. Because such presentation was quite common, women's fashion writing may have been read with the same seriousness as if male intellectuals had produced it. As Hanway reveals, fashion was now the "rightful subject of Argentinean men," with authors like Sarmiento arguing that the work of female "creatures obsessed with fashion" could not be held to the same standards, quickly adding that dress "wakes the descriptive faculties, the imagination, judgment, feminine penetration, the sentiment of artistic harmony."[84] With the added security of pseudonyms, the editorial participants of *La Camelia* managed to overcome "the contradiction between self-protection and self-expression." "Disguise in the form of literature gives protection as well as the chance to overstep the boundaries of the real and to postulate utopias," Sigrid Weigel reminds us.[85]

The first issue of *La Camelia* presents an alleged dialogue between "Eliza," a female editor using her pseudonym, and "the oldie Mr. Hermógenes, that nightmare for all women who have had the misfortune of meeting him, that sickening being who is as bothersome as the asthma that ails him."[86] Mr. Hermógenes, presumably a fictitious character, made an earlier appearance in *La Moda* as a scathing critic of inventive journalism. During a conversation with the anonymous editor of *La Camelia,* Mr. Hermógenes calls into question the true gender of the magazine's staff, claiming that men might still prefer female pseudonyms after Rosas. More important, he discredits Eliza when she tells him that she knows the editors personally. Feigning surprise at Eliza's passionate reply, Mr. Hermógenes declares that if the newspaper is truly directed by women, it won't last but a month. His response ultimately represents the currents against which *La Camelia* stood.

Although the magazine's staff consciously withheld descriptions of their own appearance, they did not hesitate to present their ideas and criticism of idealized feminine fashion. Appropriating much of the vocabulary from the previously male-dominated discourse of fashion, *La Camelia* featured a regular column called "Fashions" in which the editors reexamined the history of negative tendencies in fashion. Initially at the forefront were reports of the changes brought about by the defeat of Rosas in 1852. *La Camelia* characterized fashion under the Federalist regime as dauntingly oppressive, with little life and few colors. Immediately following the storm of tyranny, the women's fashion magazine claimed to play a significant role in liberating women from their somber lifestyles, presenting them with numerous and especially glamorous choices.

Old traditions and public spectacles that flourished in the days following independence regained their popularity. Masquerade balls, which had been outlawed by the regime, were all the rage. An article entitled "Masks" pokes fun at the neurosis of tyrants who felt it necessary to outlaw such forms of entertainment.

> This diversion was so feared by Rosas, for he believed that behind every mask lurked an enemy and within each domino, a dagger. Detested by every tyrant, this diversion has been put into practice again without any hint of disorder. May our youth continue as it has, with the decorum proper of enlightenment that will always be applauded by the beautiful sex. We women, although weak, constitute an organ of this enlightenment. We will not tire of repeating to all, "Order and liberty! Down with licentiousness, for it leads to anarchy!"[87]

Because the masked ball encountered none of the chaos anticipated by Rosas, the author drew a parallel to the Argentine nation's newly found stability and liberty. "Masks" called on women to assume a significant role in the creation and implementation of national customs. Though popularly deemed the "weaker sex," women, the article argues, constitute the moral backbone of society and, therefore, should tailor the nation's fashions and leisurely activities.

The editors of *La Camelia* promoted the concept of change inherent to the fashion system as a force that would allow the nation to rejuvenate itself continuously. Change, as the members of *La Moda* and *El Iniciador* had suggested, was necessary for all types of prosperity to materialize, whether industrial, economic, or political. *La Camelia* certainly associated moral prosperity with fashion when it described the ideal Latin American woman. For its editors, fashion writing was a means toward acquiring a youthful yet moral perspective, a way of becoming the "female friend of the new generation."[88] In the premiere issue, the editors provide the following assessment of the potential role of the fashion column:

> Do not believe that we plan to detail here all the puerility that we call Fashion—by no means. Although we are women and therefore lovers of all fashions, we are also sensible enough to overlook

frivolities, especially when fashion plates abound. Our article has a moral tendency, because we very well know that Mrs. *Morality* is the beloved sister of *Liberty* and the enemy of little Miss *Licentiousness.*— During the long period that, happily, has ended, Mrs. Morality was replaced by *Prostitution*. It is very just to see that, once she was thrown back into the dung from which she never should have left, Mrs. Morality could return from her exile and extend her charitable influence to all segments of society.[89]

Because Rosas had represented a barbaric turn toward moral indecency, the call for cultural independence and new freedoms—although strictly bound by moral limits—promised to help elevate the status of women. This same article cautions the temptation to become a "slave to fashion"; some articles even parody the obsessive nature of those who choose to sequester themselves with imprudent and uncomfortable fashions. When considering the hairstyles worn by women during the reign of Louis XV, *La Camelia* criticizes French women for having forced artificial structures into their hair or having displayed ridiculous thematic scenes. No mention is made of the more homegrown crown, the Argentine *peinetón*. Prompted by this policing of history, "Some Female Subscribers" came together to denounce the imprudent dress lengths that were transforming the fashionable females of Buenos Aires into street sweepers. They especially critiqued the luxurious extravagance of contemporary petticoats, which, at their current size, seemed to take on an entire room.

> It is the most uncomfortable feeling to have to run into posts and sweep the sidewalks of our narrow streets. It so happens that even in the stores with the most spacious counters and four or five young attendants, petticoats fill the space with their seven or eight yards of material.[90]

Although petticoats certainly granted women fashion presence, it also required them to purchase inordinate amounts of material that sequestered their bodies and spirits. "In the end," these subscribers argue, "we expect from the beautiful Argentine woman more prudence, more domestic economy, and less emission of petticoats."[91]

Through fashion writing, women criticized the dysfunctional aspects of elite fashions, while at the same time identifying the potentially contradictory desire for sartorial pleasures. Like their predecessors of

La Moda, these writers reminded readers of the need to alter European fashions to make them comfortable for a Latin American climate.

Through the act of assigning political function to garments and through the reexamination of the history of morality, gender, and dress, fashion writing proved a most effective tool in the tailoring of the nation. In early to mid-nineteenth-century Argentina, fashion writing safely imported the political ideas of revolutionary Europe to Latin America, while it simultaneously criticized the arrogance and pomposity of those readers who mindlessly obeyed the dictates of fashion. As the Young Argentine Generation forged a national identity for the emerging nation, they relied on a protocol of unveiling in which the threads of ideology were woven through seemingly innocuous descriptions of clothing. As we have seen, the fashion description of *La Moda* did not need morally loaded phrases to communicate its political message. Often the message was latent, embedded in the choice of function and value assigned to the garment, a signification that one received but did not read.[92] Through the added security of female pseudonyms, many of these authors posed as writing women. The fashion system, or so it seemed, allowed for a woman to wear her politics on her sleeve. Such a strategy did not go unnoticed by women of the post-Rosas period. Taking up paper, pen, and ink, the pioneer women of *La Camelia* surveyed the freedoms of the moment and spoke for themselves.

FIVE

Searching for Female Emancipation

"Oh! How heavy these dress jackets are!" said a sweet, whining voice close to Mauricio. And one heard the thump of heavy clothing hitting the furniture.

"By God! Is there anything more brutal than imposing on the delicate body of a woman this crushing astrakhan and the no less impossible fustian!"

It was necessary, it was precise, as Cienfuegos says, to characterize those ready-made fashion clothiers: Wort, Bowctlaw, and the likes, as crazy or having conspired against us. And with a sigh of relief:

"Ah!" the voice said. "I seem to have cast two tons off myself."

"Little do you have left to suffer," answered another, also sweet and young.

ONE DAY, a young romance writer who has lost his place to urban expansion in Buenos Aires overhears this intimate conversation coming from another bedroom in an all-women's residence hall. An "invisible houseguest" in Madame Bazan's boarding-house for middle-class women of all ages, Mauricio Ridel works on finishing a happy ending for his latest serialized novel. During the writing process, however, he finds himself distracted by the sounds and rhythms of the house, his focus carried away to the conversations in the house on fashion, family life, and female emancipation. Careful not to indicate his presence in any way (for he has agreed to respect the privacy of the women who live there), Mauricio listens in to the conversations between female residents from the comfort of his assigned room. Believing themselves removed from male listeners, the female characters of Juana Manuela Gorriti's 1888 novel, *Oasis en la vida* (Oasis in Life), openly discuss their concerns and desires in the security of enclosed spaces. The dialogue that begins this chapter demonstrates the relief that a group of unnamed women experience when removing their uncomfortable clothing. They complain about the weight and needless complexity of their fashions and even flesh out a conspiracy theory concerning a few of those crazy designers.[1] As the women contemplate the changes that tomorrow's fashions will inevitably bring, their soft, sweet voices appear punctuated by the incongruous thud of tossed garments.

For the twenty-first-century reader, the corseted waists and extremely layered body dressing of the nineteenth century might seem a unique blend of suffering and social obligation. Indeed, fashion historians have traditionally presented women of the nineteenth century as frail beings, slavishly bending to the whims of male designers. Although there has been mention of a few notable women who escaped the period's imposed moral and social expectations, the tendency has been to represent the draped female body as the immobilized victim of an oppressive fashion system.[2] Body dressing would seem to reflect the social, moral, and economic concerns of this period, demarcating the public arena and the private domain along strict gender lines.

Donald Lowe explains that female fashions were subject to continuous transformations in style, undergoing a series of revivals that were "sometimes decorative, sometimes *décolletée,* but always antiutilitarian, in order to indicate the woman's embellishing function in the public space." In comparison, male fashions tended to be "less fanciful in color and style, more utilitarian and somber," reflecting "man's rationality in the public space."[3] Although fashion once reflected the individual's status in society and class, it now organized the body according to its sex and prescribed roles within society. Given such a framework, one might read the female voices that resonate in the bedrooms of *Oasis en la vida* as an indicator of the public pressure that had forced women to regress to the domains of their households. Certainly, some female fashions would have rendered a woman unfit for work. However, these conditions certainly did not translate into the wholesale lockout of otherwise healthy women willing to roll up their sleeves and press their status as citizens.

In *Fashion and Eroticism,* Steele argues that the highly decorative and colorful garments worn by the woman of the Victorian period designated her as an important presence in an expanding public sphere. She counters the idea that nineteenth-century society may have forced women into submissive fashions and masochistic behavior, arguing that the prescriptive ideals of fashion magazines were very different from the real experiences of women. The female presence in several Latin American novels—from Mármol's *Amalia* (1851–1855) to José Martí's *Amistad funesta* (Fatal friendship) (1885)—certainly allows for connections between elaborate body dressing and a female character's strong convictions. Gorriti takes such an approach further when she unites the opinions and desires of her female characters into a single commentary on fashion. Choosing to emphasize, and not dismiss, her epoch's styles, she even entertains, albeit jokingly, the possibility of emancipation from odious men. Like the fashion column and society pages of the late nineteenth century, Gorriti's novel emphasizes the visual immediacy of the real garment. At the same time, it presents strong female voices that, emanating from private spaces, enter the domain of public consciousness with ease.

Looking to serialized fiction, the fashion lithograph, and the history of dress, this chapter examines the rhetorical force of the written garment as it pertains to late nineteenth-century Argentina. A brief definition of the "Fashion novel" leads into a discussion on the fashion and print culture of Buenos Aires. Next is an exploration of the nineteenth-century question of female emancipation in light of an interesting debate on the "oasis in life" that Gorriti initiated at a literary salon in Lima, Perú, prior to the publication of her novel. Her best-selling novel of the same title, along with the widely circulated fashion columns of Spanish author María del Pilar Sinués de Marco, help to unravel the significance of fashion writing during a moment of national reorganization and modernization. Popular magazines that appealed to literate women of all classes, with titles like *La Ondina del Plata* (Trendsetter of the River Plate), presented fixed images of beauty and comfort as if to bridge a highly commercialized and fragmented culture with the warmth of home. At the same time, these periodicals provided women with a unique forum in which to raise questions for public debate and to create an expanded version of the public sphere. Not unlike the female characters of *Oasis en la vida,* the writers of the fashion column whispered news of upcoming styles—and thereby introduced their readers to new approaches in dressing, thinking, and experiencing life.

We have already established that fashion is a carefully constructed language that one can use to prescribe limits and proclaim liberation, to establish social categories and delineate political loyalties. As Barthes suggests in *The Fashion System,* the object itself, whether a hat or coat or robe, requires a grounding that is temporal, spatial, sensory, and cultural in nature. Someone must decide what is fashion and who is fashionable, and another must convince the targeted public that such declarations only follow an obvious cultural logic. Barthes uses the term "Fashion novel" to describe any narrative that integrates written or visual signs of dress to organize the body in an overarching social framework, a concept that is integrated into this discussion on postcolonial fashion. He writes,

> The Fashion novel is organized around two equivalences; according to the first, Fashion presents the reader with an activity defined either in itself or by its circumstances of time and place (If you want to signify what you are doing here, dress like this); according to the second, it offers an identity to be read (If you want to be this, you must dress like this).[4]

Within a given cultural group, a narrative of dress thereby undergoes a series of negotiations. At first, the designer exerts some control over the initial sequence, as the historical moment of creation endows the garment with particular meaning. Motivated by her imagination, a sense of "free choice,"[5] and perhaps the advice of a fashion columnist, the consumer now decides how to wear a style, fashioning herself according to specific needs, desires, and historical moments. Such negotiations of real experience pose serious challenges for the scholar of material culture, whose work must go beyond the realm of empirical data and address the "fragmented, divergent, fluid and idiosyncratic" nature of dress.[6]

In approaching the Fashion novel, or the written or visual signs of dress, we thus face a number of questions. Leslie Rabine reminds us to ask, "Who speaks this language, to whom is it addressed, what does it mean, and how are its meanings established or transformed?"[7] In answering these questions, Rabine uncovers a surprising and unlikely partnership between the fashion magazine and twentieth-century North American feminism. While the Fashion novel clearly subjected readers to an idealized and nearly unattainable form of beauty, these "instruments of consumer capitalism" also provided an important forum for a variety of women's issues. Challenging the restrictive logic of its time, fashion narratives of late nineteenth-century Argentina enabled middle- and upper-class women to voice their assessments and differing opinions on prescribed social roles. Given the fashion writer's ability to transform lives with an imaginative twist, it should not surprise us that women authors would choose to "fashion their way to freedom" in an ever-evolving framework of the modern nation.[8] A significant power shift was underway at the level of material culture. In the Fashion novel, women were becoming more than a spectacle of modernization and, increasingly, set their *own terms* of femininity and social status.

As we have seen, the rhetoric of fashion had long addressed matters of public concern in postcolonial Argentina. Following the struggle for independence from Spain, writers of the River Plate region used the pages of early literary magazines to present more than their views on color and cut. Newspaper reporters and popular poets submitted narratives on military costume and fashionable dress when configuring a prenational subject in the attempt to disseminate political goals for an emerging nation. Staunchly divided between Unitarian and Federalist tendencies, Argentine customs had become an overarching moral question, a topic of high seriousness and public debate. For a brief time, censors had overlooked the audacious rhetoric of *La Moda,* perhaps because fashion was still perceived as a frivolous endeavor and not intrinsically political in nature. To ensure their own safety, several male authors posed as writing women, veiling their ideologies with fashion commentary.

Women authors of the nineteenth century would appropriate this same strategy to propagate their own agendas. Because they, too, used female pseudonyms and the rhetoric of fashion, several readers suspected men, and not women, to have penned such views. When newspapers such as the *British Packet* or *La Gazeta Mercantil* used their columns to ascertain the authorship of women's magazines, the authors asked their readers to take issue with their ideas rather than their sex.[9] Mary Louise Pratt argues that, although lacking political rights, women authors used these early print networks to "engage with national forms of understanding, maintain their own political and discursive agenda, and express demands on the system that denied them full status as citizens."[10] With this initiation into mainstream journalism, along with a fashionable vocabulary that envisioned independence for all members of society, women stood to gain a more pronounced access, despite numerous obstacles and male antisentiments regarding their political participation.

The pages of *La Aljaba* (The Quiver) (1830–31), *La Camelia* (The Camellia) (1852), and *La Ilustración Argentina: Museo de Familias* (The Argentine Enlightenment: Family Museum) (1853–54) emphasized new patriotic roles for women. While all valued the domestic obligations of the middle class, they also called on women to increase their presence in public and political life. *La Aljaba*'s title alluded to both the quiver that holds arrows and the fashionably bold color fuchsia that few women of the period dared to wear. Nevertheless, the magazine was not in the business of maintaining the comfort zones of its readers, audaciously announcing in 1830, "We will liberate ourselves from the injustices of men only when we do not exist among them."[11] Edited by Petrona Ignacia Rosende de Sierra, *La Aljaba* highlighted education rights for women and the oppressive nature of beauty and luxury, attempting to orient its readers to a more intelligent and healthy approach to life.[12] At this same time, the *Gymnastics Manual for the Beautiful Sex, or Essays on the Physical Education of Young Women* circulated in Buenos Aires, advocating that women partake in the spirit of independence and freedom.[13] Combining moralizing tales with illustrations of active women, this manual pressed for a woman's right to comfortable dress, physical activity, and an education. This enlightened approach to health found a forum in *La Ilustración Argentina,* which published notes on horseback riding, foreign literature, and feminist poetry alongside beauty advice. An early poem, "To Women's Emancipation," advocated a confident female presence, "Emancipate yourself proudly / Manifest

your power / And you will see that woman / Is no slave, but a God-
dess."[14] The pages of *La Camelia,* edited by Rosa Guerra, advocated
dress reform and equality for both sexes. Marifran Carlson explains,
"Fashionable women's clothing was both expensive and uncomfortable; women, the editor said, dressed like ornamental dolls. Men might
enjoy looking at them, but these fussy, fragile clothes did nothing to
improve relations between the sexes."[15] With this fresh attitude and the
promise of a lighter wardrobe, many women felt called upon to bring
about a *movement* of simple but elegant change.

By the mid- to late nineteenth century, women authors did not
feel the need to shield themselves with pseudonyms, although the
practice continued in various contexts. Juana Manso de Noronha publicly assumed all editorial duties for *El Álbum de Señoritas* (The Young
Women's Album) (1854). Both she and Eduarda Mansilla de García
signed their names to articles in the pages of *La Flor del Aire* (Flower of
the Air) (1864) and its sequel *La Siempre-Viva* (The Ever-Lively Woman)
(1864). Many issues of these magazines juxtaposed sewing patterns and
reports on the latest European styles with essays on the politics of
education and the struggle for female emancipation. "Men speak of
science, literature and progress, while women speak of fashion, fashion, fashion," Manso de Noronha bemoaned, suggesting that it was
time for women to educate themselves rather than just "live between
a crinoline and a crest."[16] Several periodicals edited by men for a female readership integrated such texts by women authors, who, in turn,
found it possible to support themselves financially with poetry and
prose. Although the overall focus of these magazines may have been
less oriented toward the sociopolitical concerns of women, various
essays on fashion suggest that women were well versed in the vocabulary of luxury and consumption.[17] Furthermore, their pages appear
to have encouraged independent decisions rather than mere fashion
prescriptions, or as one inquiry from *El Alba* (Dawn) (1868–69) put
it, "Why don't you just impose your own rules rather than following
them?"[18] Other magazines in Buenos Aires in the mid- to late nineteenth century included *La Moda Hispanoamericana* (Spanish American
Fashion) (1874); *El Correo de las Porteñas* (The Porteña Post) (1876);
Doña Mariquita (1877); *El Álbum de las Niñas* (The Girls' Album) (1877);
El Correo del Domingo (Sunday Post) (1864–68); *La Elegancia* (Elegance)

(1878); *El Álbum del Hogar* (Home Album) (1878–84); and *El Correo Americano* (The American Post) (1881). Two magazines in particular used fashion description to discuss issues of public access and the prospects for emancipation: *La Alborada del Plata* (Dawn of the River Plate) (1877–80), founded by Josefina Pelliza de Sagasta and edited by Gorriti and Lola Larrosa; and its competitor *La Ondina del Plata* (1875–79?), edited by Luis Telmo Pintos.

Despite the increasing successes of female authors, many still felt threatened by the idea of women writing, as this involved "women producing in the public sphere, often from within the domestic center, who introduce domestic issues into the place of public discussion and insist on making visible the activity of women in workplaces, politics, and commercial and social life."[19] This evaluation of Habermas's "liberal model of the bourgeois public sphere" points to the permeability of the relationship between the private and the public. When women found in domesticity a "public spirit" they could employ, the boundaries blurred.[20] Able to strike a balance between family and public life, women planted the seed for "equal standing before the law."[21] Asunción Lavrin demonstrates that the goal, which would culminate in the suffrage movement of the first half of the twentieth century, included "equal access to educational opportunities, the abrogation of nineteenth-century codes curtailing women's rights after marriage, and specific legislation for the protection of women and children."[22] While society appointed women as the symbols of family virtue and the guardians of morality, the new configuration underway in the public sphere of the late nineteenth century promised to alter women's roles and the traditional family structure.

The role of women as readers, on the other hand, was considerably less controversial. Reading, like other patterns of bourgeois consumption, was a passive activity that did not contradict the period's notion of gender expectations.[23] The changing attitudes toward female education promoted learning, and reading in particular, for achievement in the domestic sciences. "Home is the school in miniature," wrote the editor of *La Ondina del Plata*.[24] Yet for many women readers, Francesca Miller argues, education represented "the road to greater control over their lives, in both domestic and political spheres."[25] Following the formation of an Argentine Republic in 1862, the Congress had responded to high illiteracy rates and accelerated urban growth by creating a normal school system. The first national census, dated 1869, indicated a literacy rate of 25.2 percent of the male population and 18.3 percent of the female population.[26] Once appointed as the National Minister of Education in 1856, and later during his presidency (1868–74), Sarmiento expanded educational opportunities for women, viewing their involvement in public and political life as crucial to the national well-being.[27] He appointed Manso de Noronha, author and self-described *maestra* (school mistress), as the school supervisor for the province of Buenos Aires. Following his presidency, a Common Education Law (1876) finalized the transfer of control over girls' schools from the Society of Beneficence to the provincial governments. While educational goals served to complement domestic roles, as Carlson indicates, they simultaneously motivated women to become more involved in the patterning of all social roles. Rising literacy rates and the emergence of competitive markets helped the fashion magazine proliferate.[28]

In the 1880s, Argentina began a period of national consolidation when it unified Buenos Aires, the new capital, with the provinces of the interior. The gaucho and his horse, both symbols of traditional rural values, had long faded into the horizon of the pampas. Having surmounted the political tensions that so divided Argentina following independence, the country now focused its sights on economic growth, fueled by foreign investment capital, massive immigration, and agricultural exports.[29] From 1857 to 1890, the nation's population grew from 1.1 to 3.3 million, with most immigrants settling in the capital.[30] Economic booms from 1884 to 1889 earned Buenos Aires its reputation as the Paris of South America, as the cityscape began to resemble the center of European fashion in terms of its customs and architecture. Guy writes, "Fashionable stores, cafés, restaurants, and banks soon dotted the elegant downtown, adding to the glamour and glitter of this apparently opulent capital."[31] Buenos Aires, a city previously viewed as *la gran aldea* (the grand village), stood transformed with all of its allusions to luxury, consumerism, and international capitalism.[32]

At a time when a proliferation of publics became evident, luxury took on a fraudulent and discomforting role. The upper classes, in an attempt to reflect their political and economic privilege, had phased out "the enclosed and guarded family style of the 1870s" with lavish celebrations and other public forms of consumption. Members of the elite classes in the Southern Cone had often been drawn to goods from Europe when placing themselves at the center of modernity; markers of "status" allowed them to "stand out from their less cultured, less modern, compatriots by fervently embracing everything European and especially French and English."[33] Wealthier inhabitants in Argentina, in particular, sought to mark their increasing importance in the global order. "In dress, art collections, furniture, table service and carriages, the Argentine elite were determined to equal or outdo the wealthy of Europe," James R. Scobie writes.[34] Displays of affluence helped set apart *la gente decente* (well to do), who made up only 5 percent of the population of Buenos Aires, from the growing middle class and *la gente de pueblo* (the working classes).[35] With the arrival of new immigrants, the black mourning dress that had prevailed in the cityscape, a consequence of the yellow fever epidemic of the early 1870s, gave way to a myriad of foreign styles. For women, dresses had become a bit more flexible, although they still incorporated layered skirts and trains that required bustles of an exaggerated shape and numerous hooks to draw the weighted materials up and to the back. The dandies of the Generation of 1880 (the governing elite), such as Lucio Mansilla and Manuel Quintana, carefully attended to the details of etiquette and other fineries, appearing at the newly founded social clubs with black tuxedos and white gloves. The novelties of Parisian fashion had become a symbol of high status and Argentine fashion magazines anticipated the most popular of European styles.

Because of the accelerated pace of economic expansion, however, members of the nouveau riche and even newly arrived immigrants began to imitate bourgeois styles.[36] With the emergence of the fashion lithograph, modistes contemplated the distinctiveness of European dress, copied its design, and then commissioned seamstresses to piece the garment together with a sewing machine.[37] The working-class men and women of Buenos Aires turned to the study of Parisian fashions for success in the workplace. A commentary in *El Correo del Domingo* titled "Inmigrantes: casi una novedad" (Immigrants: almost a novelty) trails the new immigrant on his arrival to the city of Buenos Aires, pointing to his blue beret and the scarves and short, colorful dresses of his wife and daughters. Within a few months, the article continues, the immigrant will have erased the outward signs of his foreign past.

> Before the year ends, men will have thrown off their berets, cotton clothing and espadrilles, and women will have changed their short dresses and signature scarf for dresses that are more or less in fashion. A little bit more and they will be rich, and maybe the women will look to the lithographs of Paris for clothes that they never knew in France.[38]

As the immigrant discarded those fashions that marked his predominantly rural background, like the *boina* (beret) and *alpargata* (espadrilles), he adopted the coat and tie.[39] This kind of access to social mobility created a great deal of anxiety for members of the upper classes who feared losing their power and prestige in an immigrant revolution.

As Julián Martel portrays in *La Bolsa* (The Stock Market), Buenos Aires had become a place where the employee could dress like his millionaire employer.[40] In one section of the novel, the reader follows a fashionable ballerina on her way to enjoy the parks of Palermo on a Sunday afternoon. While dressed to make a distinguished impression on this special excursion, Martel drowns her presence in a sea of opulent carriages.

> On a sunny Sunday they descend to the riverbank of the Recoleta and they turn toward Alvear Avenue until reaching Palermo. Among them, Lucrecia, the withdrawn ballerina with her haughty luxury, is trying to impress others with her velvet dress in garnet, that masterwork from the scissors of Madame Carrau. There go our heroes, all wrapped up in the whirlwind that confuses the carriage of the prostitute with the majestic landau belonging to a respectable family, and the slow vehicle of small-time clerk, who is rich without anyone knowing why, made proud by the arrogant colt of the young flirt.[41]

In this epoch of materialist wealth and bourgeois insecurity, the fashionable female body found itself increasingly regulated and sculpted for distinction. In 1870, the corset reappeared for the *talle avispa* (wasp waist) style, a look that stayed in vogue until the beginning of the twentieth century.[42] This style dramatically changed the proportions of women's bodies, with the average Argentine woman's waist shrinking dramatically from about 25 to 27.5 inches (63–70 cm) to between

17 and 19.5 inches (43–50 cm), a size some women kept even during pregnancy.[43] Penelope Byrde describes the pose that a corseted and bustled woman kept, known as the "Grecian bend," which pushed "the head and bust forward but moved one's hips and rear backwards."[44] A tight-laced corset rendered a woman inactive, her petite waist functioning as an indicator of her family's social status. Yet while one strove for this fashionable presence, anything too lavish was viewed in bad taste. "Although women were widely regarded as morally superior to men," Steele explains, "they were also regarded, in some sense, as morally feeble; the 'proper' and 'modest' dress provided them with a protective shield."[45] Women felt great pressures to adhere to the rules of modest behavior, at times undergoing extreme physically discomfort, as the corset wreaked havoc with internal organs. Because prostitutes often set the terms of fashion, it was difficult to achieve psychological comfort through fashion. Writing in the same period, Havelock Ellis revealed that this legislated modesty was an "agglomeration of fears" that made for extreme self-consciousness, even when it aimed to do exactly the opposite. "Garment-conditioned prudery is self-contradictory and eventually self-defeating," he ultimately concluded.[46]

The apprehensiveness toward luxurious feminine display in the public arena provided Argentine women authors with a precarious challenge. Feminine style seemed to regulate a woman's movement, encouraging her to assume domestic roles that kept her tucked away at home with her children and family. At the very least, an affluent woman might serve her family as an ornamental appendage of pleats and puff. Furthermore, symbols of high fashion ultimately rendered invisible the identities of the very women who had made them. To piece together sartorial pleasures, seamstresses endured such long hours, low wages, and miserable working conditions that many turned to prostitution for a less burdensome life. Argentine poet Evaristo Carriego (1883–1912) sadly remembers this social problem in "La costurerita que dio aquel mal paso" (The seamstress who took that wrong step)."[47] For working-class women, who found themselves relegated in both the public and the private spheres, an oasis of life may have seemed a mirage. By 1888, the year when Gorriti published her *Oasis en la vida,* women found themselves at a fashion crossroads. The affordability of the sewing machine allowed women to choose between homemade dresses or ready-made clothing. The advent of comfortable textiles, built-in bustles, and the rejection of the crinoline skirt helped women feel a bit more comfortable in their dresses. Two years later, despite the economic crash of 1890, the *fashionistas* of Buenos Aires continued to plot a shift in vision. Lengthened bodices, uncorseted waists, and deep jewel-like tones revealed a confident and relaxed concept of elegance. The Fashion novel, just as Gorriti suggested, prefigured the struggle for more equitable roles for women. Its movement would gain special momentum by the very end of the nineteenth century.[48]

Like the fuchsia heralded in *La Aljaba*'s title, the female reader of the nineteenth century embraced the bold presence of new styles. She could admire them and envision using them, but she did not always wear them. Lavrín explains that the historian may not always be able to quantify the motivations of women and the kinds of political lives they desired. How, then, to unravel those "behavioral norms" and the tensions that women felt as they struggled to gain rights *and* preserve their femininity?[49] Although the Fashion novel does not grant us definitive answers, it does shed light on the concerns and triumphs of women who reflected on the restrictive nature of their social roles. Through fashion writing, authors could embrace the feminine styles of the day as they worked to piece together a narrative of emancipation. Employing discursive strategies not unlike those found in Gorriti's *Oasis en la vida,* women imagined a refuge inspired and changed by their alternative designs.

With the chaos of modernization, where exactly did one find their harbor of strength and salvation? The idea of an oasis in life first surfaced at the well-known literary soirees held at the home of Gorriti in Lima, Perú. An Argentine native, Gorriti had moved to Perú with her two daughters following a difficult separation from Manuel Isidoro Belzú, a military official who became the president of Bolivia in 1848.[50] These evening gatherings, at times lasting until three o'clock in the morning, included at least fifty male and female participants who read their works of creative fiction, debated treatises on women's education,[51] smoked cigars, and performed séances by moonlight.[52] Following her return to Buenos Aires, Gorriti again posed the question of what constitutes an oasis, "the perfume of happiness," in the pages of *La Alborada del Plata,* a magazine under her editorial leadership.

In a thoughtful discussion on the oasis in life, Mercedes Cabello de Carbonera (from Perú), Florencia Escardó, and Larrosa (from Uruguay) touched on the importance of serenity and self-realization in an increasingly complex and materialistic society.[53] An essay by Cabello de Carbonera set the soul free amidst the temptations of life to uncover the essence of the oasis, arguing that nature grants all the capacity to search for meaning and contentment.[54] Her extensive commentary on the self-reliance that authorship afforded her gave strong indicators to the reader that writing could serve as one's oasis in life. Escardó would focus on the sacrifices undertaken to maintain the oasis. When meeting diversions and pleasures such as "the bustle of the salon, the joy of long walks, illusions, conceit, the vanity of youth," maintaining one's spiritual focus on the home might seem especially great.[55] Escardó reminded her reader that maintaining peace at home was well worth the struggle, as nothing compared to the love and happiness of family. Larrosa, who would edit the magazine during its second run, also directed her readers to the delights and comforts of home. She writes, "The one who loves the home has a delicious oasis from which to amuse the spirit when faced with the bitter moments of life and changes of fortune."[56] Incorporating both liberal and conservative views, Gorriti explored the question of self-realization and, in the process, expanded the debate on female emancipation. From *La Alborada del Plata,* readers gained an appreciation for the diversity of views and personal motivations that underscored the search for happiness.[57]

One decade later, Gorriti, Argentina's first female professional novelist,[58] would insert herself as a character in her own *Oasis en la vida,* a social novel on the importance of "work, perseverance and savings."[59] Written toward the end of a most prolific career, the publication of this book absolved Gorriti of all debts and thereby reinforced the message found on its title page: *sine labore nihil* (without work, nothing).[60] Masiello explains, "From its introduction to final resolution, the book emphasizes the world of financial exchange and the possibility of profit and security in a society founded on materialist values."[61] Printed by the Compañía Sud-Americana de Billetes de Banco and with its interests in mind, the novel depicts a city in flux. Returning to his native Argentina from France, Mauricio finds the Buenos Aires of his childhood transformed by the thriving economy and a population explosion.

He feels an overwhelming sense of patriotism for his country although he grew up in a French boarding school that his stepmother forced him to attend. While away, his stepmother forces Mauricio's father into a faulty business venture that leaves him bankrupt and ultimately leads him to commit suicide. Having lost his inheritance, Mauricio thus returns to the city that will make his new fortune. A sign announcing La Buenos Aires insurance company, "powerful association that has at its core the strongest national and foreign capital," provides a protective backdrop to this orphan's meditations.[62] Despite the turmoil of urban expansion, La Buenos Aires helps guide the characters of the novel to their refuge, calming unnecessary fears and anxieties. In dedicating her novel "A la Buenos Aires," Gorriti gives thanks to the insurance company who commissioned the work but also incorporates an image of the growing capital and its female inhabitants. Appearing at a moment of great economic prosperity for Argentina, the novel highlights an emerging middle class whose promise of upward mobility offers great hope to the hard-working Mauricio.

The novel's dedication continues with some preliminary words by S. Vaca-Guzmán, Argentina's minister of economy to Bolivia, who links Gorriti's premise of the oasis of life to the creation and accumulation of wealth.[63] Under the title of "Political Economy," he combines the seemingly contradictory forces of Christian doctrine and positivist science to make sense of the new materialist values that predominate the culture. Vaca-Guzmán describes Argentina's political economy as "that venerated matron" or "this moralistic tutor for society," as if to establish a new guiding mother for Mauricio and all modern orphans.[64] He situates Gorriti in the highest realm of American intellectuals, commending her for the ability to put an attractive dressing on an otherwise dry and challenging topic.[65]

> Creative intelligences have the ability to transform and embellish ideas that pass through the spirit; it would appear that they possess that revitalizing gift of sensual Spring that makes everything beautiful, covering all with flowers and the luster of clouds.
>
> If one still does not believe such an assertion, I invoke as witness, with my support, the present book.
>
> Its author proves, with the attractive dressing of the novel, the benefits of work, perseverance and savings. Never before has such

an economic theme been handled with such charm, with the most graceful mischief, nor with the most natural and unaffected intrigue.[66]

Such an introduction from someone who most probably was not a proponent of women's rights must have pleased Gorriti immensely. Vaca-Guzmán's words placed *Oasis en la vida* in the context of Argentina's political and economic transformations, thereby undermining boundaries that traditionally relegated "male discourse" to the public sphere and female voice to the private sphere. Furthermore, the introduction validated a heavily commercialized enterprise: Advertisements for delicious juices and sensational candies in addition to La Buenos Aires insurance policies abound. Appropriating the language of consumerism, Gorriti promoted images of active, independent female characters "on the rise."[67]

As a *maestra* and advocate of women's rights, where would Gorriti position herself in the *Oasis en la vida?* Several first-person mentions allow her to appear alongside the female protagonist, Julia López, and to move along the development of the plot. In chapter 14, Gorriti allows her clothing to drop to the floor with a thud. Her voice criticizes the social codes that force women into uncomfortable dresses as if to bar them access from the public arena. As her friend Julia changes into more comfortable dinner attire, she, too, sheds extremely heavy layers. One can imagine the laughter of the many readers who knew that Gorriti preferred to appear in masculine trousers—à la George Sand—while about in downtown Buenos Aires.[68]

Contemplating the final sequence of his romance novel, Mauricio finds his attention diverted to the "faint sounds of voices and skirts" next door.[69] Throughout the novel, Mauricio finds himself distracted by the activity and strong opinions of the female residents. He listens to their desires for emancipation and imagines the French designs they describe. The discourse on fashion often takes on the qualities of a foreign language, with some of the more challenging vocabulary appearing in italics, implying that Mauricio, like any "unenlightened" fashion reader, probably doesn't understand them. As previously examined, the women hypothesize that fashion will soon revolutionize their lives with lighter and more liberating styles. "Ha! Ha! Ha! I'm casting aside all that is bad, as you can already see," Julia remarks as she puts on a self-made design.[70] At this point, the eavesdropping Mauricio realizes that he is in love with Julia, who he has admired since first sighting her in France. An orphan like Mauricio, Julia has returned to Buenos Aires following a notable career in Europe as a pianist.[71]

Taking advantage of the liberties that an all-female boardinghouse allows, the residents subscribe to the most important newspapers, dress in their own designs, and play the tunes of "Women's Emancipation."[72] The twenty residents of all ages and backgrounds—widows, young professionals, and one retired school director—find friendship and support in each other. Together they ponder questions related to female emancipation, debating biblical misquotations used to regulate women and the image of the domestic angel. One woman affirms, "Emancipated or not, woman will always reign as queen." An older resident opposes emancipation on the grounds that women might become as tyrannical as men. The residents eventually refute this comment, deciding that their neighborhood has already yielded its share of tyrannical females. For Mauricio, this mosaic of voices represents little more than "a noisy invasion."[73] Gorriti juxtaposes this sensation with a real offensive when she has a burglar enter a window that very night to steal the money and jewels of the residents. Mauricio rushes heroically to the rescue, breaking his status as the "invisible houseguest" and getting stabbed in the process. In the days that follow, the residents nurse him back to health and give up the freedoms they normally enjoy without a male presence.[74] One voice advises the residents, "Now, let us assimilate our looks as much as possible to the latest lithograph of *The Season,* and with all our buttons and bows, we will sit down at the table with our handsome guest."[75]

In chapter 31, Gorriti makes a final appearance as a witness to Mauricio and Julia's wedding. Written with a dialogic technique similar to that of our opening quote, the reader understands the consensus but does not necessarily know who has articulated it. One does know, however, that the participants of this dialogue are those female guests who, following the wedding, return to their residence hall and share news of the event with others. As the women set down their fans and take off their hats and gloves, they re-create the image of Julia López on her wedding day. The precious wedding dress, the intricate butterfly fan—all the details point to a fashion lithograph "of the latest design."[76] The guests evaluate the bride's good fortune, noting the list of prominent leaders who attended the wedding. The few women in attendance, with the exception of Gorriti, are not identified.

> "Few women: all very elegant."
> "But what a large entourage of gentlemen! All the press: General Mitre, Bartolito, Dávila, Lainez, Vedia, Laurencena, Lalanne, Walls, Ribaumont, Ortega, Alberú, Mulhall and so many others."
> "Eduardo Coll was also there. And Emilio Casares was the best man and they say he gave an awesome gift to the bride."
> "Many literary figures: General Sarmiento, Santiago Estrada, José María Zuviria, Bolivian minister Dr. Vaca Guzmán and so many others, dear, who I don't know. We could hardly fit in the chapel."[77]

Following this entourage of male public figures, the narrative sheds its dialogic approach and continues with a unified sermon by a priest who details the importance of savings, hard work, and a reliable insurance company. It ends with a moment of sweetness between the bride and groom, "two spirited devotees of work." Gorriti promptly interrupts this romanticized vision of complete security with the joyous cries of the female guests. She writes, "Everyone cried. I cried, too."[78] The tears break the hegemonic narrative of the ceremony, a strategy that encourages the reader to consider all points of view and to break with the framing provided by Vaca-Guzmán's "Political Economy." Gorriti concludes *Oasis en la vida* by viewing the male leaders of the epoch through the eyes of many women and on their own terms.

This late nineteenth-century Fashion novel reflected carefully the onslaught of economic transformations brought about by bureaucratic modernization. By including Vaca-Guzmán and herself as characters in a social novel on the importance of savings and hard work, Gorriti entered a public debate on materialism and female economic autonomy. Turning to the rhetoric of fashion, she discussed the prospects of female emancipation in a society wrought by change. Incorporating a diversity of voices, Gorriti asked her readers to embrace the challenges and hard work that the premise of female emancipation entailed. In a world ruled by economic experts and advertisers, a woman would have to rely on her confidence and her own decisions to forge beyond her oasis in life.

Fashion engaged many of the social changes brought about by modernization, linking the rhetoric of publicity to a consumer's private desires and reflecting the increasing complexity of women's lives. *La Alborada del Plata* and *La Ondina del Plata* also marketed this new language of fantasy and self-transformation. Under the premise of improving its readership's wardrobes, the magazines published reviews of Parisian fashion plates. Fashion columnists worked to educate readers on their uses, helping them to appropriate styles for a Latin American climate and to make sense of the overwhelming number of options: combinations for travel by train, garments for evenings at the opera house, outfits for high tea, dresses for excursions to the countryside. In the creation of consumer fantasies, dress would seem to have played a prominent role in granting women "access to publicness."[79] Might one argue that the plethora of consumer choices contributed to a more flexible notion of the public sphere?

Figurines, engraved fashion plates, present an interesting challenge to this question. Publicity campaigns in magazines often presented women as ornamental appendages, grouping them together in manicured gardens, beach boardwalks, and elaborate mansions. A more humorous nineteenth-century fashion plate places two women in a rowboat, dressed for a tranquil lake adventure but drifting aimlessly without oars. As in *modernista* poetry and prose, the female form seemed a precious jewel tucked away in an extravagant palace.[80] These commercialized images, often colored by hand, outlined trends on color and cut for the fashion inspired. Vyvyan Holland described early fashion illustration as a process that showed people "the right kind of clothes for them to wear to be abreast of the fashion of the moment," while also predicting "what the fashionable person will be wearing in the near future."[81] Anticipating the future, the fashion plate thus rendered an ideal for the body, allowing each reader to accept, alter, or reject its image of perfection.[82] Responding to lithographs of contemporary European fashions, Argentine women would have appropriated and transformed numerous styles, deciding when to use the image as a model and when to deviate from its designs.

Because *figurines* advertised a particular pattern or style, the description that accompanied the engravings provided the late nineteenth-century reader with clear instructions on how to piece together her garment. Accustomed to predominantly visual approaches to fashion, the twenty-first-century reader may prefer to gloss over such lengthy

Fashion plate depicting women's visiting dresses. Published in *La Torre de Oro* 13 (1873): 102–3. Courtesy of Biblioteca Nacional, Buenos Aires, Argentina.

detail. But this information was extremely important for the home seamstress, as the following description from *La Ondina del Plata* illustrates:

> Princess dress of a snow-covered grey and brown silk. —The front of the dress provides a silk cover that buttons to the side. This part of the cloth disappears under the puff behind, where it then falls to the right and creates a pleated skirt. A trimming in grey cloth, adorned with lace and tassels, runs along the edges of the front cover as well as the fragment of brown silk. The other side of the dress is all snow-covered grey, which intersects the section made of brown silk and falls like a pleated skirt in the back. The middle portion of the back is striped with a border of grey material and the tail of the dress is gathered at the bottom. Adorned with ruffles, the tail is also of silk: one of the ruffles is fastened at the hem. The small silk purse bears the same lace adornment; its buttons, like the ones of the dust jacket, are of a pearl grey. Silk sleeves with lace boots. The wing, lifted on only one side, is fastened with a fantasy-style plume. Outlining the crown of the hat, clasps and feathers.[83]

Broken down into parts, the description of this princess-style dress presented a very fragmented yet detailed approach to ornamentation. It divided the female body into the corresponding sections of the dress: the front (parallel to the sleeves, the collar), the many parts of the back, and the sides. As the reader carefully considered each section, she may have lost sight of the complete dress. Furthermore, the dress was not enough. Special accessories, such as the gray pearl buttons, a matching purse, or the plumed fantasy hat, added to the impressive flow of pleats and puff.

Bridging the novelties of fashion with matters of common sense, the fashion columnist presented creative ideas for homemade designs. Realizing that luxury had limits, she also had women consider the benefits of the fashion magazine to the prosperity of one's family. Under the heading of "Real Life," Sinués de Marco writes,

> From the lithographs that fashion presents, take what you agree with: modify, add, match one style with another. Faced with the precise explanations, try to make your own accessories by yourselves and you will find that your families will realize that the fashion magazine, instead of being a burden, is of great practical value for you and other women.[84]

To demystify fashion for themselves and their families, many Argentine women in the capital and the provinces turned to the writings of Sinués de Marco, who was highly regarded throughout her native Spain and Latin America for her Christian conduct manuals. As Spain's first female professional author, Sinués de Marco found herself placed alongside other Hispanic writers in the pages of *La Alborada del Plata* and its competitor, *La Ondina del Plata,* "the middle-class women's newspaper that most vocally supported female emancipation."[85]

While scholars of Latin American literature have viewed Sinués de Marco as a figure staunchly opposed to the premise of feminist emancipation, the recent scholarship of Ignacio Sánchez-Llama and María Cristina Urruela helps clarify this position by taking into account the later evolutions of her work.[86] Early in her career, Sinués de Marco espoused the moral values deemed of national importance by Isabel II (1843–68). Following her marriage to a well-known Spanish journalist and playwright, José Marco, she published a series of conduct manuals,[87] including the best-selling *El ángel del hogar* (Domestic Angel) (1859), which circulated widely throughout Latin America. Despite a seemingly contradictory belief in female self-sacrifice, Urruela explains that, "time and again Sinués presented herself explicitly as a woman writer in favor of educating women and furthering their role as productive members of society."[88] She would defend the professional status of women authors and female economic autonomy throughout her life. Her magazine with the same title of her best-selling conduct manual, *El Ángel del Hogar,* would support the progressive agenda of the revolutionary Spanish government of 1868, when all other women's periodicals aligned themselves with the Spanish monarchy.[89] By 1872, she edited a transatlantic fashion newspaper titled *La Torre de Oro* with offices in Sevilla and Buenos Aires.[90] New editions of her books continued to appear in Buenos Aires, Lima, and Mexico.[91] Three years later, following a much publicized separation from her husband, Sinués de Marco left Madrid and set up shop in Paris, penning fashion columns for *El Correo de la Moda* (1851–93) and essays for *El Imparcial* (1867–1933), a liberal Spanish newspaper.

In *La Ondina del Plata,* Sinués de Marco offered solicited advice to readers with a conversational style. "I am going to give you some friendly advice, as is all of my advice, dear readers,"[92] her column on "Fashion" began. Faced with so many *figurines,* some women must have felt unsure about their options.[93] Like Gorriti, Sinués de Marco reminded her reading public of the value of hard work and savings, values that did not necessarily affirm the goals of high fashion. She writes,

> In order to be a truly elegant woman, distinguished, and even eccentric sometimes, there is no need for financial ruin.

> Simplicity attracts sympathies and even admiration, and this admiration does not bear bitter fruit but instead might make others imitate you.

> You should love fashion as if it were a friend; but you should not offer her sacrifices as if she were a deity.[94]

While the *figurines* promoted a particular vision of artificial beauty, the thoughtful consumer needed to contemplate her own identity and self-presentation. Could fashion not reflect the emotional intelligence and intellectual capacity of its wearer?[95] By providing sensible and rational explanations, the fashion columnist helped her readers domesticate the chaos of choice. Finding elegant statements in every woman's closet, she reminded her readers that the pursuit of the oasis in life did not require a costly dress.[96]

The rhetoric of fashion of late nineteenth-century Argentina defined the specific features of dress, re-creating the "puff" train and the immigrant arrival's blue beret. With fashion lithographs, readers imagined a new range of applications and especially the fashions of Europe imported to Argentine soil. As a visual sign, these *figurines* served, as Barthes has explained in another context, "to propose a model which is a copy of reality but also and especially to circulate Fashion broadly as a meaning."[97] Each garment thus unfolded according to its own logic, allowing writers to assign function and value to an otherwise neutral article. In earlier years, the rhetoric of fashion had imported the enlightened ideas of Europe. Women authors later used the vocabulary of fashion to establish, although somewhat problematically, a public forum in which they could discuss their aspirations and exercise a limited control over the perception of gender. In the pages of *La Alborada del Plata* and *Oasis en la vida,* Gorriti encouraged her contemporaries to explore the prospect of female emancipation. Sinués de Marco focused on the pragmatic issues that her readers faced when making choices for themselves and their families. Gorriti pushed for more comfortable clothing; Sinués de Marco aspired to make women feel comfortable with individualized designs. Into the twentieth century, the Fashion novel continued to provide a forum for a myriad of opinions on female emancipation, allowing all to contemplate triumphs and plot challenges in the search for the oasis in life.

EPILOGUE *Counter-Couture*

A FEW YEARS INTO THE TWENTY-FIRST CENTURY, a walk in downtown Buenos Aires on a summer afternoon reveals a trend for solidarity-inspired styles.[1] The relaxed fashions of today contrast sharply with those of previous decades, when strict codes imposed clean-cut looks for men and feminine designs (such as skirts and dresses) for women. Very little has been written about the political nature of clothing from this period, although dress was indeed used to regiment the population during dictatorship. In "Scattered Bodies, Unfashionable Flesh," Fabricio Forastelli remembers, "My first memories of fashion date back to the 1970s, precisely the moment when fashion becomes 'moda': that is, a statement that unveils the repetition and the triviality always present in the nature of violence. Back then, people wearing pants too tight or their hair too long would be stopped by the police and publicly punished."[2] Forastelli's memories remind us that individual and collective forms of dress disclose powerful emotions. The unwritten but regulated dress codes of the late 1970s and early 1980s served to control the populace at large; any disruptive practices of such codes called into question the legitimacy of power.

At around this same time, on April 30, 1977, a courageous group of women banded together to demand information about their missing family members and protest human rights violations. The Asociación Madres de Plaza de Mayo (Mothers of the Plaza de Mayo), known for their weekly marches around a monument commemorating the first revolutionary government installed by patriots, initially wore morning robes and house slippers as if to register visually that they longed to be at home caring for their families. They often walked alone or in pairs to avoid arrest, unlike today's gatherings that assemble large groups. The Mothers usually carry with them the black and white photographs of their "disappeared" children. Because the military regime labeled their children enemies of the state, the Mothers remember when few dared march in solidarity with them, let alone recognize their struggle. The Mothers have since gathered to march together every Thursday afternoon to keep alive the memory of their children and grandchildren. They have become the leaders of a peaceful movement against the brutality of military dictatorship and for independence from all forces of domination.[3]

One usually recognizes a Mother of the Plaza de Mayo by the white shawl that she wears, the name of her beloved child cross-stitched in blue thread on the back corner. Worn during marches and at other

Members of the Mothers of the Plaza de Mayo (Línea Fundadora) in front of Casa Rosada during a Thursday march around the revolutionary monument, 2004. Photograph courtesy of Sarah Smith.

public events, the white shawl initially served to help the Mothers identify each other in large crowds; it eventually became an internationally recognized symbol of consciousness in the struggle for human rights in Argentina. During the Dirty War, while several associations organized a Mother's Day march, the Catholic Church called on one million Argentine youth to pilgrimage to Luján, Argentina, a town some 43.5 miles (67 km) from Buenos Aires, with a cathedral that houses a famous statue of the Immaculate Conception, the Virgin of Luján. Known as the patron saint of Argentina, the Virgin of Luján is reputedly the source of several miracles, having allegedly healed the afflicted and disappeared at one location only to reappear in another. Protesting the fact that the Church had overlooked if not fully condoned the actions of the military regime, the Mothers of the Plaza de Mayo decided to make the pilgrimage on behalf of their missing children. Realizing that it would be extremely difficult to find each other in the waves of people making their way to Luján, Hebe de Bonafini remembers that the Mothers of the Plaza de Mayo collectively decided to wear the pale white cotton diapers of their children on their heads.[4] This same white shawl appears as an icon on the books, posters, pins, and handkerchiefs that the Mothers sell today at the Plaza de Mayo to fund human rights causes. Images of the shawl have also been painted around the same monument of independence at which the Mothers began their movement some thirty years ago.

After the economic collapse of 2001 in Argentina, the politically active have performed a new nation by wearing Arte y Confección (art and confection) t-shirts and other clothing produced in factories that were abandoned by their owners, like Brukman, and that workers have reclaimed.[5] The fifty-eight seamstresses of Brukman, who had long produced quality men's suits, found their plight at the forefront of national debates, a recent presidential campaign, and an entire social movement. The seamstresses were owed back wages and benefits, but the owners had abandoned the enterprise, leading Forastelli to argue that "dress may be the very performance that helps us calculate the ruins of the local amidst the ashes of the economic global market."[6] Dressed in their blue smocks, the seamstresses recovered the factory in order to continue working and control the terms of production but were then treated "as if sewing a grey suit were a capital crime."[7] Many of the Mothers of the Plaza de Mayo, standing out in large crowds with their white shawls, marched with the seamstresses of Brukman and other protestors at the factory site in vehement opposition to the forced removal of the seamstresses from the worksite.[8] Because such mobilizations were highly publicized and covered by the media, protestors sometimes wore printed t-shirts with political slogans and images of revolutionary figures to assert what was on their minds.[9] Several present at this demonstration also wore baseball caps, tennis shoes, and jeans, all of which probably served as a layer against the cold and did not necessarily represent an incongruous political statement.[10] A few wore a black and white kaffiyeh, a cloth headdress for Arabic men also used as a radical leftist accessory, as a scarf. Since the height of the repression occurred in the late autumn, jeans and dark-hued sweatshirts prevailed—with the sweatshirts unzipped to reveal newly designed political t-shirts beneath.

Inexpensively printed cotton t-shirts announced solidarity with the Brukman workers and set wearers apart from those wearing the logo sportswear sold in the fashion districts of Buenos Aires. The artists of the Taller de Serigrafía Popular recall printing at the very site of the demonstration designs with three different colors of ink.[11] Often, they used the old t-shirts that a few demonstrators had gathered from their closets to recycle. Some protestors took off the very shirt they had been wearing and waited patiently for an affiliated artist to stamp it with a political design.[12] New messages of resistance marked the moment with unique patterns, such as imaginary stitches for a sewing machine to follow, the parts of a sewing machine, and a sale ticket announcing that "Brukman belongs to the people." The Arte y Confección t-shirts made in 2003 quickly became an important urban expression for supporters of the right-to-work movement in Argentina to get the word out about critical events and to unite artists, intellectuals, university students, and textile workers under a common cause. Eventually, the words "Work, dignity and social change" not only appeared on t-shirts but also graced the sides of handbags, handkerchiefs, and jean jackets worn throughout the city.

During the destruction and renovation that anticipated the transformations of globalization, Jean Franco argues that the "lettered city" set the stage for a cultural clash between those who advocated artistic freedom (and U.S. cultural interventions often presented the defense of freedom against censorship) and those who defended a Soviet-style "pragmatic realism" based on class struggle.[13] Since the late twentieth century, apocalyptic landscapes have haunted Latin American cultural productions as emblems of historical failure. Rapid growth and modernization, utopias and shattered dreams—the consequent "trauma of subjectivity within globalization" presents discordant fragments that upset a reader's sense of identification,[14] with several cultural productions exposing "the trope of disorder, of spontaneity and chance."[15] Yet while Franco finds literature buried in the rubble of the "lettered city," this epilogue suggests that the impact of fashion in today's Argentina prevails as strongly as it has during previous historical junctures.

Contemporary political struggles in Argentina have brought about significant shifts in the way fashion is designed, made, consumed, and understood. The lessons of the past remain extremely relevant, however, for they evoke an ongoing process rooted in the spirit of independence. As *Couture and Consensus* shows, discordant fragments of material culture have disrupted political agendas and plotted alternatives

Graffiti of the local and global: "Hello Kirchner" in downtown Buenos Aires, 2004. Photograph courtesy of Sara Gilmer.

since colonial times. Through appearance and the rhetoric of dress, individuals and entire communities brought to fore questions of consent, independence, and modern citizenship. Several current fashion practices also seek to establish consensus, push for liberation from tyrannical practices, and negotiate a stronger position for individuals in society at large. In an increasingly complex world, postcolonial fashion can be as relevant to the past as it is in the present. It is true, however, that "gaucho pants" and plastic *peinetones* worn on Independence Day no longer serve as symbols for those who found their access to the public sphere denied consistently. When worn, these material culture appropriations instead serve as a kind of logo for Argentine national identity.

Unlike the *chiripá* of Don Segundo Sombra,[16] which has long faded into the horizon of the pampas along with this prototype of the gaucho, Argentine fashion is an Internet click away. At this juncture of global "sameness,"[17] "Moda argentina" has been critical in Argentina's political and economic recovery. An Internet search reveals that several brands weathered the crash at the beginning of the twenty-first century by marketing their designs abroad, especially to the United States, one of the largest importers of clothes in the world. Kosiuko, an Argentine company that markets skateboard chic infused with Asian design, sent free samples of its designs to U.S. celebrities and made headlines throughout Latin America when Britney Spears donned their sexy garb in the video "Overprotected." Argentine ponchos, originally of indigenous origins, were "made for export" as part of a global consumption pattern that included celebrity clients like Jennifer Aniston, Jessica Simpson, and Martha Stewart.[18] Major department stores like Dillard's, JCPenney, and Macy's marketed the "new" gaucho pants to a mass market. One could even "Dress Gaucho at Target."

While Argentine fashion rested on a destroyed textile industry in the 1990s, as Ana Torrejón indicated in a 2001 interview,[19] the creative designs of those responding to the influx of global goods and the expansion boom of more recent years have transformed culture and the economy. A few years following the devaluation of the Argentine peso, the textile sector apparently became one of the fastest growing industries in the nation. New fashion districts emerged in the heart of Buenos Aires, like Palermo Viejo and Palermo Hollywood touted in fashion magazines worldwide. The government of the City of Buenos Aires subsidizes fashion by circulating maps to tourists wishing to locate "up and coming" design studios and sponsoring the newly established Buenos Aires Fashion Week. Unlike the nineteenth century, when high fashion used to "trickle down" to the masses, today's fashion industry calculates the intense speed of "trickle up."[20] To compete in the global marketplace, Argentine coolhunters canvas neighborhoods for "street cool," which sometimes means that international clothing companies will eventually market the very trends back to the marginalized youths who invented them. Aspects of the "style" of anti-consumption that is currently the rage, for instance, was most likely inspired by the impoverished young inhabitants of the *villas miserias* (misery villages) on the outskirts of urban areas.[21] The rising status of the Argentine textile industry allows national designers to create trends and tap into these patterns of consumption. Furthermore, the apparel industry now has the ability to conceptualize and market a garment— from the moment the coolhunter identifies a trend to the placement of a finished product on a store shelf—in one week.[22] In Argentina, this process plays itself out within the parameters of national industry, revealing that Mike González's account of Latin American apparel for the *Encyclopedia of Contemporary Latin American and Caribbean Cultures* may already be obsolete. In 2000, González claimed that the majority of clothing in Latin America was produced in China, Taiwan, Korea, and the Philippines, believing that these countries had "supplanted, by the even more profound exploitation of their labour, many of the sweatshop industries that produced cheap clothing in Latin America through the 1960s and 1970s."[23] In Argentina, however, most clothing is now produced nationally, with Brazil and China competing for segments of this expanding market.

Some designers, working within the parameters of the Mercosur trading block, insist that the continuing recovery will entail the integration of local forms of knowledge into business practices and the creation of competitive markets for local products.[24] The recently established nongovernmental organization Raíz Diseño is a transnational network based in Chile that represents Latin American designers. Emerging from Identidades Latinas,[25] an endeavor initiated in Argentina, Raíz Diseño projects as "lifestyle" the values of fair trade and environmental and social responsibility. Affiliated members of the fashion industry and research institutions work together with indigenous communities to ensure representation in the design process, an innovative approach that has recently gained the approval of the UNESCO Alliance for Cultural Diversity. The goal is that fashion invest the wearer with enhanced meaning and provide the consumer with sustainable alternatives to the machine of mass production and consumption.[26]

While alternatives to the current dynamics of the global fashion industry have sprouted during economic crisis, it is also clear that many Argentines still gravitate toward European labels. Quino, the pseudonym for Mendozan comic artist Joaquín Salvador Lavado, unravels this quandary with humor when he depicts a middle-class fashion victim affected by the crisis.[27] Here the female subject recycles "national news" by tearing apart the newspapers she no longer needs. She whistles a call to the hangers in her armoire and, when they come flying, she dresses them in imaginary replicas of haute couture. Sweetly arranging each shred of paper, she refers to each hanger as "Usted," the formal version of second-person address in Spanish. Finally, she adds a designer name for each article: "Piercar Dén" for Pierre Cardin, "Gior Gioarmani" for Giorgio Armani, "Cocó Shanell" for Coco Chanel, "San Lorán" for Yves Saint Laurent, "Cris Tiandior" for Christian Dior (the French designer remembered in Argentina as Eva Perón's favorite), and "Pacórra Bán" for Paco Rabanne. The incorrect placement of accents on Pacórra Bán notes the degree of dislocation: This female subject desires access to the haute couture of Basque designer Paco Rabanne, with her whistles obviously trying to stay "in tune" with the "latest news" from Europe rather than the realities of her homeland. The new status of the Argentine middle class in the global economy thus resigns this female subject to a "knock-off" winter coat made from recycled fragments of reports on "Robbery," "Death," and soccer matches. In some sense, the concerns of this particular woman remind the viewer of Teodelina Villar, the character Jorge Luis Borges developed in "El Zahir,"[28] who "pursues perfection in the momentary" but whose "external source of fashion makes it impossible to establish secure connections with it."[29] In the case of Quino's cartoon, however, the protagonist is incapable of establishing secure connections both abroad and in her home country. The portrayal also brings to mind the contradictions on which the image of Eva Perón rests in Argentina: Evita's closets were filled with hundreds of designer garments to project an image of social ascension to which few members of the working classes she represented could aspire. It is a contradiction that has also surfaced recently in Argentine politics, with the look of President Cristina Fernández de Kirchner—especially her penchant for high fashion and elaborate gemstones—strongly criticized for being incongruous with the stark economic realities of the nation.[30] Quino's cartoon depicts an empty armoire until the dressed hangers fly back to inhabit their space. Alone in a bare room, the woman realizes with horror: "It must be tough to be a hanger in a middle-class home that does not resign itself to the crisis carrying away its highest ideals!" With ironic humor, Quino represents fashionable dreams as "old news" or torn fragments at odds with the realities of the Argentine nation.

On the sidelines of the Argentine Workers' Movement, 1996. Photograph by the author.

"Buenos Aires, I think, is out of joint with its own material representation; it cannot be any other way," Forastelli writes in the conclusion to *The Latin American Fashion Reader*.[31] When chronicling dress, body, and culture, on the anniversary of the Argentine political crisis, the cultural critic made some striking observations: As an Argentine emigré returning to Buenos Aires and his native Córdoba, he fully expected to find "guerilla fashion" announcing revolution in the streets. But where were those black berets, like the ones Che Guevara once touted, or the khaki pants of a Subcomondante Marcos? Instead, Forastelli documented a sea of printed t-shirts and logo-laden sportswear at one manifestation;[32] he apparently even sighted a counterfeit pair of Calvin Klein jeans. Despite the fact that poverty remains a critical issue for Argentina, and much disparity exists between those who have purchasing power and those who experience extreme poverty, most urban inhabitants have remained adamant about their access to imported styles advertised on television and in music videos. At the height of the crisis, Argentina imported more silicone implants than any other country in the world.[33] Fashionably thin bodies that provoked the recent Sizes Law in the province of Buenos Aires, or what government leaders called the "tyranny of tiny tiny sizes,"[34] also provide a striking contrast with the real hunger experienced by segments of the population who rely on soup kitchens. Such contradictions are hardly unique to Argentina, of course, but one must at least recognize this reality when archiving distressing juxtapositions of material representation in contemporary life.

At the staging of an unemployed workers' mobilization, Forastelli joined a group of transvestites who no longer dressed like they did in 2000, or if we take Ana Gabriela Álvarez's study of "The City Crossdressed" as an example: "in six inch heels, tight-fit clothing that requires constant readjustment so that it can cover anything at all, make-up that has to be constantly touched up to keep it even, given that when one sweats its runs."[35] A few years later, transvestites now resisted wearing the clothes that once provoked their arrest as dictated by city police ordinances, specifically the article illegalizing "those who appear in public in the clothes of the opposite sex."[36] Lohana Berkins, one of the founders of the Argentine Transvestite Association, told Forastelli, "Now we dress without glamour, like any other sweaty worker in the streets."[37] At this juncture, sartorial expressions reflected the solidarity among unemployed workers, transvestites, and other marginalized groups in crisis.

The role that Argentine fashion plays in rearticulating the past, empowering sectors of the population, enacting change, and "producing" cultural meaning is significant. For this reason, contemporary design now challenges the idea of "efficient" models of mass production and consumption that neglect the spirit of political transition. A recent collection by Flavia Angriman, a professor at the Institute of Art and Fashion in Buenos Aires, is just one example of this reflection. Through fashion design, Angriman explores the psychological responses to authoritarianism and crisis. Her sketches integrate muted representations of silence, presence, voice, and national self-understandings. In 2001, she presented a sportswear collection constructed from fragmented but not necessarily separate visions of maternity, mourning, and the wounds of the soul.[38] Fully aware of the pitfalls of rendering the pain of dictatorship and the politics of crisis artistically, Angriman evoked the power of citizenship in reconstructing memories and imparted on her designs the emotional pulse of urban life. Her understated skirts, for instance, call to mind the triangular shapes of the shawls worn by the Mothers of the Plaza de Mayo and the freedom of movement. At least three sketches for shirts with long, flared sleeves integrate one to six X-shaped patterns delicately fashioned with bandages, symbols of urgency and care that initiate the healing process. The colors depicted by Angriman's sketches convey somber and understated hues, although visual disharmony erupts onto this pattern as if to overpower some of the more muted pieces. Angriman was extremely careful with the ways in which she represented the spirit of resistance artistically, aiming to disallow the collection of any pretentiousness.[39] While one might argue that such creative imaginings inescapably fix one's gaze on the trauma of the Dirty War, this collection ultimately asks the wearer to acknowledge a national past and reconsider contemporary struggles through active presence in the cityscape. Fashion announces change, and like the very style it represents, it is always the latest news.

Negotiating the promise of the future while facing the memory of dictatorship, visual artist María Silvia Corcuera Terán continues to map the nation's political tensions onto the *peinetón,* protective layers, and

Flavia Angriman, *Design Sketches*, 2001. Courtesy of the designer.

the shawls of mothers from around the world who appeal for justice on behalf of their families. In *The Supplicant,* a wood sculpture of an inverted crimson comb is also like a trough used in the north of the country to grind grains for popular foods or to wash clothing. From this structure emerges the city of Buenos Aires, turning history on its head and emphasizing the migrations on which urban life rests. As a creative endeavor worn collectively in the postcolonial moment, the *peinetón* called into question those political interests that did not bear in mind equity for all citizens. In the nineteenth century, the rhetoric of fashion disrupted authoritarian practices that limited the participation of certain segments of the population. The potential for fashion to inspire creative agency continues to inspire many Argentine authors, designers, and artists alike. The symbols of political consciousness in Argentina, whether the *peinetón,* crimson-coded poncho, white shawl, or stamped t-shirt, continue to extend the symbolic dimensions of "representation" and reverberate with new messages and meanings. As scholars unravel the political dimensions of dress in Latin America, the terms of couture and consensus will help bring to light the significance of mapping these often overlooked and truly dynamic facets of Argentine cultural history.

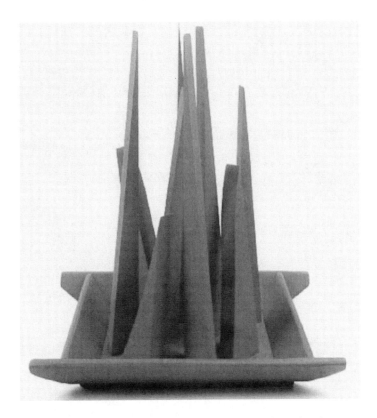

María Silvia Corcuera Terán, *The Supplicant,* 2002. Painted wood sculpture.
Courtesy of the artist.

Notes

Introduction

1. "Cultura," *La Nación,* December 12, 2001.

2. Translated by Mary Peabody Mann, this book appeared in 1868 (New York: Macmillan, no date).

3. See Diana Sorensen's insightful work on *Facundo and the Construction of Argentine Culture* (Austin: University of Texas Press, 1996). She writes, "It is interesting to see how national identity can be observed from the vantage point of a classic and its readings, how they constitute a repertory of conflicting interpretations, and the extent to which polemics can provide a model for understanding cultural formation" (5).

4. The Pink House, home to the executive branch of the Argentine government, is also known as the "presidential palace."

5. Daniel James, "October 17th and 18th, 1945: Mass Protest, Peronism and the Argentine Working Class," *Journal of Social History* 21.3 (Spring 1988): 441–61. See pages 452–53 in particular. As James explains in his analysis of the events of October 17 and 18, 1945, a "festive, familial atmosphere" prevailed. He cites an article published on October 19, 1945, in *La Capital* as one "based strongly in historical fact": "The majority of the public who marched in the many different columns did so in shirt sleeves. One could see men dressed as *gauchos* and women as peasants ... boys who turned the *avenidas* and plazas into roller skating rinks, and men and women dressed outrageously, carrying placards of Perón, with flowers and cockades tacked onto their clothes and posters. Men on horseback and youngsters on bicycles with ill matching clothes, singing ditties and breaking out in hurrahs" (450).

6. Dalmiro Sáenz, *Yo te odio, político* [I hate you, politician] (Buenos Aires: Planeta, 2001), 8.

7. Ibid.

8. Ezequiel Martínez Estrada, *X-ray of the Pampa,* trans. Alan Swietlicki (Austin: University of Texas Press, 1971), 250. An economic collapse in that same decade would initiate many different readings of consumption patterns in Argentina. In the conclusion, we take up the question of Teodina Villar, the fictitious socialite portrayed in "El Zahir" by Jorge Luis Borges.

9. Amid the clanging of pots of *asambleístas* (protestors from neighborhood assemblies), the final strophes of "Martín Fierro está furioso" beg the listener to avoid confusing the true countryman with the bandit who took Argentina for what it had. The song ends with a national embrace ("this land hugs us / we will not leave our home") that illegitimates the status of the same politicians mentioned in Sáenz's book.

10. A *piquetero* is a member of the unemployed worker's movement in Argentina. Silvia Tandeciarz writes, "In addition to organizing massive demonstrations to protest their lack of work, piqueteros use roadblocks that interrupt the flow of goods and people to call attention to their situation." See page 167 of her article titled "Citizens of Memory: Refiguring the Past in Postdictatorship Argentina," *PMLA* 122.1 (January 2007): 151–69. *Descamisados* refers to the "shirtless workers," especially those who toiled over long hours of industrial labor, to whom Juan Perón had appealed for support and wished to represent, and for whom the luxurious figure of Eva Perón (herself of working-class origins) represented the promise of transformation. Fabricio Forastelli discusses the shift in the representation of workers from peronista to *piquetero* in "Lo pobre lindo," available at http://www.berlinsur.org/pages/miradas/pobrelindo.htm (accessed January 1, 2010). Detailing a city out of synch with its own material representation, he also describes the luxurious red carpet that linked the fashion district of Buenos Aires shortly after the crisis. Forastelli argues that this carpet symbolically represents the connections between members of more affluent sectors who somehow managed to hide their wealth during the crisis. Forastelli's argument counters the idea espoused by Gilles Lipovetsky that fashion represents the "ultimate phase of democracy" because the red carpet and related fashion marketing campaigns following the crisis forged an exclusive status for wealthy urban inhabitants that did grant access or represent the dire needs of the majority of the population. See Lipovetsky, *The Empire of Fashion: Dressing Modern Democracy,* trans. Catherine Porter (Princeton, N.J.: Princeton University Press, 1994), 10.

11. *Nunca más: informe de la Comisión Nacional sobre la desaparición de personas,* published in 1984, estimated nine thousand cases of executions, tortures, and other human rights violations. For the complete report, see http://www.nuncamas.org. News and human rights organizations report that this figure is probably closer to thirty thousand.

12. Personal interview with the author, Buenos Aires, 2001.

13. See, in particular, the work of H. D. Fernández L'Hoeste, "Between Comic Strips and Literature: On Fragmentation and Identity in Ricardo Piglia's *La Argentina en pedazos*," available at http://www2.gsu.edu/~forhdf/piglia.html.

14. The panelists included Fabricio Forastelli, Francine Masiello, Regina A. Root, and Silvia Tieffemberg.

15. Francine Masiello, *The Art of Transition: Latin American Culture and Neoliberal Crisis* (Durham, N.C.: Duke University Press, 2001), 5.

16. Luis Roniger, "Human Rights Violations and the Reshaping of Collective Identities in Argentina, Chile and Uruguay," *Social Identities: Journal for the Study of Race, Nation and Culture* 3.2 (1997): 221–47. See page 221 in particular.

17. Susana Rotker, *Captive Women: Oblivion and Memory in Argentina*, trans. Jennifer French (Minneapolis: University of Minnesota Press, 2002), 9.

18. For glimpses of the Rosas period, see in particular "Cadaveres" [Cadavers]. The apparel of Eva Perón is rendered neobarroque in "El cadaver de la nación" [The nation's cadaver]. Both poems are published in Néstor Perlongher, *Poemas completos* (Buenos Aires: Editorial Seix Barral, 2003).

19. See César Aira's *El vestido rosa; Las ovejas* (Buenos Aires: Ada Korn Editora, 1984). For more on this novel, set in the time of the expeditions of Roca, see Corina S. Mathieu, "*El vestido rosa* de César Aira: ¿Puro cuento o novela?" *Romance Languages Annual* 5 (1993): 469–71. Graciela Montaldo has placed the work of Aira as a response to the context of this "neoboom of 'historical novels'" in "An Obscure Case: Bizarre Aesthetics in Argentina (Books, Culture Industries and Fictions)," *Journal of Latin American Cultural Studies* 9.2 (2000): 181–92.

20. In fact, Mina Roces and Louise Edwards suggest that the gendered politics of dress in the Americas have striking parallels with the Asian context. Roces and Edwards argue that "'[a]ppeals to 'tradition' became powerful forces for political change and 'national dress' often served to advance radical causes" (4). See their introductory chapter to *The Politics of Dress in Asia and the Americas* (East Sussex, United Kingdom: Sussex Academic Press, 2007).

21. Arnold Bauer, introduction to the "Material Culture," ed. Judith Ewell, special issue, *Americas: A Quarterly Review of Inter-American Cultural History* 60.3 (January 2004): 317–23. See page 318.

22. Ibid., 317.

23. Ross Jamieson, "Bolts of Cloth and Sherds of Pottery: Impressions of Caste in Material Culture of the Seventeenth Century Audiencia of Quito," in "Material Culture," ed. Judith Ewell, special issue, *Americas: A Quarterly Review of Inter-American Cultural History* 60.3 (January 2004): 431–46. See page 433.

24. Ibid., 432.

25. Ibid., 434. For a framework concerning the scholarly integration of the material and social aspects of clothing and textiles, Susanne Küchler and Daniel Miller, eds., *Clothing as Material Culture* (Oxford: Berg Publishers, 2005).

26. Karen Tranberg Hansen, "The World in Dress: Anthropological Perspectives on Clothing, Fashion, and Culture," *Annual Review of Anthropology* 33 (2004): 369–92. See page 370. Doris Sommer has written an insightful discussion on the potential for creative culture to serve as a vehicle for agency in the Americas, "Art and Accountability," *Review: Literature and Arts of the Americas* 71, 38.2 (2005): 261–76. See also http://culturalagents.org.

27. Tranberg Hansen, "The World in Dress," 370.

28. Ibid. Tranberg Hansen's astute observations lead us to ask: Are scholars of fashion studies maximizing the potential of the interdisciplinary and pan-disciplinary qualities of research that is also grounded in international contexts?

29. Yuniya Kawamura, *Fashion-ology* (Oxford: Berg Publishers, 2005).

30. Susana Saulquin, *La moda en Argentina* (Buenos Aires: Emecé, 1990), 35.

31. Benedict Anderson, *Imagined Communities* (London: Verso, 1991), 5–7.

32. For a comprehensive overview of these questions, see Seminar on Feminism and Culture in Latin America, ed., *Women, Culture and Politics in Latin America* (Berkeley: University of California Press, 1990); Sara Castro-Klarén and John Charles Chasteen, eds., *Beyond Imagined Communities: Reading and Writing the Nation in Nineteenth-Century Latin America* (Washington D.C., Baltimore, and London: Woodrow Wilson Center Press and the Johns Hopkins University Press, 2003); and Nancy Appelbaum, Anne S. Macpherson, and Karin Alejandra Rosemblatt, eds., *Race and Nation in Modern Latin America* (Chapel Hill and London: The University of North Carolina Press, 2003).

33. Antonio Cornejo Polar, *Escribir en el aire: Ensayo sobre la heterogeneidad socio-cultural en las literaturas andinas* (Lima: Centro de Estudios Literarios "Antonio Cornejo Polar" [CELACP], 2003), 99.

34. Juana Manso de Noronha, *Compendio de la historia de las Provincias Unidas del Río de la Plata* (Buenos Aires: Angel Estrada, 1881), 30. Also see the version of Domingo Faustino Sarmiento's school textbook, originally published in Chile in 1842 and used in Argentine schools in the late nineteenth century: *Método de lectura gradual* (Paris: Librería de Ch. Bouret, 1882).

35. Thomas C. Holt, "The First New Nations," in *Race and Nation in Modern Latin America,* ed. Appelbaum, Macpherson, and Rosemblatt, x.

36. Diana Sorensen uses these same words in her intriguing discussion of Domingo Faustino Sarmiento's liminality and the narrative of cultural resistance. See "Postcolonial Liminality: Sarmiento and Metropolitan Cultures," in *Studies in Honor of Enrique Anderson Imbert,* ed. Nancy Abraham Hall and Lanin A. Gyurko (Newark, Del.: Juan de la Cuesta, 2003), 108. Like other members of his generation, Sarmiento attempted to translate imaginatively "the general principles and propositions of hegemonic knowledge into local forms. But, at times, their marginal location gave them the freedom to appropriate, transform, adapt and adopt these forms." Ibid., 110. In this context, see also Francine Masiello, *Between*

Civilization and Barbarism: Women, Nation and Literary Culture in Modern Argentina (Lincoln: University of Nebraska Press, 1991).

37. Arnold Bauer writes that the Spanish Crown issued a series of statements to emphasize the delineations of dress according to caste hierarchies, denouncing the ostentatious dress of mestizas, but not the luxurious presence of clergymen. See his book on *Goods, Power and History: Latin America's Material Culture* (Cambridge: Cambridge University Press, 2001). Mariselle Meléndez emphasizes the transgressive qualities of dressing like another caste during the colonial period in "Visualizing Difference: The Rhetoric of Clothing in Colonial Spanish America," in *The Latin American Fashion Reader,* ed. Regina A. Root (Oxford: Berg Publishers, 2005), 17–30. Rebecca Earle argues that sumptuary legislation was enacted throughout Latin America in the eighteenth century as a result of the dramatic increase in racial reclassifications through dress. Such laws were discarded with the retreat of Spanish colonialism. See "Luxury, Clothing and Race in Colonial Spanish America," in *Luxury in the Eighteenth Century: Debates, Desires, and Delectable Goods,* ed. Maxine Berg and Elizabeth Eger (Hampshire, United Kingdom: Palgrave Macmillan, 2003), 219–27.

38. Bauer, *Goods, Power, and History,* 112.

39. By the late nineteenth century, the garments of founding fathers would appear represented in illustrated magazines throughout the Americas without any hint of the owner, as if the aura of the garments now on display in a museum represented some higher truth. For similar depictions of Simón Bolívar's uniform, for instance, see the *Papel periódico ilustrado* from late nineteenth-century Colombia.

40. William Katra, *The Argentine Generation of 1837* (Cranbury, N.J.: Associated University Presses, 1996), 19.

41. John Lynch, *Argentine Dictator Juan Manuel de Rosas, 1829–1852* (Oxford: Clarendon Press, 1981), 13–15.

42. Mark D. Szuchman, *Order, Family, and Community in Buenos Aires, 1810–1860* (Stanford, Calif.: Stanford University Press, 1988), 7, translation added.

43. The Brigadier General Cornelio de Saavedra Historical Museum has on display an intriguing collection of the messages placed within top hats during this period.

44. See page 481 of "The Leading Lady," a fashion spread set in Buenos Aires, in the March 2006 issue of *Vogue* magazine.

45. The "collective catalogue" of headdresses and other postcolonial material artifacts can be found at http://www.acceder.buenosaires.gov.ar/acceder/index .htm. Be sure to click on "Moda e indumentaria" (Fashion and dress) to survey this online collection. The primary collections of *peinetones* in Argentina have been housed at the Saavedra Museum and the Isaac Fernández Blanco Museum of Spanish American Art. Some of the latter museum's combs were damaged or destroyed on July 18, 1994, following the bombing of the Argentine Israelite Mutual

Association (AMIA) near the museum site. The bombing of the AMIA, in later years attributed to the Hezbollah, killed eighty-five people and injured hundreds.

46. See, for example, Eduardo Gudiño Kieffer's "Cuentos con peinetones," a brief collection of short stories depicting women and their combs published in *El peinetón* (Buenos Aires: Ediciones de Arte Gaglianone, 1986), 53–81.

47. *La Argentina,* December 5, 1830, no. 6, p. 12.

48. Torrejón believes strongly that *Elle* (Argentina) is about the projection of attitude. Torrejón was interviewed in "La moda en los medios," *DeSigniS* 1 (October 2001): 267–70. See page 270.

49. See Julio Ramos's chapter on "Decorar la ciudad" in *Desencuentros de la Modernidad en América Latina: Literatura y política en el siglo XIX* (Mexico City: Fondo de Cultura Económica, 1989), 112–42.

50. The Saavedra Museum discovered that the Federal ribbons worn by members of the Zemborain family in a Cayetano Descalzi portrait had been hidden by overpaint. The crimson ribbons worn by the female subject were hidden underneath blue paint.

51. For a similar view that involves approaching the study of a porcelain plate, see the work of Jorge F. Rivas P., "The Pineapple Plate," trans. Isabela Villanueva, *Review: Literature and Arts of the Americas* 72, 39.1 (May 2006): 74–76. Rivas P., who catalogs Latin American furniture in the collection of the France Mayer Museum in Mexico City, admits that a scholar can "never know the complete history" of a piece but she or he can begin to unravel a brief history and its relation to a larger historical context.

52. Sadly, many of the artifacts and archival materials that I consulted in Argentina for this project in the 1990s were difficult to locate. Items once available in library and museum catalogues were conserved improperly due to lack of funds, discarded as libraries moved collections or registered information online, or simply missing. It was often suggested to me that materials had been sold to private collections throughout the world during the 1980s, a period of massive inflation.

1. Uniform Consensus

1. Esteban Echeverría, *La Cautiva: El matadero* (Buenos Aires: Kapelusz, 1995), 85–86.

2. David Viñas once told me that "The Slaughterhouse" could very well have been titled "Elogio del matambre" (Praise for matambre). *Matambre,* which quite literally means that it "kills hunger," is a rolled and stuffed flank steak that is boiled or baked but traditionally served cold. In this context, it implies an elitist narrative, as told by the *gente decente* (well to do) to distinguish them from those associated with raw meat. I would like to thank Professor Viñas for his guidance when I began the research for this chapter at the University of Buenos Aires.

3. Cristina Iglesia, "Mártires o libres: Un dilema estético. Las víctimas de la

cultura en *El matadero* de Echeverría y en sus reescrituras," in *Letras y divisas: Ensayos sobre literatura y rosismo*, ed. Cristina Iglesia (Buenos Aires: Eudeba, 1998): 25–35. See page 25.

4. Ibid. These connections are also made in Tulio Halperin Donghi's discussion of "El matadero" in "Argentina's Unmastered Past," *Latin American Research Review* 23.2 (1988): 3–24.

5. The decree mandating the use of the crimson insignia went into effect on February 3, 1832. The decree can be found listed under that date in Pedro de Angelis's *Recopilación de leyes y decretos promulgados en Buenos Aires desde el 25 de Mayo de 1810 hasta fin de Diciembre de 1835* (Buenos Aires: Imprenta del Estado, 1836).

6. Lawrence Langner, *The Importance of Wearing Clothes* (Los Angeles: Elysium Growth Press, 1991), 128.

7. Michel Foucault, *Discipline and Punish* (New York: Vintage Books, 1995), 164.

8. For more information on the military corps and their leaders in command, see Ignacio Nuñez, *Noticias históricas de la República Argentina* (Buenos Aires: 1857).

9. During the war for independence, African Argentines made up the infantry and gauchos the cavalry. See Lynch, *Argentine Dictator*, 105.

10. This description is dated March 19, 1812. Cited in Enrique Udaondo, *Uniformes militares usados en la Argentina desde el siglo XVI hasta nuestros días* (Buenos Aires: Pegoraro Hermanos, 1922), 147.

11. Lynch, *Argentine Dictator*, 29.

12. For the original Spanish version of the poem, see Fermín Chávez, *La vuelta de Don Juan Manuel* (Buenos Aires: Dirección de Impresiones del Estado y Boletín Oficial de la provincia de Buenos Aires, 1991), 23.

13. Foucault, *Discipline and Punish*, 140.

14. Nancy Hanway, *Embodying Argentina: Body, Space, and Nation in Nineteenth Century Narrative* (Jefferson, N.C.: McFarland and Company, 2003), 11.

15. Unitarians losing their property were sometimes forced into military conscription. Lynch writes that no one dared challenge a wrongful classification. It is interesting to note that Unitarian authorities had also confiscated property prior to the Federal regime. See Lynch, *Argentine Dictator*, 64–66.

16. *British Packet*, no. 159 (September 5, 1829): 1.

17. Certain uniforms underwent quick alterations so that they could not be mistaken for any Unitarian affiliation. A decree published on August 8, 1835, revised the Federal navy uniform, declaring, "cerulean blue or green are out, the requirement being that the cap take on a crimson hue."

18. See chapter 23 of Paz's *Memorias póstumas* (La Plata: Imprenta La Discusión, 1892). It would be interesting to link this gloved hand to the complex workings of power. The idea of the "Federal touch" was already prominent in women's fashion circles, where ladies had their gloves stamped with the image of Rosas.

19. Ibid., 530–31.

20. Ricardo Cicerchia has recently studied the relationship of the linking of

Arab armed rebels to the gaucho insurgents in Sarmiento's work, arguing that the Argentine statesman's racialized vision of national constitution sought a "forced harmony" that took its cue from the "signs of Civilization" of anti-Spanish Europe. See 679 of his article on the "Journey to the Centre of the Earth: Domingo Faustino Sarmiento, a Man of Letters in Algeria," *Journal of Latin American Studies* 36.4 (November 2004): 665–86.

21. Donghi, "Argentine Counterpoint: Rise of the Nation, Rise of the State," in *Beyond Imagined Communities,* Castro-Klarén and Chasteen, 46.

22. *El Iniciador* made the sky the official insignia of the Generation of 1837. See page 186 of the periodical for this declaration.

23. *Tirteo,* no. 5, 1.

24. *Tirteo,* no. 4, 29–31.

25. Originally published in *Tirteo* in 1841, this poem can be found in Juan María Gutiérrez, *Poesías* (Buenos Aires: Imprenta y Librería de Mayo, 1869), 56.

26. The light blue sky figured prominently in descriptions that commented on or pressed for political and religious freedoms. José María Ramos Mejía remembered, "I have known the city of Buenos Aires all dressed in crimson, when it was just out of the hands of Rosas. To find a blue ray it was necessary to look at the sky on a nice spring day, for even the colors of the flag had disappeared." See his essay on "La negrada federal," *Rosas y su tiempo* (Buenos Aires, 1907).

27. José Rivera Indarte, *Rosas y sus opositores* (Buenos Aires: Imprenta de Mayo, 1853), 159–60.

28. Ibid., 160–61.

29. For the actual decree, see de Angelis, *Recopilación,* 1117–18. An accessible version of this document and excerpts of other decrees have been compiled by Jorge Myers in *Orden y virtud: El discurso republicano en el régimen rosista* (Bernal, Argentina: Universidad Nacional de Quilmes, 1995), 127–28. For more on the use of the insignia and its various modifications through time, see Adolfo Saldías, who dates its usage to the struggle for independence: *Historia de la confederación argentina: Rozas y las facultades extraordinarias* (Buenos Aires: Editorial Americana, 1945), 7–8.

30. Rosas modified Argentine mourning traditions, believing that men and women should not be required to purchase expensive outfits at a time of war. He therefore instituted the use of black ribbons, such as the one required of citizens to commemorate the death of Rosas's wife, Doña Encarnación. Saldías writes that men wrapped the black ribbons around their left arm, whereas women used them to fashion a bracelet for their left wrist. See Saldías, *Historia de la confederación,* 809.

31. To access this example in the Saavedra Museum archives, see what is cataloged under 13-2-1852.

32. José Luis Busaniche, *Rosas visto por sus contemporáneos* (Buenos Aires: Hyspamérica, 1986), 125.

33. To access such notices on the distribution of insignias, see the Archivo

Histórico de la Provincia de Córdoba, Gobierno, 1835, vol. 143, f. 346. I would like to thank Seth Meisel for sharing this fascinating discovery with me.

34. *La Gazeta Mercantil*, July 18, 1835.

35. The Rosas regime symbolically upheld its social order by antagonizing nonconformists. This presented a problem to foreigners who required access to public buildings and who did not feel it appropriate to pledge allegiance to the regime. The *British Packet*, while recognizing some unresolved factual inconsistencies, describes the mob-style harassment that diplomats and their families faced on November 14, 1835: "Females who have on their clothing the least portion of blue, are hooted and pursued in the streets and on the promenades. The daughter of the French Vice-Consul [DeVins de Peysac], a young girl of 13 years of age, was obliged to hide a blue bonnet, which she could neither wear abroad, nor even let be seen at home to the Federal visitors" (no. 482, 2). For more about these tensions, see Andrew Graham-Yooll's anthology of the accounts of diplomats who served during the regime, *Así vieron a Rosas los ingleses, 1829–1852* (Buenos Aires: Rodolfo Alonso, 1980).

36. Manuel Gálvez, *Vida de don Juan Manuel de Rosas* (Buenos Aires, 1965), 457–58.

37. Lynch, *Argentine Dictator,* 164.

38. Ibid., 164–65.

39. Ibid., 184.

40. Eugenio Rosasco, *Color de Rosas* (Buenos Aires: Editorial Sudamericana, 1992), 195.

41. *Registro Oficial,* May 27, 1835, 128.

42. Saldías, *Historia de la confederación,* 157.

43. Rosasco, *Color de Rosas,* 197.

44. Ibid., 252.

45. S. Samuel Trifilo, *La Argentina vista por viajeros ingleses: 1810–1860* (Buenos Aires: Ediciones Gure, 1959), 115–16.

46. For more on the theatrical representation of the Confederation, see Raúl Castagnino, *El teatro en Buenos Aires durante la época de Rosas* (Buenos Aires: Instituto Nacional de Estudios de Teatro, 1944); and Mariano G. Bosch, *Historia del teatro en Buenos Aires* (Buenos Aires: no date).

47. As stated previously, authorities were known to destroy green and blue decorations, as these were believed to be spatial extensions of the self. For a more extensive study on the decoration of everyday objects and the iconography of the Rosas period, see Juan Pradere, *Juan Manuel de Rosas: Su iconografía. Reproducción de óleos, acuarelas, grabados, litografías, viñetas de imprenta, monedas, porcelanas, curiosidades, etc.* (Buenos Aires, 1914). In a history of the fan in Uruguay, Horacio Arredondo analyzes ones with images of Rosas in uniform that had circulated for propagandistic purposes. See his *Temas de Museo: Abanicos* (Montevideo: Imprenta "El Siglo Ilustrado," 1928), 59–61. The examples show how the owner of a seemingly insignificant object could transform her possession into a compromising political message.

48. William Henry Hudson, *Far Away and Long Ago* (London: Eland Books, 1982), 108–9.

49. The police department of Buenos Aires held raffles to benefit Federalist military efforts. Clothes were the most frequent prizes, given away each *fiesta de patria,* the twenty-fifth of May. Items included men's and women's clothing imported from Europe and other specialties, such as hair combs, umbrellas, and silk handkerchiefs.

50. See María Sáenz Quesada's interpretation in *Mujeres de Rosas* (Buenos Aires: Emecé, 2005).

51. Elizabeth Garrels, "La lucha por el cuerpo muerto de Facundo: Reflexiones sobre la necrofilia política y la construcción de la masculinidad en el libro de Sarmiento," in *La literatura iberoamericana en el 2000: Balances, perspectivas y prospectivas* (Salamanca, Spain: Ediciones Universidad de Salamanca, 2000), 905–12. See page 907.

52. The *chiripá* was a precursor to *bombachas,* which became an international sensation when marketed by the industry a few years ago as "gaucho pants." For more on the poncho, see Ruth Corcuera's work: "Ponchos of the River Plate: Nostalgia for Eden," in *The Latin American Fashion Reader* (Oxford: Berg Publishers, 2005), 163–75; and *Ponchos de las tierras del Plata* (Buenos Aires: Fondo Nacional de las Artes and Verstraeten Editores, 2000). Richard W. Slatta also describes the "Material Culture: Housing, Clothing, Food, Recreation" of the gaucho in his book, *Gauchos and the Vanishing Frontier* (Lincoln: University of Nebraska Press, 1983), 69–90. For the River Plate context, see Fernando O. Assunçao, *Pilchas criollas* (Buenos Aires: Emecé, 1991).

53. Rosas cited in Lynch, *Argentine Dictator,* 109.

54. Lynch, *Argentine Dictator,* 110.

55. See Tomás de Iriarte and his depiction of Rosas as "a miserable gaucho without any glorious service record or antecedents" in *Memorias: Luchas de Unitarios y Federales y Mazorqueros en el Río de la Plata* (Buenos Aires: Ediciones Argentinas, 1947), 224–26. Iriarte criticizes the poncho-clad caudillo for being a cunning fox in "honest gaucho costume."

56. Hudson, *Far Away and Long Ago,* 127.

57. Ariel de la Fuente, *Children of Facundo: Caudillo and Gaucho Insurgency during the Argentina State-Formation Process (La Rioja, 1853-1870)* (Durham, N.C.: Duke University Press, 2000), 148, 149.

58. Unitarian counterattacks used "identity camouflage" to expose the atrocities of the regime. The disguises employed by Daniel Bello in Mármol's *Amalia* and the female co-optation of uniform in Juana Manso de Noronha's *Misterios del Plata* [Mysteries of the River Plate] offer intriguing discussions of uniform for strategic purposes.

59. John Lynch, *Caudillos in Spanish America, 1800–1850* (Oxford: Clarendon Press, 1992), 190.

60. Lynch, *Argentine Dictator,* 23.

61. Gauchos often "hoped that their new shoes and clothing would survive the campaign so that they could return home better furnished," writes La Fuente, *Children of Facundo,* 94–95.

62. See Ernesto Celesia, *Rosas: Aportes para su historia* (Buenos Aires: Ediciones Peuser, 1954), 454.

63. *British Packet,* April 11, 1829: "Parts of the country have become the prey of the most horrid excesses. *Foul murder stalks abroad* almost with impunity" (no. 140: 3).

64. This undated poem published by the Imprenta del Comercio was titled "Así es el mundo, vidita" and is housed in the Saavedra Museum archives.

65. Lynch, *Argentine Dictator,* 236 and 262.

66. Mirta Zaida Lobato, *La Revolución de los Restauradores, 1833* (Buenos Aires: Centro Editor de América Latina, 1983), 72–73.

67. Juan María Gutiérrez, *La literatura de mayo y otras páginas críticas,* ed. Beatriz Sarlo (Buenos Aires: Centro Editor de América Latina, 1979), 38.

68. Ricardo Rojas explains that the collection of poems circulated without a cover or index and without listing an editor or publisher, suggesting that it was a clandestine volume. See his "Prólogo," in *La lira argentina, o Colección de piezas poéticas dadas a luz en Buenos Aires durante la guerra de su independencia* (Buenos Aires: Librería La Facultad, no date), 8.

69. Rosas's preferred literary genre was apparently poetry. Popular folklore recounts how he freed a prisoner who, in an attempt to save his own life, dedicated to Rosas a poem about a *bienteveo* bird. Rosas authored a poem that he had inscribed on the San Francisco Church tomb of Estanislao López in Santa Fe. See José Luis Muñoz Azpiri, *El poema Rosas de John Masefield: La leyenda del Restaurador cantada por el poeta nacional de Inglaterra* (Buenos Aires: Editorial Universitaria de Buenos Aires, 1970), 7.

70. Doris Sommer, *Foundational Fictions. The National Romances of Latin America* (Berkeley: University of California Press, 1991), 9. Sommer focuses her analysis of the Argentine context on the heterosexual union of Amalia and Eduardo Belgrano in Mármol's novel, *Amalia,* published after the defeat of Rosas and prior to the formation of the nation-state. Several decades earlier, Federalist popular poetry had attempted to consolidate the Confederation through heterosexual unions, with the significant exception that all Unitarians be excluded from this process.

71. Celesia, *Rosas,* 411–18.

72. Anderson, *Imagined Communities,* 7.

73. Lynch, *Argentine Dictator,* 183.

74. See, for example, the reply of María Retazos in *El Torito de los muchachos* to what a "man of the fraternal order" writes in *El Clasificador* (no. 13, 1–2).

75. Josefina Ludmer, *The Gaucho Genre: A Treatise on the Motherland,* trans. Molly Weigel (Durham, N.C.: Duke University Press, 2002), 15–18.

76. Lehman, "The Gaucho as Contested National Icon in Argentina," in *National Symbols, Fractured Identities: Contesting the National Narrative,* ed. Michael E. Geisler (Lebanon, N.H.: Middlebury College Press and University Press of New England, 2005), 149–71. See page 162.

77. Luis Soler Cañas, *Negros, gauchos y compadres en el cancionero de la federación (1830-1848)* (Buenos Aires: Ediciiones Theoría, 1958), 50.

78. Schvartzman, "A quién cornea *El Torito*: Notas sobre el gauchipolítico Luis Pérez," in *Letras y divisas,* ed. Iglesia, 13–23. His explanation appears on page 23.

79. *British Packet,* no. 207 (August 7, 1830): 3.

80. Several antagonistic poems followed, like the ones published in *El Gaucho.* See no. 29, 2–4 and 40.

81. Ponchos and other clothing for the Argentine market had been imported from England since 1765, according to Enrique Taranto and Jorge Marí. See their *Argentine Textiles* (Buenos Aires: Maizal Ediciones, 2003), 81. During the first half of the nineteenth century, Birmingham and Manchester produced ponchos for the River Plate region that were sometimes finished in Buenos Aires.

82. *El Gaucho* 3 (Buenos Aires: Imprenta del Estado, 1830–1833): 2–3.

83. Domingo F. Sarmiento, *Facundo: Civilization and Barbarism,* trans. Kathleen Ross (Berkeley: University of California Press, 2003), 237.

84. Ibid., 236–37.

85. The verses do represent what happened historically. See Katra, *The Argentine Generation of 1837,* 16.

86. This particular poem was published in *El Gaucho,* August 18, 1830, no. 6, 2. In *Amalia,* Mármol portrays the Federal compadre as a barbarian misfit who appropriates fashionable customs and degrades their value.

87. Szuchman, *Order, Family, and Community,* 8.

88. The Federal uniform, especially in the early part of the Rosas period, subjected its wearer to a lot of attention. "The Federal Water-seller" for instance, used descriptions of the civilian uniform and patriotic decoration to emphasize the pride of the Federalist working class: "My dress conforms / To my social status / Poor (of course) / But Crimson." See *El Gaucho,* no. 20, 3.

89. *El Gaucho,* no. 20, 17.

90. *El Gaucho,* no. 20, 19.

91. Héctor Pedro Blomberg, ed., *Cancionero federal* (Buenos Aires: Ediciones Anaconda, 1934), 41–43.

92. See "Lista del equipage de un Unitario que está de novio," *De cada cosa un poquito* (Buenos Aires: 1830–31), no. 22, 1–2.

93. A rare exception appears in the poem published in *El Torito de los Muchachos* (Buenos Aires, 1830), no. 19, 2. Federalists sing to women in "Bellas Unitarias" in the hopes that they will win hearts for the Federalist cause.

94. *El Gaucho,* no. 21, 2–3.

95. See Rosasco, *Color de Rosas,* 221.

96. This appears, for instance, in the *Anuario para el año 1857,* an almanac published in Buenos Aires five years after the defeat of Rosas. Popular almanacs explained that a well-populated beard implied a good-natured and regular temperament. According to this logic, any other inclination on the part of a man implied that he was effeminate. "The man without a beard is not a man. Women can not grow beards because the heat that men possess to help produce one dissipates in women with the flow of menstruation" (15).

97. For more on the role of the spectator in "The Slaughterhouse," see Iglesia, "Mártires o libres," 26.

98. Foucault, *Discipline and Punish,* 111.

99. "Canción del violín" [Violin song] (Buenos Aires: Imprenta del Estado, no date). This song is archived in the Saavedra Museum.

100. *El Gaucho,* no. 2. This particular issue was only one page long.

101. These posters are normally on permanent display in the Saavedra Museum.

102. The title of this poem was "Vayan estos versitos de siguidillas para cantarlos en Tahapuí."

103. *El Toro de Once* (Buenos Aires, 1830), no. 14, 2.

104. *El Torito de los Muchachos,* no. 3, 3.

105. Schvartzman, "A quién cornea *El Torito,*" 23.

106. Lynch, *Argentine Dictator,* 261.

107. Rivera Indarte reveals that the name of and the concept for the Mazorca was imported from Spain by Tiburcio Ochoteco, a young man who had traveled to Cádiz in 1822 and learned of a similar society. It is clear that the Mazorca sometimes acted on police reports describing inappropriate dress.

108. For several Unitarian authors, the Mazorca became an overarching metaphor for the corruption and injustice of the regime. Juana Manuela Gorriti, for instance, represents a Mazorca leader who accidentally murders his only daughter in her short story "La hija del mazorquero."

109. This incited acts of vandalism and terrorism, which scandalized British and French diplomats. In a letter to Viscount Palmerston, John Henry Mandeville (who arrived in Argentina in 1836) painted a portrait of mass terror directed against the property and lives of diplomats, who were not avid supporters of the Federalist regime and therefore suspected for being Unitarians.

110. Dated April 25, 1835. *Revista de Derecho, Historia y Letras* (Buenos Aires), vol. 61.

111. The poem was later published in *La Gazeta Mercantil* on June 30, 1835, further emphasizing its public nature. See Saldías, *Historia de la confederación,* 154.

112. Salessi *(Médicos, maleantes y maricas)* connects this river of blood to the political debates regarding hygiene, rivers, body fluids, and the yellow fever epidemic that circulated in 1871, when "The Slaughterhouse" was published.

2. Dressed to Kill

1. Hélène Cixous, "Sonia Rykiel in Translation," in *On Fashion,* ed. Shari Benstock and Suzanne Ferris (New Brunswick, N.J.: Rutgers University Press, 1994), 95–99. The quotation appears on page 99.

2. Helen M. Cooper, Adrienne Auslander Munich, and Susan Merrill Squier, *Arms and the Woman: War, Gender, and Literary Representation* (Chapel Hill: University of North Carolina Press, 1989), xiii.

3. The anonymous author claimed to be a woman in her thirties. See *La Argentina,* February 23, 1831, no. 16, 13.

4. Ibid., 15.

5. Benstock and Ferris, "Introduction" to *On Fashion,* ed. Benstock and Ferris, 4.

6. Ibid.

7. See Szuchman, *Order, Family, and Community,* 8.

8. Isabel Cruz de Amenábar discusses this critique in the context of Chile in *El traje: Tranformaciones de una segunda piel* (Santiago: Ediciones Universidad Católica de Chile, 1996). See, in particular, page 174.

9. Mariselle Meléndez, "Eighteenth Century Spanish America: Historical Dimensions and New Theoretical Approaches," *Revista de Estudios Hispánicos* 35.3 (October 2001): 615–32. See page 616.

10. Susana Dillon, *Mujeres que hicieron América: Biografías transgresoras* (Buenos Aires: Editorial Catari, 1992), 152.

11. The role of the *cuartelera* is not well documented during the Rosas period, despite its significance to the cause and representation in canonical works. Recall the solitary figure of María in Echeverría's *La cautiva* [The captive], for instance. María washes her beloved Brian's uniform and tends to the needs of the troop when she falls captive to indigenous peoples defending their territory during a period of brutal expansionism that would continue into the last decades of the nineteenth century. Echeverría uses the tragic deaths of María and the soldier she attempts to save, Brian, to critique the failure of the Desert Campaign initiated by Rosas. Historically speaking, however, the campaign was extremely successful for Rosas and his supporters. In *The Generation of 1837,* Katria writes, "Rosas made available thousands of square kilometers of land for new settlements and the expansion of the country's prospering cattle industry" (42).

12. Vera Pichel, *Las cuarteleras* (Buenos Aires: Planeta, 1994), 133.

13. La Fuente, *Children of Facundo,* 92.

14. *La Gazeta de Buenos Aires,* vol. 2, 1004.

15. Hanway, *Embodying Argentina,* 114.

16. Szuchman, *Order, Family, and Community,* 37.

17. Mariquita Sánchez, *Recuerdos del Buenos Ayres virreynal* (Buenos Aires: Ene Editorial, 1953), 15.

18. *La Gazeta Ministerial,* no. 3, 226.

19. Rotker, *Captive Women,* 29.

20. Szuchman, *Order, Family, and Community,* 73. According to Szuchman, these fashion enterprises included the making of silk hats.

21. *La Gazeta de Buenos Aires,* no. 3, 63.

22. Halperín Donghi, "Argentine Counterpoint," 51.

23. *La Gazeta de Buenos Aires,* vol. 3, 68.

24. Szuchman, *Order, Family, and Community,* 13.

25. Ibid., 109.

26. *La Argentina,* January 9, 1831, no. 11, 15.

27. Saulquin, *La Moda,* 44.

28. For one example, see *La Argentina,* January 16, 1831, no. 12, 12.

29. Lynch, *Argentine Dictator,* 175.

30. José Mármol wrote this in *La Semana* in 1851. Cited in Saulquin, *La Moda,* 46.

31. Hanway, *Embodying Argentina,* 30.

32. *La Cotorra.* Issue dedicated to women (no number or date), 5. This periodical likely dates to the 1840s.

33. Ibid., 1. The last strophe plays with the word *pareceres,* which translates as either *views* or *appearances.*

34. Because Rosas continued the order of colonial times, punishments were often as harsh for those who broke the law—whether gauchos or members of the military—as they were for Unitarians. Szuchman, *Order, Family, and Community,* 62.

35. Udaondo, *Uniformes militares,* 187. Argentine women also played a pivotal role in the creation of the military uniform in the years following the Rosas period. This ended in 1856, when the country acquired a large shipment of red uniforms left over from the Crimean War. Although no assembly had been required, the government distributed the uniforms under the guise of being homemade. A scandal ensued when it was discovered that Argentine women had not made this ready-to-wear uniform, further demonstrating the importance that society attributed to the patriotic seamstress.

36. *La Gazeta Mercantil,* no. 1524, 4.

37. For example, see the "Aviso de policía," *El Progreso de Entre Ríos* (Gualeguaychú), March 21, 1849, 6.

38. *La Gazeta Mercantil,* no. 1545, 2.

39. See *El Progreso de Entre Ríos,* March 1, 1849, 1.

40. *La Argentina,* January 30, 1831, no. 14, 12.

41. *British Packet,* no. 1079 (April 24, 1847): 1.

42. Szuchman, *Order, Family, and Community,* 145.

43. Ibid.

44. Alberto Julián Pérez, *Los dilemas políticos de la cultura letrada: Argentina—Siglo XIX* (Buenos Aires: Ediciones Corregidor, 2002), 68.

45. *El Progreso de Entre Ríos,* no. 61, 2.

46. Most churches of the period did not have pews.

47. See *El Federal Entreriano,* April 27, 1848, no. 244, 4.

48. *La Argentina,* July 3, 1831, vol. 2, no. 4, 8.

49. Katra, *The Generation of 1837,* 30.

50. Julián Pérez, *Los dilemas políticos,* 77.

51. In *Argentine Dictator,* Lynch writes, "Slave numbers were certainly depleted during the wars of independence, when emancipation was offered in return for military service; but this tended to lead to death rather than freedom" (119).

52. Ibid., 121. The Constitution of 1853 finally abolished slavery in Argentina. See also Daniel Schavelzon, *Buenos Aires Negra: Arqueología histórica de una ciudad silenciada* (Buenos Aires: Emecé Editores, 2003), 40.

53. Lynch, *Argentine Dictator,* 121.

54. Ibid.

55. Hanway, *Embodying Argentina,* 10.

56. Lynch, *Argentine Dictator,* 55 and 40, respectively.

57. Ibid., 114.

58. Oscar Chamosa, "To Honor the Ashes of their Forebears: The Rise and Crisis of African Nations in the Post-Independence State of Buenos Aires, 1820–1860," *Americas* 59.3 (January 2003): 347–78. See page 352.

59. This is Katra's explanation of Juan Bautista Alberdi's views. See Katra, *The Generation of 1837,* 37. Although some people of color fought as members of the Unitarian army, most supported Federalist policies. Service records reveal the names of various African Argentine soldiers who offered their service to either side. Domingo Sosa, Felipe Mansilla, and Casildo Thompson distinguished themselves in their military service to Urquiza during the Battle of Caseros. See Luis Soler Cañas, *Negros, gauchos, y compadres en el cancionero de la federación (1830–1848)* (Buenos Aires: Ediciones Theoría, 1958), 40–41. On the Federalist side, Rosas exercised a great deal of power over the make-up of the military, granting many privileges to African Argentines. On the other hand, high-ranking military officials suspected of sympathizing with Unitarians were often demoted by Rosas to the battalion for people of color.

60. Katra, *The Generation of 1837,* 113.

61. La Fuente, *Children of Facundo,* 146.

62. See, for instance, the official list of Buenos Aires–based organizations and their contributions to the war against the Unitarians dated "10 del mes de América de 1842," but published on June 25, 1842, in *La Gazeta Mercantil.*

63. George Reid Andrews, *Afro-Latin America, 1800–2000* (Oxford: Oxford University Press, 2004), 99.

64. Ibid.

65. Chamosa, *"To Honor the Ashes,"* 348. In 1825, the original ten associations splintered, becoming more than fifty by 1835.

66. Ibid., 350.

67. Ibid., 358.

68. For the entire poem, see Cañas, *Negros, gauchos y compadres,* 30–32.

69. George Reid Andrews, *The Afro-Argentines of Buenos Aires, 1800–1900* (Madison: University of Wisconsin Press, 1980), 97.

70. The painting, completed in the 1860s, is often referred to as "El candombe en 1838."

71. Schavelzon, *Buenos Aires Negra,* 27.

72. On this practice in Buenos Aires, see Lynch, *Argentine Dictator,* 128.

73. Chamosa, *"To Honor the Ashes,"* 363.

74. It has been suggested that the origin of the word was derived from "hablar como embozalado" (muffled speech) and, in South America, "bozal" (one who speaks broken Spanish). Contemporary linguists are more apt to categorize this language as an Afro-Hispanic pidgin or Creole language. John Lipski, for example, has found that popular songbooks, pamphlets, and street vendor calls of the nineteenth century often represented stereotypical linguistic expressions rather than merely depicting the way many African Argentine slaves spoke. See John M. Lipski, *A History of Afro-Hispanic Language: Five Centuries, Five Continents* (Cambridge: Cambridge University Press, 2005).

75. See *La Gazeta Mercantil,* December 5, 1831.

76. Chamosa, *"To Honor the Ashes,"* 357.

77. *El Negrito* and *La Negrita* complement the poetic narratives of *El Gaucho* and *La Gaucha.*

78. Héctor Pedro Blomberg mentions this when discussing another version of the same poem in *Cancionero federal* (Buenos Aires: Anaconda, 1934), 16.

79. Scholars will note that this anonymous poem with the call from Juana Peña differs from the one translated in *The Argentina Reader,* ed. Gabriela Nouzeilles and Graciela Montaldo (Durham, N.C.: Duke University Press, 2002), 93–94.

80. La Fuente regards this as the "slow process of nation formation." See *Children of Facundo,* 115 and 117.

81. Ludmer, *The Gaucho Genre,* 17–18.

82. La Fuente, *Children of Facundo,* 94–95.

3. Fashion as Presence

1. Because Unitarians had a predilection for French fashion and political philosophies, this term referred to them.

2. *British Packet,* no. 216 (October 9, 1830): 1.

3. See Claudia López and Horacio Botalla, "El peinetón en Buenos Aires, 1823–1837," *Boletín Histórico del Instituto de la Ciudad de Buenos Aires* 8 (1983): 9–47.

4. *British Packet* 7, no. 348 (April 20, 1833): 2–3.

5. See Marcela Taletavicius's analysis of late-twentieth-century fashion in

90-60-90: Aventuras y desventuras del mundo de las modelos (Buenos Aires: Espasa Calpe, 1995).

6. Castagnino documents the marked presence of the *peinetón* in his discussion on fashion in the theater during the Rosas period. See chapter 4 of *El teatro en Buenos Aires.*

7. For more on this theory, see López and Botalla, "El peinetón en Buenos Aires."

8. See Lynch, *Argentine Dictator,* 135 and 140, for his discussion of this shift in the marketplace.

9. Ibid., 130.

10. E. E. Vidal, *Picturesque Illlustrations of Buenos Ayres and Monte Video Consisting of Twenty-Four Views: Accompanied with Descriptions of the Scenery and of the Costumes, Manners, &c. of the Inhabitants of Those Cities and Their Environs* (London: R. Ackermann, 1820), 49.

11. Ibid.

12. López and Botalla, "El *peinetón* en Buenos Aires," 11–12.

13. *British Packet* 6, no. 271 (October 29, 1831): 3.

14. *El Monitor,* no. 152, 2–3.

15. Ibid., 2.

16. *British Packet* 6, no. 290 (March 10, 1832): 3. This represents a contradictory stance in the editorial vision, as the newspaper's headquarters served as a major outpost for information regarding European fashions. One might even credit the *British Packet* for introducing the corset to Buenos Aires and for providing women with access to special lithographs from *The World of Fashion.* The *British Packet* also circulated fashion dolls that provided women with instructions on how to wear the latest fashions from Europe, such as "the figure of a young lady en Corset. (Our fair readers must not blush, there is nothing to offend the most rigid modesty.) . . . In order to save all further explanation as to the mode of dressing and undressing the pretty puppet, we have given it away to a young lady, who has promised to cherish and take great care of it" (no. 318, 2).

17. *British Packet* 7, no. 348 (April 20, 1833): 2–3.

18. Eduardo Gudiño Kieffer, *El peinetón* (Buenos Aires: Ediciones de Arte Gaglianone, 1986), 10.

19. A war with Brazil over land entitlement led, ultimately, to the conception of Uruguay in 1828, when a British treaty proposed its creation to separate Argentina and Brazil. See David Rock, *Argentina 1516–1987: From Spanish Colonization to Alfonsín* (Berkeley: University of California Press, 1987), 103.

20. Masiello, *Between Civilization and Barbarism,* 20.

21. Ibid., 20.

22. Ibid., 23. Also see Francine Masiello, *La mujer y el espacio público: El periodismo femenino en la Argentina del Siglo XIX* (Buenos Aires: Feminaria Editora, 1994).

23. Sizable hair accessories appeared in other regions of the Southern Cone, from neighboring Montevideo to mountainous Mendoza. The symbolic value of each merits study, and it is likely that such styles evoked presence similar to that of the *peinetón*. The Mendoza headdress, for example, appears to have possessed the vertical height, but not the horizontal span, of the *peinetón*.

24. The fashion column highlighted recipes for homemade products that promised hair growth and the aesthetic improvement of hair follicles. Women appear to have expressed concern over the heaviness of their *peinetón*, which sometimes pulled out otherwise healthy hair. Usually, these recipes required staple goods available in most homes: eggs, milk, vinegar, broth. A few concoctions involved a lengthy creation and application process. For anyone desiring to create the most popular recipe for hair growth, I include the instructions here but do not guarantee results: "*To make the hair grow.* Take four ounces each of chicken broth, hemp seed oil and honey. Melt the mixture in a pot and beat it until it has the consistency of a pomade. Nourish the crown of the head for eight days straight." See *El Iris,* no. 4, 3–4. There is little information regarding the effectiveness of such recipes, but one can only imagine the horror associated with one mixture of aged eggs and vinegar. See *El Iris,* no. 4, 3–4.

25. Saulquin, *La Moda,* 41 and 43.

26. See "El Veinticinco de Mayo, Jaleo a los Hombres," no date (but probably around 1833). A poem in *El Gaucho* from this period explains that, because of the humble status of the fatherland, a gaucha should not spend all of her money and energy on dressing up for patriotic festivities. Remembering those who fought for liberty sufficed.

27. See *La Argentina,* March 6, 1831. Also discussed in Botalla's "Acerca de los peinetones," in *Extravagancias de las porteñas: Los peinetones* (Buenos Aires: Museo de Arte Hispanoamericano "Isaac Fernández Blanco," November–December 1997), 7–10.

28. *La Gazeta Mercantil,* no. 2355, 2.

29. *La Argentina,* January 20, 1831, no. 14, 14. Also see February 6, 1831, no. 15, 4.

30. *British Packet* 7, no. 356 (June 15, 1833): 3.

31. *La Argentina,* no. 19, 14.

32. The editorship of *La Argentina* was assessed in the early twentieth century by the noted historian of journalism Antonio Zinny, who attributed it to Manuel de Irigoyen. This assessment was contested by Ismael Solari Amondarain in 1936, whose research revealed that the editor was Petrona Ignacia Rosende de Sierra, an Urguayan author involved with the competing *La Aljaba.* Néstor Tomás Aúza sides with the idea that Irigoyen disguised his writing as female, but he does not provide any evidence beyond Zinny's assessment. See "El caso de un redactora que no era tal," in Aúza's *Periodismo y feminismo en la Argentina, 1830–1930* (Buenos Aires: Emecé, 1988), 21–25. Regardless of the editor's identity, *La Argentina* clearly

advertised itself as a magazine edited by women. Furthermore, the staff at other periodicals believed that women penned articles for its pages on subjects as seemingly diverse as politics and fashion. As the introductory issue explained, "It will seem a novelty to have a female journalist, but it is time to begin if we are to have influence. For the most part, men have strayed and it is imperative to bring them to reason. . . . We will touch every subject, feeling everyone's hurts, without offending any citizen of our country. We will criticize what we feel merits censure." See the first issue of *La Argentina*, 1–2. Following a period of doubt regarding the gender of *La Argentina*'s editor, the *British Packet* later maintained a regular correspondence with a person they called "Mrs. Editor." The English newspaper's correction read: "Byron has somewhere written, 'Sweet is revenge—specially to woman.' *La Argentina* of Sunday last has reprehended us for doubting that the said periodical was edited by a lady. It seems that in this supposition we have been mistaken, we therefore ask pardon of *La Señora Redactora*." See the *British Packet* 5, no. 222 (November 20, 1830): 2.

In the course of its publication, *La Argentina* would respond regularly to *La Aljaba*, another, more short-lived women's magazine. Janet Greenberg asserts that *La Aljaba* was edited by Rosende de la Sierra although the readers of the period would likely have believed that male authors ran the enterprise. See Greenberg, "Towards a History of Women's Periodicals in Latin America, 18th–20th Centuries: A Working Bibliography," in *Women, Culture, and Politics in Latin America*, ed. Seminar on Feminism and Culture in Latin America (Berkeley: University of California Press, 1990), 182–231. Hoping to wipe out its competitor, *La Argentina* published several editorials claiming that *La Aljaba* had mistakenly identified them as "machos" and "without us ever having deserved such treatment." See *La Argentina*, January 23, 1831, no. 13, 7. The archives suggest that *La Argentina* forced *La Aljaba* out of circulation with a negative publicity campaign that panned the quality of the latter magazine's poetry.

33. *La Argentina*, no. 20, 10.

34. Szuchman, *Order, Family, and Community*, 22.

35. Ibid., 104.

36. Ibid.

37. Cited in María del Carmen Tomeo, "La moda: Esa dulce tiranía," *Todo es Historia, Buenos Aires*, no. 30. Also cited in Saulquin, *La Moda*, 42.

38. *La Argentina*, no. 21, 8.

39. Botalla, "El peinetón en Buenos Aires," 7. My thanks also to Seth Meisel, who helped me compile the information necessary for this price comparison.

40. *British Packet* 6, no. 271 (October 29, 1831): 3.

41. *El Iris*, no. 97, 3.

42. The poem originally appeared in 1833 and was republished in *La Gazeta Mercantil*. See no. 2923, 2.

43. *La Argentina,* November 7, 1830, no. 2, 10.

44. Lynch, *Argentine Dictator,* 145.

45. Ibid., 147. Lynch writes that Corrientes prohibited the sale of foreign clothing and footwear in 1831.

46. Ibid., 140–41.

47. See Alejo González Garaño's "Una típica moda porteña, los peinetones creados por Manuel Masculino," *La Prensa,* January 1, 1936, 1.

48. Because this correspondence met with such success, other dailies either republished it or began their own versions of fashionable battles between the sexes. The readers of Montevideo newspaper *El Investigador* continued this debate between the lovely Argentine lady and Don Cid and even proclaimed "¡Abajo Peinetas!" [Down with the Combs!]. See *El Investigador,* no. 25, 209–11 and no. 2, 13–16.

49. This segment of the poetic correspondence appears in *El Iris,* no. 44.

50. See *El Iris,* no. 48.

51. *La Gazeta Mercantil,* no. 1962, 2.

52. *La Gazeta Mercantil,* no. 2923, 2.

53. The article, "Spirit of the Public Journals," appears in the *British Packet* 7, no. 312 (March 9, 1833): 2–3.

54. *British Packet* expands on the Poor Christian's allusion in a later issue: "The following account of the Giralda, will show if the comparison was just:—'The Cathedral at Seville has a fine campanile, 350 feet high, which was built in 1568, by Guever the Moor. This tower is called La Giralda, from its brazen figure bearing that name;—this figure, though it weighs a ton and a half, turns with the wind'" (*British Packet* 11, no. 538 [December 10, 1836]: 3).

55. "Fulmination against Fashionable Combs," *British Packet* 7, no. 356 (June 15, 1833): 3.

56. *British Packet* 10, no. 474 (September 19, 1835): 3.

57. *British Packet* 9, no. 417 (August 16, 1834): 3.

58. Donna J. Guy, *Sex and Danger in Buenos Aires: Prostitution, Family, and Nation in Argentina* (Lincoln: University of Nebraska Press, 1991), 2–3.

59. Ibid., 49.

60. A printed copy of "Lo que cuesta un peinetón" [What a *peinetón* costs] is cataloged and ordinarily on display at the Saavedra Museum.

61. Ibid., stanzas 1–6.

62. Ibid., stanza 5.

63. Ibid., stanzas 7–46.

64. Ibid., stanza 23.

65. Ibid., stanzas 36–37.

66. A printed copy of "El que paga el peinetón" [He who pays for the *peinetón*] is cataloged at the Saavedra Museum.

67. Ibid., stanza 1.

68. Ibid., stanza 4.

69. Ibid., stanza 17.

70. Ibid., stanza 12.

71. Ibid., stanza 5.

72. Ibid., stanza 6.

73. Ibid., stanza 11.

74. Ibid., stanza 18.

75. Alejo González Garaño, "Prólogo," *Trages y costumbres de la provincia de Buenos Aires: 36 litografías coloreadas* by Bacle (Buenos Aires: Viau, 1947), 14.

76. Bacle organized a select group of artists that included many of his students: Arthur Onslow (author of the first series of lithographs of the *Trages y costumbres de Buenos Aires* series), Hipólito Moulin, Carlos Enrique Pellegrini, J. F. Guerrin, Julio Daufresne, and Adrienne Pauline Macaire. Macaire, who was also Bacle's wife, later dedicated her efforts to the Ateneo, an elite school for young women. Bacle's enterprises perhaps enabled Argentina to publish an illustrated weekly long before Spain could do so.

77. The publications produced by the Imprenta del Comercio included Rivera Indarte's *Diario de anuncios y publicaciones oficiales de Buenos Aires* and several popular pamphlets such as *El Arrepentimiento de un Unitario, El Gaucho Federal,* and *Don Juan Manuel de Rosas.* Bacle also designed the cover of the *Himno de los Restauradores,* an official book of Federalist hymns composed by Rivera Indarte.

78. Bacle, "Higiene: Uso del corsé," *El Recopilador* (Buenos Aires: 1835), 166.

79. Bacle, *Diario de anuncios y publicaciones oficiales,* March 9, 1836. See also Botalla, "Acerca de los peinetones," *Extravagancias de las porteñas,* 10.

80. *La Argentina,* no. 6, 13–14.

81. *La Argentina,* no. 9, 15–16.

82. For more on the presence of the *peinetón* in the theater, see Castagnino, *El teatro en Buenos Aires. La Argentina,* no. 12, 14, also chronicles the fashion extremes witnessed in theater balconies:

> My friend: All extremes are faulty. The other night I saw a young woman in the theater whose *peinetón* and hairstyle almost reached the ceiling. While criticizing such excess with a friend, another young and very scholarly woman referred us to the following epigram, as if it were her own.

> I once saw in Paris
> a hairstyle so sublime
> that it was a neighbor
> to the wing of a roof.
> When two fighting cats
> saw the hairstyle,
> they jumped over to continue the fight,
> and no one felt a thing.

83. Barbara Creed discusses the vagina dentata in the context of film, but she could very well have analyzed the *peinetón*. See *The Monstrous-Feminine: Film, Feminism and Psychoanalysis* (London: Routledge Press, 1993).

4. Fashion Writing

1. Lipovetsky, *The Empire of Fashion*, 33.

2. Norman Holland, "Fashioning Cuba," in *Nationalism and Sexualities,* ed. Andrew Parker, Mary Russo, Doris Sommer, and Patricia Yeager (London: Routledge, 1992), 150.

3. Benedict Anderson's concept of an imagined political community proposes that citizens and their governing bodies commonly share an imaginary ideal of the nation.

4. *El Corsario,* no. 1, 1.

5. Ibid., 2.

6. Nicholas Mirzoeff, *Bodyscape: Art, Modernity, and the Ideal Figure* (London: Routledge, 1995).

7. Ibid., 75.

8. Ibid., 58.

9. Ibid., 93.

10. Richard Wrigley, "The Formation and Currency of a Vestimentary Stereotype: The Sans-culotte in Revolutionary France," in *Dress, Gender, Citizenship: Fashioning the Body Politic,* ed. Wendy Parkins (Oxford: Berg Publishers, 2002), 19–47. See page 39 in particular.

11. Ibid., 19.

12. Aileen Ribeiro, *Dress and Morality* (Oxford: Berg Publishers, 2003), 120. The papacy even denounced such dress as immoral.

13. Ibid., 120. Such a shift may also have initiated the sober styles of male fashion of later decades. Ribeiro suggests, for instance, that male fashions now integrated less of a range of colors. The focus was instead on cleanliness and the whiteness of linen, a luxury few could afford (see 113).

14. Barbara Vinken, *Fashion Zeitgeist: Trends and Cycles in the Fashion System* (Oxford: Berg Publishers, 2005), 12.

15. Ibid., 9.

16. "Soon the Phrygian cap was discarded and the badge alone was considered a sufficient sign of patriotism," writes Halperin Donghi, with the majority of the population suspecting anyone without the badge—but especially members of the Creole elite—as a Spanish sympathizer ("Argentine Counterpoint," 44).

17. Katra points to Juan Bautista Alberdi's maxim: "We must first define a philosophy before we can hope to achieve a nationality." Juan Bautista Alberdi, *Obras*

completas, vol. 1 (Buenos Aires, "La tribuna nacional," 1886). Cited in Katra, *The Generation of 1837,* 51.

18. Katra, *The Generation of 1837,* 137.

19. Marzena Grzegorczyk, *Private Topographies: Space, Subjectivity, and Political Change in Modern Latin America* (New York: Palgrave Macmillan, 2005), 72.

20. *El Mártir o Libre,* no. 9, 2–3.

21. Ibid.

22. One is sure to find echoes here of Ricardo Piglia's interpretation of the faces of enmity during this period. Literary strategies from the opposition fictionalized the "barbarian," in this case Rosas, in order to understand his brutal existence as one of political unfinishedness. "One must enter the enemy's world, imagine his interior dimensions, his true secrets, his way of being. The other must be made known in order for him to become civilized." "Sarmiento the Writer" in *Sarmiento: Author of a Nation,* ed. Tulio Halperín Donghi, Iván Jaksic, Gwen Kirkpatrick, and Francine Masiello (Berkeley: University of California Press, 1994): 127–44. Quote on page 133.

23. *El Grito de los Pueblos,* 1831, 1–2.

24. For a more elaborate discussion on this question of incomplete democracy, see Nicholas Shumway, *The Invention of Argentina* (Berkeley: University of California Press, 1991), 151.

25. *La Mariposa,* no. 18, 137.

26. Ibid., 139.

27. Ibid., 138–39.

28. Ibid., 137.

29. David Viñas, *Literatura argentina y política: De los jacobinos porteños a la bohemia anarquista* (Buenos Aires: Editorial Sudamericana, 1995), 95–104.

30. José Mármol, *Cantos del peregrino,* ed. Elvira Burlando de Meyer, critical edition (Buenos Aires: EUDEBA, 1965). For a poetic discussion of the civil war and the color of hope, see the third song of the 1849 manuscript of the *Cantos del peregrino.* For the allusion to the mothers of freedom, see the sixth song of the 1889 version.

31. Roland Barthes, *The Fashion System* (New York: Hill and Wang, 1967), 10.

32. Ibid., 13.

33. Written language, Barthes continues, "conveys a choice and imposes it, it requires the perception of this dress to stop here (i.e., neither before nor beyond), it arrests the level of reading at its fabric, at its belt, at the accessory which adorns it. Thus, every written word has a function of authority insofar as it chooses—by proxy, so to speak—instead of the eye. The image freezes an endless number of possibilities; words determine a single certainty" (ibid.).

34. Ibid., 231.

35. Fredric Jameson, *The Political Unconscious: Narrative as a Socially Symbolic Act* (Ithaca, N.Y.: Cornell University Press, 1981).

36. Barthes, *The Fashion System*, 232.

37. Shumway, *The Invention of Argentina*, 126.

38. Ibid., 127.

39. See Myers, *Orden y virtud*, 44. Alberdi's articles for *La Moda*, although mostly critical of the Rosas regime, can also be viewed as supportive. Félix Weinberg believes that the admiration displayed for Rosas was a ruse on Alberdi's part, designed to attract Rosas to the precepts of the young generation. *El salón literario de 1837* (Buenos Aires: Librería Hachette, 1977), 97–110.

40. Alberdi believed that democratic institutions, for instance, would come about with "decades of social interaction." Katra, *The Generation of 1837*, 51 and 54.

41. Ibid., 48.

42. There were a total of five bookstores in Buenos Aires around 1830 and ten by 1836. Ibid., 44.

43. Valerie Steele, *Fashion and Eroticism: Ideals of Feminine Beauty from the Victorian Era to the Jazz Age* (Oxford: Oxford University Press, 1985).

44. *La Moda,* no. 1, 1.

45. In 1837, Alberdi elaborated on these ideas in his essay "Fragmento" [Fragment] when he wrote: "We should cleanse our spirit of all false colors, of all borrowed clothing, of all imitation, of all servility. Let us govern ourselves, think, write and proceed in all things, not through imitation of any other people on earth, no matter what people's prestige, but exclusively according to the demands of the general laws of the human spirit and the individual laws of our national condition." Juan Bautista Alberdi, *Obras completas,* 8 volumes (Buenos Aires: "La tribuna nacional," 1886 [1837]), 111–12.

46. Juan María Gutiérrez, "La vida y la obra de Esteban Echeverría," in Echeverría's *Obras completas* (Buenos Aires: Zamora, 1972), 23. Cited in Katra, *The Generation of 1837*, 53.

47. Katra, *The Generation of 1837*, 54.

48. *La Moda,* no. 1, 2.

49. Ibid., 3.

50. Masiello, *Between Civilization and Barbarism*, 23.

51. *La Moda,* no. 3, 3.

52. Ibid.

53. Oría, "Prólogo," in *La Moda,* facsimile edition (Buenos Aires: Guillermo Kraft, 1938), 38.

54. *La Moda,* no. 3, 4. Cited in Masiello, *Between Civilization and Barbarism*, 24.

55. *La Moda,* no. 14, 1–2.

56. Ibid., no. 4, 3.

57. That is, "dice *replubica* por república, *treato* por teatro" (ibid.).

58. Ibid.

59. *La Moda,* no. 15, 1.

60. Ibid.

61. Ibid., 2. See his "Signs of a Gentleman."

62. Ibid., no. 5, 1.

63. Shumway, *The Invention of Argentina,* 128.

64. *La Moda,* no. 21, 3.

65. Ibid., no. 18, p.1.

66. Ibid.

67. *El Iniciador,* vol. 1, no. 9, 198.

68. Lipovetsky, *The Empire of Fashion,* 33.

69. Ibid., no. 12, 253.

70. Ibid., no. 10, 210.

71. See the last issue of *El Iniciador,* vol. 2, no. 4, 76.

72. Ibid., vol. 2; no. 2, 37.

73. Ibid., no. 1, 1–2.

74. See page 199 of *El Iniciador.*

75. Ibid., no. 3, 53.

76. Ibid.

77. Ibid., no. 3, 54.

78. Ibid., no. 3, 53.

79. Ibid.

80. Greenberg, "Towards a History," 192.

81. *La Camelia,* no. 1, 1.

82. Rita Felski, *Beyond Feminist Aesthetics* (Cambridge: Harvard University Press, 1989), 12.

83. "Angeles en el hogar argentino: El debate femenino sobre la vida doméstica, la educación y la literatura en el siglo XIX," *Anuario del IEHS* 4 (1989): 265–91. See page 276.

84. Hanway, *Embodying Argentina,* 138. See, in particular, her discussion of Sarmiento in the section on Eduarda Mansilla. Sarmiento and most other male intellectuals did not believe that women could be as invested in the nation-building process. In Sarmiento's eyes, Hanway writes, women served to awaken refinement in men.

85. Sigrid Weigel, "Double Focus: On the History of Women's Writing," trans. Harriet Anderson, in *Feminist Aesthetics,* ed. Gisela Ecker (Boston: Beacon Press, 1985), 67.

86. *La Camelia,* no. 1, 4.

87. *La Camelia,* no. 2, 2.

88. *La Camelia,* no. 1, 3.

89. Ibid.

90. Ibid., no. 6, 3.

91. Ibid.

92. Barthes, *The Fashion System,* 231–32.

5. Searching for Female Emancipation

1. Interestingly enough, Gorriti chooses to use the word *nosotros,* suggesting that both men and women aspire for ideal bodies and clothes with which to shield them.

2. See, for instance, Stephen Kern's study of *Anatomy and Destiny: A Cultural History of the Human Body* (New York: Bobb-Merrill Company, 1975) and Helene E. Roberts' essay "The Exquisite Slave: The Role of Clothes in the Making of the Victorian Woman," *Signs: Journal of Woman in Culture and Society* 2 (Spring 1977): 554–69. Steele writes, "It is absurd to blame clothing for limiting women, and pointless to blame 'men' or 'society' for *forcing* women to wear restrictive or 'feminine' dress" (*Fashion and Eroticism,* 246).

3. Lowe, *History of Bourgeois Perception* (Chicago: University of Chicago Press, 1982), 96.

4. Barthes, *The Fashion System,* 249.

5. I write this with the understanding that one's sense of "free choice" may or may not be real.

6. Efrat Tseelon addresses the need for attention to sartorial diversity in order to resist stereotypes in the realm of fashion research. She especially questions the validity of the qualitative and quantitative divide that permeates this interdisciplinary field. See her "Clarifications in Fashion Research," in *Through the Wardrobe: Women's Relationships with Their Clothes,* ed. Ali Guy, Eileen Green, and Maura Banim (Oxford: Berg Publishers, 2001), 253. For an analysis of the historical presentation of style, which C. Evans and M. Thornton believe has not accounted for the way in which "worn fashion generates meaning," see "Fashion, Representation, Femininity," in *Feminist Review* 38 (1991): 48–66.

7. Rabine, "A Woman's Two Bodies: Fashion Magazines, Consumerism, and Feminism" in *On Fashion,* ed. Benstock and Ferris, 59.

8. I borrow this turn of phrase from Guy, Green, and Banim: "The fashion system is fluid enough to show 'gaping seams' which allow women some control over their clothed images and identities, spaces which permit personal agency and negotiated images" (*Through the Wardrobe,* 7).

9. Zoila writes, "It seems like I can already see some young men with a sardonic laugh at the same time they declare, 'What childishness! The girls with a newspaper!'—Regardless of these funny stories, go forth *compañeras,* I will help you with all my soul and we will make them understand what we know, what

we are worth, that is: We will humiliate them." Eliza narrates a conversation with Don Hermógenes, who believes that the editor is a man using a series of female pseudonyms (*La Camelia*, no. 1, 4).

10. Pratt, "Women, Literature, and National Brotherhood" in *Women, Culture, and Politics*, 52.

11. *La Aljaba* (Buenos Aires: Imprenta del Estado, 1830), 1. Nestor Tomás Aúza believes that a group of nameless women edited *La Camelia*, despite popular attribution to Rosa Guerra. See *Periodismo y feminismo en la Argentina, 1830–1900* (Buenos Aires: Emecé, 1988), 166–68. The magazine does indeed use the pronoun "we" when discussing opinions on topics as diverse as literature and equal rights. See also Masiello, *La mujer y el espacio público;* Greenberg, "Towards a History; and Lily Sosa de Newton," *Narradoras argentinas (1852–1932)* (Buenos Aires: Editorial Plus Ultra, 1995).

12. The luxurious pursuits had reached such an extreme that Rosende de Sierra considered it "ruinous of abundance; damaging to domestic tranquility; a clash with good reason and ridiculous to the situation of the country" (*La Aljaba*, no. 8, 3).

13. Published in London by R. Ackerman, Strand, and distributed throughout Mexico, Guatemala, Colombia, Perú, Chile, and Buenos Aires, President Rivadavia used this *Gimnástica del bello sexo, o ensayos sobre la educación física de las jóvenes* to introduce the concept of physical education for women to the River Plate region. From the advertisements of newspapers, as well as one signed copy of this manual in the private library of Ricardo Rodríguez Molas, we know that the second edition (published in 1827) circulated in Buenos Aires after 1830. Very little is known of its author; Rodríguez Molas ascertains that he was a Spanish native exiled in England. See Rodríguez, "La gimnasia femenina como arma de la ilustración," *Río Negro*, February 10, 1993, 11.

14. *La Ilustración Argentina: Museo de Familiás*, no. 8, 121–22. Signed B. H.

15. Marifran Carlson, *¡Feminismo! The Woman's Movement in Argentina from Its Beginnings to Eva Perón* (Chicago: Academy Chicago Publishers, 1988), 60–61.

16. *La Siempre-Viva*, June 16, 1862, front page. The July 9, 1864, issue argued that Argentine women were suffering beneath their luxurious clothes rather than taking the steps necessary to secure an education.

17. For an interesting view of material culture, technological advancement and changing domestic roles, see the editorial comments found in *Búcaro Americano* (1896–1908), a magazine published in Buenos Aires and edited by Clorinda Matto de Turner. The Peruvian author documents the way in which telephones, sewing machines, electric massagers, and hairdryers were transforming the daily lives of urban women. Bonnie Frederick comments on the international scope of Matto de Turner's enterprise, explaining that in the magazine's pages "women everywhere were writing literature and urging expanded women's rights." Fred-

erick, *Wily Modesty: Argentine Women Writers, 1860–1910* (Tempe: Arizona State University Center for Latin American Studies Press, 1998), 28.

18. *El Alba,* 1868, no. 1 (first issue), 11.

19. Seminar on Feminism and Culture, *Women, Culture and Politics,* 175.

20. Several scholars point to the porous nature of the public sphere in the nineteenth century, particularly when it concerns women's issues. See Craig Calhoun's edited volume on *Habermas and the Public Sphere* (Cambridge, Mass.: MIT Press, 1992), in particular Mary Ryan's essay on "Gender and Public Access: Women's Politics in Nineteenth-Century America," 259–88, and Seyla Benhabib's "Models of Public Space," 73–98. When following Habermas's model, Benhabib reinforces the idea that "participation is seen not as an activity only possible in a narrowly defined political realm but as an activity that can be realized in the social and cultural spheres as well" (86).

21. Asunción Lavrín, "Final Considerations," in *Latin American Women: Historical Perspectives,* ed. Asunción Lavrín (Westport, Conn.: Greenwood Press, 1978), 316. Guy describes a civil code passed in 1871 that treated women as minors "completely under the control of their husbands or fathers." Women could not "manage their own money or property; nor could they work without patriarchal permission. Furthermore, until the 1913 Ley Palacios, family heads who forced women into prostitution committed no crime that affected their rights of *patria potestad* as defined by the civil code" (*Sex and Danger in Buenos Aires,* 44).

22. Lavrín's "Final Considerations," 316. In the context of early twentieth-century feminism, she writes, "Suffrage was a goal, but almost as a derivative of the larger goal of legal equality."

23. Seminar on Women and Culture, *Women, Culture, and Politics,* 175.

24. Telmo Pintos, "La mujer: habilitada para la enseñanza," *La Ondina del Plata,* August 1, 1875, 301; cited in Frederick, *Wily Modesty,* 49. For an insightful discussion of education and "The Angel in the House," see Frederick, *Wily Modesty,* 45–49.

25. Francesca Miller, *Latin American Women and the Search for Social Justice* (Hanover, N.H.: University Press of New England, 1991), 44.

26. Twenty years later, Rock continues, "although conditions varied greatly among the regions, in some areas education, housing, and consumption standards bore comparison with the most-advanced parts of the world" (*Argentina 1516–1987,* 118).

27. Carlson, *¡Feminismo!,* 66 (see chapter on "Education for Women in Nineteenth Century Argentina"). For more information on Sarmiento's contradictory views on the question of female emancipation, see Elizabeth Garrels in "Sarmiento and the Woman Question: From 1839 to the *Facundo,*" in *Sarmiento: Author of a Nation,* ed. Tulio Halperín Donghi, Iván Jaksic, Gwen Kirkpatrick, and Francine Masiello (Berkeley and Los Angeles: University of California Press, 1994), 272–93.

See also Tulio Halperín Donghi's essay in the same volume, "Sarmiento's Place in Postrevolutionary Argentina," which offers a unique vision of this education project as a "gospel of renewal" (19–30).

28. Roberto Cortés Conde discusses the transformations of this marketplace in "Sarmiento and Economic Progress: From *Facundo* to the Presidency," in *Sarmiento: Author of a Nation*, 114–23.

29. James R. Scobie, *Buenos Aires: Plaza to Suburb, 1870–1910* (New York: Oxford University Press, 1974), 213. Rock points to the transatlantic boom in commerce and the export of sheep wool starting in the 1850s. Sheep, it appears, outnumbered people and cattle for the second half the nineteenth century. By the late 1880s, Rock estimates a ratio of thirty sheep for every one Argentine (*Argentina 1516–1987*, 133).

30. Rock, *Argentina 1516–1987*, 132. Rock writes, "By the late 1880s the nation's population was increasing threefold every thirty years. Argentina was now becoming a society of white immigrants and large cities" (118). The census of 1869 indicates 1,836,590 inhabitants. In 1914, the number of inhabitants had grown to 7,885,237. Income levels also boomed as a result of international commerce, with gold prices rising from $7.80 in 1870 to $19.70 in 1910. Saulquin describes how the period's affluence converted Calle Florida into the city's most well-known pedestrian mall for window-shopping and fashionable purchases (*La Moda*, 48).

31. Guy, *Sex and Danger in Buenos Aires*, 37.

32. Lucio López addresses this transformation of Buenos Aires from a provincial village to a materialistic urban center in his social novel of the same name. *La gran aldea* appeared in serialized form in *Sud-América* in 1884 (Buenos Aires: Centro Editor de América Latina, 1992).

33. Benjamin Orlove and Arnold J. Bauer, "Chile in the Belle Epoque: Primitive Producers, Civilized Consumers," in *The Allure of the Foreign: Imported Goods in Postcolonial Latin America*, ed. Benjamin Orlove (Ann Arbor: University of Michigan Press, 1997), 113–49, 118.

34. Scobie, *Buenos Aires*, 234.

35. Scobie discusses the social structure of late nineteenth-century Argentina, defining *la gente decente*, the emerging interests of the middle class, and *la gente de pueblo* (who, as Scobie indicates, made up the other 95 percent of the population of Buenos Aires) in his chapter on "Social Structure and Cultural Themes" (*Buenos Aires*, 208–49).

36. Such imitation had been unheard of previously. Susan Socolow has addressed those legal documents that used dress and other social conventions to denote racial status in the Spanish colonies. See "Acceptable Partners: Marriage Choice in Colonial Argentina, 1778–1810," in *Sexuality and Marriage in Colonial Latin America* (Lincoln: University of Nebraska Press), 209–46. By the late nineteenth century, however, dress codes did not distinguish race and class in the same

way. Because society did not challenge the well-dressed man, working-class males wore coats and ties. This also served to distance themselves from the low status of their foreign-born parents. See Scobie, *Buenos Aires,* 220 and 232.

37. Lily Sosa de Newton writes that the modiste was often foreign-born. See "El trabajo de la mujer" in *Las argentinas ayer y hoy* (Buenos Aires: Ediciones Zanetti, 1967), 210.

38. *Correo del domingo: Periódico literario ilustrado* (Buenos Aires: Imprenta del Siglo, 1885), December 3.

39. The beret and espadrilles made their way to the rural regions of Argentina, where farmers then adopted them (Saulquin, *La Moda,* 57).

40. Julián Martel, *La bolsa* (Buenos Aires: Imprenta Artística "Buenos Aires," 1898).

41. He continues, "There goes an entire society like an immense apocalyptic vision raised by agio and speculation, celebrating the most scandalous orgy of luxury that Buenos Aires has ever seen and will ever see." Cited in Saulquin, *La Moda,* 58.

42. The uncorseted waist and "natural style" of North American dancer Isadora Duncan most likely helped bring about this change in Argentina. See Saulquin, *La Moda,* 53.

43. Ibid., 51. Leigh Summers explains that the taboos of Victorian culture forced women to keep a pregnant body from view. See Summers, "Corsetry and the Invisibility of the Maternal Body," in *Bound to Please: A History of the Victorian Corset* (Oxford: Berg Publishers, 2001), 37–61.

44. Penelope Byrde, *Nineteenth Century Fashion* (London: B. T. Batsford Limited, 1992), 66 and 68.

45. Steele, *Fashion and Eroticism,* 130. Frederick highlights the symbolic language that alludes to female modesty in *El Álbum del Hogar.* The Spanish author Sinués de Marco, for instance, compares the modest woman to a violet, "an unobtrusive flower often hidden under the leaves of larger, showier flowers," as if to show that "a woman-violet should be silent, self-effacing, and out of the public eye" Frederick, *Wily Modesty,* 47. The question of Sinués de Marco's feminism appears later in this essay.

46. Cited in Bernard Rudofsky, *The Unfashionable Human Body* (Garden City, N.Y.: Anchor Press, 1974), 26.

47. *Selección de poemas de Evaristo Carriego y otros poetas* (Buenos Aires: Centro Editor de América Latina, 1968), 34. Wages for sewing had always been low, in part because most women knew how to perform such a task. Guy writes, "For poor women in the capital city, domestic service and sewing at miserable wages were the major alternatives to prostitution" (*Sex and Danger in Buenos Aires,* 42).

48. Just two years after the publication of *Oasis en la vida,* for example, Cecilia Grierson became the first women to receive the country's medical degree,

and Eufrasia Cabral and Elvira Rawson were the first women to address publicly feminist concerns at the Plaza de Mayo.

49. Lavrín, "Final Considerations," 304 and 315.

50. Frederick, *Wily Modesty,* 160–61. Many scholars have written on Gorriti's life and creative fiction. Aside from the excellent sources already listed, see Mary Berg, "Juana Manuela Gorriti," in *Escritoras de Hispanoamérica,* ed. Diane Marting (Bogotá: Siglo Veintiuno, 1992), 231–45; Cristina Iglesia, ed., *El Ajuar de la patria: Ensayos críticos sobre Juana Manuela Gorriti* (Buenos Aires: Feminaria Editora, 1993). For a more fictionalized account of history, see Martha Mercader, *Juanamanuela, mucha mujer* (Buenos Aires: Editorial Sudamericana, 1980) and Analía Efron, *Juana Gorriti: Una biografía íntima* (Buenos Aires: Editorial Sudamericana, 1998).

51. Gertrude Yeager, "Juana Manuela Gorriti: Writer in Exile," in *The Human Tradition in Latin America: The Nineteenth Century,* ed. William H. Beezley and Judith Ewell, (Wilmington, Del.: Scholarly Resources, 1989), 114–27. See pages 123–24 in particular. During these years, Gorriti supported her children and herself with income from a girl's school and an elementary school that she founded.

52. Thomas C. Meehan, "Una olvidada precursora de la literatura fantástica argentina: Juana Manuela Gorriti," *Chasqui: Revista de literatura latinoamericana* 10.2–3 (February–May 1981): 3–19. See page 7.

53. All essays mentioned in this paragraph can also be found in Masiello, *La mujer y el espacio público.*

54. Cabello de Carbonera, "Los oasis en la vida," *La Alborada del Plata* 4 (December 9, 1877): 32.

55. Florencia Escardó, "El oasis en la vida," *La Alborada del Plata* 6 (December 23, 1877): 45–46.

56. Lola Larrosa, "El Hogar," *La Alborada del Plata* 5 (December 16, 1877): 33–44.

57. Without question, many of the views held by women authors were extremely conservative. As one widely circulated manual encouraged, "Work, economy and savings sustain the home and ensure that its well-being transmit satisfaction and joy to all members of the family." See Emilia M. Salzá, *La economía doméstica al alcance de las niñas* [Domestic economy for girls] (Buenos Aires: Librería del Colegio, 1901), 48. Gorriti provided a forum for all of those voices, as if she realized that open discussion on matters of interest and concern to women would promote—and not stifle—the quest for female emancipation.

58. R. Anthony Castagnaro, *The Early Spanish American Novel* (Las Americas, 1971), 91.

59. Gorriti, *Oasis en la vida,* 6

60. Masiello, *Between Civilization and Barbarism,* 129.

61. Ibid., 126. Masiello continues, "A novel whose principal objective is to urge readers to place their savings in the banking institutions of America and to

confirm their faith in the future by purchasing life insurance, *Oasis en la vida* integrates modern materialism with a call to strengthen the home economy."

62. Gorriti, *Oasis en la vida,* 43.

63. He writes these words on December 22, 1887.

64. Ibid., 6.

65. Ibid.

66. Ibid.

67. Masiello, *Between Civilization and Barbarism,* 125.

68. Scholars mention this cross-dressing only briefly. See Nina M. Scott, "Juana Manuela Gorriti's *Cocina ecléctica*: Recipes as Feminist Discourse," *Hispania* 5.2 (May 1992): 310–14. See page 311. Meehan writes that her cross-dressing began in the 1850s, when she organized the literary soirees at her home in Lima ("Una olvidada precursora," 7).

69. Gorriti, *Oasis en la vida,* 56.

70. Ibid., 59. When Gorriti compliments Julia for the comfortable simplicity of her robe and then asks who made it, the resident replies, "Who would it be? Julia López, your servant."

71. Out of respect for her recently deceased father, Julia only wears black garments. "Happy you," Gorriti quips, "who can emancipate yourself from the odious tutelage of the modistes" (ibid., 58).

72. Gorriti attributes this melody to Ortiz Zeballos.

73. Ibid., 66. Throughout the novel, Gorriti portrays the sounds that Mauricio hears with choppy sentences such as "Laughter, the moving of furniture, the opening of the piano."

74. Again, Mauricio views this female presence as an invasion. Upon awakening, Mauricio finds his space overtaken by women, but by now he enjoys the kindhearted attention. "At that moment, those who had been strolling in the garden invaded the room, with full scarves and double skirts with the beautiful roses of Spring that spread themselves out on Mauricio's bed, over furniture and even the flooring." Ibid., 96.

75. Ibid., 98.

76. Ibid., 110.

77. Ibid., 110–11.

78. Ibid., 114.

79. Michael Warner, "The Mass Public and the Mass Subject," in *Habermas and the Public Sphere,* ed. Craig Calhoun, 384.

80. Rubén Darío's *Azul* was published in 1888, the same year that *Oasis en la vida* appeared.

81. See Vyvyan Holland, *Hand Coloured Fashion Plates, 1770–1899* (Boston, Mass.: Boston Book and Art Shop, 1955), 21. Holland was a prominent fashion

lithograph collector also known for being the son of Oscar Wilde, one of the period's most dramatic dressers.

82. See Ann Hollander's *Seeing through Clothes* (Berkeley and Los Angeles: University of California Press, 1978), 321.

83. *La Ondina del Plata* (Buenos Aires, 1876–79), 622.

84. Ibid., 6.

85. Frederick believes that *La Alborada del Plata* was a more conservative periodical that celebrated the domestic angel or the type of woman who had "sacrificial tendencies" and worked toward "self-erasure" (*Wily Modesty*, 46).

86. In *Wily Modesty*, Frederick depicts her as a "leading promoter of the domestic angel" concept. Masiello sees her as a feminist in *Between Civilization and Barbarism*, but notes her ultraconservative tendencies in *La mujer y el espacio público*. Urruela provides a new historical perspective in her essay on "Becoming 'Angelic': María Pilar Sinués and the Woman Question," *Recovering Spain's Feminist Tradition*, ed. Lisa Vollendorf (New York: The Modern Language Association of America, 2001).

87. Her moral stories found in *La ley de Dios* (1858) and *A la luz de la lámpara* (1858), officially endorsed by Spanish religious and government authorities, were even incorporated for use in public instruction. Despite the conservative neo-Catholic approach of her conduct manuals and serialized novels, Sinués de Marco did not escape criticism. Women authors often found themselves in a precarious public role, their private lives as scrupulously reviewed as their written work. As Sánchez-Llama suggests, the "manly realist" tendencies of the late nineteenth-century cultural histories that assigned inferior status to works by women authors based on biological premises alone were ultimately responsible for discounting the status that Sinués de Marco achieved in her lifetime. See his essays on "María del Pilar Sinués de Marco y la cultural oficial peninsular del siglo XIX: del neocatolicismo a la estética realista," *Revista Canadiense de Estudios Hispánicos* 23.2 (Winter 1999): 271–88; and "El 'varonil realismo' y la cultura oficial de la Restauración en el fin de siglo peninsular: el caso de María del Pilar Sinués de Marco (1835–1893)," *Letras peninsulares* 12.1 (Spring 1999): 37–64.

88. Urruela, "Becoming 'Angelic,'" 162.

89. Sánchez-Llama, "María del Pilar Sinués de Marco," 277–78.

90. The title of this magazine refers to the golden tower of a castle in Sevilla, Spain, its tiles reflecting the Andalusian sun. *La Torre de Oro* was referred to as a "periódico dedicado a las damas" (newspaper for the ladies), highlighting the subjects of "Educación, Labore, Literatura, Economía Doméstica."

91. Urruela, "Becoming 'Angelic,'" 161.

92. *La Ondina del Plata*, 6.

93. In their exploration of the roots of fashion anxiety, Alison Clarke and Daniel Miller affirm, "Individuals are frequently too anxious about the choices to be made to proceed without various forms of support and reassurance. Where

possible, support involves close friends and family who are trusted to give advice reflecting care and concern." See "Fashion and Anxiety," *Fashion Theory* 6.2 (June 2002): 191–213. See page 209.

94. *La Ondina del Plata,* 7.

95. A letter to Sinués de Marco's unmarried brother reiterates this belief. She writes, "Trust me, in choosing your soul mate, do not look for the extremes but instead seek out the modest, Enlightened woman who is the beautiful daughter of progress and civilization. Remember, my dear brother, that affirmation of mine that you find so silly: 'There are always old-fashioned lithographs.' Yes, I repeat, there are even really bad ones" (ibid., 247).

96. Sinués de Marco's column abounded with advice for family and dear friends, encouraging fashion victims to contemplate the simplicity of life and offering useful suggestions to those in "what to wear" despair. When one friend ponders what to wear to an important social gathering, the column re-creates their conversation. Using a dialogic approach that will remind readers of Gorriti's *Oasis en la vida,* she writes,

> "What shall I wear?" she expressed upon entering. "What dress will I don? My husband is under financial distress and so I don't even dare ask him for anything. . . . My God! What compromise!"
>
> "Don't you have a white cotton dress?" I asked.
>
> "Why, yes, but what do I do with that? I already wore it to another house a few nights ago."
>
> "And what does that matter? Do you have to wear a different dress each day?"
>
> "So it is, or I can't go!"
>
> "I do not see it this way. They have invited you to their house and therefore they appreciate you and you should go. They know that you are not rich: Is that a fault? Can someone require this of you?"
>
> "But I will be so criticized."
>
> "By the stupid. And *who* cares about them? Put on your dress with the transparent white cloth and the jasmine brooch. You would be worthy of censorship if you opted for an extraordinary brand of luxury, especially since your husband possesses a modest fortune. Trust me, and maybe you'll be happy you listened to me."

Although Sinués de Marco misses the event due to some unforeseen ailment, the grapevine reveals that guests of the opulent ball admired the youthful freshness of this friend's dress (*La Ondina del Plata,* 6).

97. Barthes, *The Fashion System,* 10.

Epilogue

1. Victoria Lescano, *Followers of Fashion: Falso Diccionario de la Moda* (Buenos Aires: Interzona Editora, 2004), 36.

2. Fabricio Forastelli, "Scattered Bodies, Unfashionable Flesh," in *The Latin American Fashion Reader,* ed. Regina A. Root (Oxford: Berg Publishers, 2005), 284.

3. The Mothers of the Plaza de Mayo are divided into two factions: the Línea Fundadora, the founding group, which focuses on archiving information on what happened to the "disappeared" to bring to justice those responsible for the kidnappings and murders; and the group of the Mothers of the Plaza de Mayo led by Hebe de Bonafini, who seek to carry out the revolutionary goals to which their children had ascribed. The former group still marches from 3:30 to 4:00 p.m. on Thursdays. The latter group has founded a human rights university a short distance away from the building in which the Argentine Congress meets. For more on the Mothers of the Plaza de Mayo, see the work of Diana Taylor, in particular *Disappearing Acts: Spectacles of Gender and Nationalism in Argentina's "Dirty War"* (Durham, N.C.: Duke University Press, 1997).

4. Hebe de Bonafini, speech given as president of the Association of the Mothers of the Plaza de Mayo, Buenos Aires, July 6, 1988.

5. "Arte y Confección" refers to a series of cultural and political events organized to express solidarity with the plight of the Brukman seamstresses and the workers' movement in Argentina. Organizers took issue with the fact that cultural events sponsored by city government tend to be juried and to overlook the creative contributions of workers. Contributing artists at the first event from May 27 to June 1, 2003, offered the viewing public many different ideas on creative agency and its role in asserting solidarity with the Brukman seamstresses. Custom-made clothes thus became part of a collective work activity that presented a viable alternative to the generic production process used to create most fashion brands.

6. Forastelli, "Scattered Bodies," 288.

7. Naomi Klein, "Argentina's Luddite Rulers," *Globe and Mail* (Canada), April 24, 2003, A17.

8. Ibid. Klein's report indicates what occurred at the Balvanera worksite from April 18 to 21, 2003:

> Police had evicted the workers in the middle of the night and turned the entire block into a military zone guarded by machine guns and attack dogs. Unable to get into the factory and complete an outstanding order for 3,000 pairs of dress trousers, the workers gathered a huge crowd of supporters and announced it was time to go back to work. At 5 p.m., 50 middle aged seamstresses in no-nonsense haircuts, sensible shoes and blue work smocks walked up to the black police fence. Someone pushed, the fence fell, and the Brukman women, unarmed and arm in arm, slowly walked through.
>
> They had only taken a few steps when the police began shooting: tear gas, water cannons, first rubber bullets, then lead. The police even charged the Mothers of the Plaza de Mayo, in their white headscarves embroidered with the names of their "disappeared" children. Dozens of demonstrators were injured and police fired tear gas into a hospital where some had taken refuge.

For a selection of photographic images of the seamstresses and supporting demonstrators, see: http://argentina.indymedia.org/news/2003/05/108349.php and http://www.poloobrero.org.ar/marcha/brukman2/index.htm.

9. Victoria Lescano, "Estampado popular," *Página/12*, June 6, 2003; available at http://www.pagina12.com.ar/diario/suplementos/las12/13-659-2003-06-08.html. (*Página/12* is one of Argentina's main newspapers.) Interestingly enough, the manner of representing revolutionary gestures has become somewhat iconic. When an artist's workshop stamped on t-shirts the image of Darío Santillán with long hair, a beard, and arms extended, many confused this image with that of other revolutionary figures, such as Che Guevara or even Jesus. Santillán was a *piquetero,* a member of the unemployed worker's movement, who, along with a friend, was gunned down and killed by police at an antiglobalization demonstration on June 26, 2002.

10. As many scholars have already wondered: If dress is implicated in a political project, then how does one begin to read Western-style dress?

11. The Taller de Serigrafía Popular was founded by Diego Posadas and Mariela Scafatti. Due to the popularity of the printed t-shirts at various demonstrations in Buenos Aires, Lescano writes that the two workshop founders later enlisted the help of other artists, including Magdalena Jitrik and Karina Grainieri. Lescano, "Estampado popular."

12. Ibid.

13. The "lettered city" is a term coined by Angel Rama and which Jean Franco uses in her most recent work to refer to the influential role of the Latin American intellectual during the Cold War. For the English translation of Rama's work originally published in 1983, see Rama, *The Lettered City,* ed. and trans. John Charles Chasteen (Durham, N.C.: Duke University Press, 1996). See in particular, Franco, *The Decline and Fall of the Lettered City: Latin America in the Cold War* (Cambridge, Mass.: Harvard University Press, 2002).

14. Franco, *The Decline and Fall,* 221.

15. Ibid., 191.

16. Don Segundo Sombra was a character in the 1926 novel of the same name by Ricardo Güiraldes.

17. Margaret Maynard, *Dress and Globalization* (Manchester: Manchester University Press, 2004). See the chapter on "Dress and Global 'Sameness,'" 32–49.

18. Worn upon release from jail, in the case of Martha Stewart, who soon marketed the style as the "Martha Stewart Coming Home Poncho."

19. Torrejón interviewed by Olga Corna, "La moda en los medios," *DeSignis* 1 (October 2001): 267–70, 269.

20. Susana Saulquin offers an interesting perspective on dressing the postmodern body in her article on "El cuerpo como metáfora," *DeSignis* 1 (October 2001): 169–84.

21. See Guy Brighton, "Cool Hunting Las Villas Miseria," January 10, 2006, available at http://www.psfk.com/2006/01/cool_hunting_la.html.

22. Maynard, *Dress and Globalization,* 35.

23. Mike González, "Clothing and Dress," in *Encyclopedia of Contemporary Latin American and Caribbean Cultures,* ed. Daniel Balderston, Ana López, and Mike González (London: Routledge, 2000).

24. Given that Mercosur represents "a market of 361 million people with a GDP of $973bn, exporting $181bn of goods and services," as the BBC indicates in one profile, this goal is like the environmental movement, connecting the local to the global, one effort at a time. See BBC News, "S America launches trading bloc," December 9, 2004, http://news.bbc.co.uk/2/hi/business/4079505.stm; as well as http://www.mercosur.int/msweb/.

25. Designers Celaine Refosco of Brazil and Laura Novik of Argentina, also a design management professor, founded Identidades Latinas in 2003. See Luján Cambariere, "Redes latinas," *Página/12,* December 10, 2005, http://www.pagina12.com.ar/diario/suplementos/m2/10-839-2005-12-10.html. Raíz Diseño, founded by Laura Novik and Spanish designer Alex Blanch, emerged in 2007. José Korn, who coordinates the Plan Nacional de Diseño de Chile [National Plan for Chilean Design], and Maricarmen Oyarzun, the coordinator of Araucanía Textil, are also directors of this nongovernmental organization. According to its mission statement, Raíz Diseño promotes fashion design that works in conjunction with community development endeavors. The organization addresses diverse cultural, economic, and social realities and targets specifically the countries of Argentina, Brazil, Colombia, and Uruguay.

26. Laura Novik and Alex Blanch, "Buen diseño, buen negocio," *ARQ* Chile 62 (December 2006): 15–17.

27. "I don't believe humour can alter anything, but sometimes it can be the little grain of sand that acts as a catalyst to change," Quino told *UNESCO Courier* journalist Lucía Iglesias Kuntz ("Quino, On the Funny Side of Freedom," http://www.unesco.org/courier/2000_07/uk/dires.htm).

28. This story was published in *El Aleph* in 1949.

29. Benjamin Orlove and Arnold J. Bauer, "Giving Importance to Imports," in *The Allure of the Foreign: Imported Goods in Postcolonial Latin America,* ed. Benjamin Orlove (Ann Arbor: University of Michigan Press, 1997), 11.

30. While President Fernández Kirchner associated her glamorous style with Eva Perón by appearing in front of images of the late Peronist leader, the opposition began to question whether images of abundance of a "Queen Cristina" or the "CFK look" were appropriate at a time of inflation, political unrest, and intense social division. These sentiments were also expressed much later, when the president asserted that farmers protesting massive tax increases on agricultural exports were involved in a "strike for abundance" that she has characterized as insensitive to the urban poor.

31. Forastelli, "Scattered Bodies," 286.

32. In another context, Elizabeth Wilson has argued that the structural frag-

mentation of contemporary dress began with the reduction of clothing to the minimal form of sportswear. Might it not be possible to extend this analysis to those fragments of fashion that are sociopolitical in nature? See "Moda y estudios culturales," Elizabeth Wilson interviewed by Katie Lloyd Thomas and Guillermo Olivera, *DeSignis* 1 (October 2001): 285–89, 287.

33. See John Carlin, "High-flying, Adored and Siliconised," *Observer* (February 12, 2006), available at http://observer.guardian.co.uk/woman/story/0,,1705316,00.htm.

34. In Argentina, "most shoppers needing larger clothing wind up picking among frumpy product lines at down-market vendors scattered throughout the province's barrios." The *Wall Street Journal* reports that plus sizes are extremely expensive. For those who happen to be a size 10 or above, the best option is shopping at Wal-Mart, one of the only stores that would carry these sizes before the Sizes Law. Spearheaded by Mabel Bello, the director of the Association for the Fight Against Bulimia and Anorexia, the push for the Sizes Law began in the 1990s. Responding to the high rates of eating disorders in Argentina, which are among the highest in the world, the provincial congress passed this law in 2001. In 2007, a store that did not carry all sizes also risked a fine of $170,000. See M. Moffett, "In Argentine Province, Fashion Police Say Small Isn't Beautiful," *Wall Street Journal* (Eastern edition), November 26–27, 2005, A1, A6.

35. Ana Gabriela Álvarez, "The City Cross-dressed: Sexual Rights and Rollbacks in De la Rúa's Buenos Aires," trans. Philip Derbyshire, *Journal of Latin American Cultural Studies* 9.2 (2000): 137–53. Her description of transvestite dress appears on page 147.

36. Ibid., 141. This ordinance is commonly referred to as Article 2F.

37. Forastelli, "Scattered Bodies," 286. Lohana Berkins is an internationally recognized activist who has been a crucial figure in the gay, lesbian, bisexual, and transsexual rights movement in Argentina. In 1995, when I interviewed Berkins in Buenos Aires, she told me about a "fashion" protest she had initiated when jailed for dressing in clothes authorities deemed as acceptable only for women. Berkins was therefore issued male attire, which she reconfigured into a dress in her cell.

38. I would like to thank Laura Novik for her generous comments and assistance in compiling sketches by Flavia Angriman.

39. Correspondence between Flavia Angriman, Laura Novik, and the author, December 2006.

Index

African Argentines: in Argentine poetry, 53, 54, 56–58, 59; Buenos Aires societies of, 53–54, 178n62, 178n65; *candombes* of, 54, 55, 57, 179n70; integration into Argentine society, 59; linguistic stereotypes of, 179n74; militias of, 57–58; during Rioplatense revolution, 169n9; in Rosas's propaganda, 58–59; Rosas's relationship with, 54–55, 57, 58–59, 178n59; in Unitarian army, 178n59; unity among, 57. *See also* women, African Argentine

Aira, César, xxi; *El vestido rosa,* 165n19

Alberdi, Juan Bautista, 178n59; association with *La Moda,* 106, 112, 114, 187n39; on democracy, 187n40; with *El Iniciador,* 115; on imitation, 187n45; on national customs, 112, 114; on national philosophy, 185n17

Allende, Isabel, xiv

Álvarez, Ana Gabriela, 158

Amalia (Mármol), 26; compadres in, 21, 174n86; crimson in, 44; dress code in, 13; heterosexual union in,

173n70; political identity in, 103; power of fashion in, 113; Unitarians in, 103, 172n58; women characters of, 127

Amazons, 36

Anderson, Benedict: on imagined community, 20, 185n3; on nation-building, xxii

Andrews, George Reid, 54, 55

Angelis, Pedro de, 48

Angriman, Flavia: *Design Sketches,* 160; sportswear collection of, 159

Aniston, Jennifer, 154

Anuario para el año 1857, 175n96

Argentina: citizens' foundational role in, 101–2; civil code (1871), 191n21; Common Education Law (1876), 133; competitive markets in, 133; conspicuous consumption in, 134, 135–36; Constitution of 1853, 178n53; consumption patterns in, 164n8; discourse on prostitution in, 81; eating disorders in, 201n34; economic booms in, xxviii, 134, 192nn29–30; economic crises in,

ness of, 40; legal limitations on, 69, 191n21; luxurious consumption by, 73–74; male parental authority over, 43–44; middle-class, xxix; mobility of, 37; in nation-building process, 40–42, 188n84; as ornaments, 143; patriotism of, 40; physical education for, 190n13; political engagement of, xxvii, 35–36, 47, 61, 130; political subjectivity of, xxvi; political vanity of, 36, 44, 61; *porteñas,* 62, 87, 91; public comments on, 84; in public sphere, 43, 47, 61, 67, 69, 70–72, 80–81, 86–87, 93; as readers, 132–33; resistance through fashion, xvii–xviii; in Rioplatense revolution, xxvi, 36, 38–42; role in cultural formation, 49; role in postcolonial society, 59–60, 75–76; soldiers, 36, 38–40; under Spanish colonialism, 37–38; Unitarian, 44; use of *chignon,* 65; use of European fashion, 143; working-class, 136

women authors, Argentine: *British Packet* on, 129–30, 182n32; conservatism of, 194n57; contesting of norms, 120; economic autonomy of, xxix, 138; editorship of *La Camelia,* 119–20, 121, 124; fashion rhetoric of, 96, 129–30; professional status of, 146; pseudonyms of, 129, 131; in public sphere, xxviii, 119–20, 196n87; threat to men, 132

women's rights: counter-sphere of, 120

women's rights, Argentine: in education, 130, 132–33, 190n13, 190n16, 191nn26–27; in fashion writing xxviii–xxx, 118–19, 129, 130–32, 145, 147; femininity and, 137; following independence, 45–47; Gorriti's advocacy of, 140, 141, 142; Sarmiento on, 191n27; suffrage, 191n22

wool: export of, 192n29

workers' movements, Argentine, 152, 157

working class, Argentine: clothing of, xiv–xv, xvi, 134, 135, 193n36; Federalist, 174n88; and *gente decente,* 134; support for Perón, xv–xvi, 164n10; unemployed, 158–59, 199n9; women, 136

World of Fashion: lithographs from, 180n16

Wrigley, Richard, 99

Zemborain family: Federalist ribbons of, 168n50

Zinny, Antonio, 181n32

REGINA A. ROOT is associate professor of Hispanic studies at the College of William and Mary.